MACMILLAN
WORK OUT
SERIES

Work Out

German

GCSE

The titles
in this
series

MACMILLAN
WORK OUT
SERIES

Work Out

German

GCSE

E. J. Neather

Editorial Consultant

BETTY PARR

MACMILLAN

First published in 1986 by
THE MACMILLAN PRESS LTD
Houndmills, Basingstoke, Hampshire RG21 2XS
and London
Companies and representatives
throughout the world

ISBN 0–333–44007–2

A catalogue record for this book is available
from the British Library.

Printed in Malaysia

First edition reprinted once
Second edition 1987
10   9   8   7   6   5
00   99   98   97   96   95

Contents

Series Editor's Preface

Work Out German has been planned for adults and older teenagers with a basic knowledge of spoken and written German and a wish to become more proficient in the language and better informed about those who speak it. The book and cassette are intended for students working, with or without a teacher, to attain a good grade in the General Certificate of Secondary Education. The Course will also serve the needs of students of more modest linguistic ability, who aim at lower grades in the examination and wish to concentrate on understanding and using the spoken language, or learning to read with confidence rather than to write.

Work Out German has two main objectives. The first is to provide a sound and interesting programme, in which the study of authentic materials will serve as a basis for studying the language in a realistic context and will give an insight into different aspects of life in West Germany, with a glimpse of other German-speaking countries. The second is to offer specific help to students preparing for an appropriate public examination, in the belief that the development of sound standards of work in the language skills will bring success in examinations to those who work effectively.

All the teaching, including the grammatical explanations and exercises, is based on carefully selected texts and recorded conversations, which exemplify the correct use of spoken and written German, and illustrate important elements of grammar and syntax. Every care has been taken to use the language in sensible situations and to avoid the bizarre statements often evoked by ill-judged questions posed out of context. A key to the exercises and an excellent grammar summary, with its invaluable index, are contained in Part II. A guide to pronunciation and the accompanying cassette will help the student to understand and use the spoken language with greater confidence.

One section of the book concentrates on the General Certificate of Secondary Education, about which much authoritative information is now available. An account of methods of assessment and of different types of oral and written tests is followed by sample materials and by much clear and helpful advice for those preparing for the new examination.

The author's very full and clear introduction gives details of the book and cassette, and suggests effective ways of using them. This section deserves the most careful attention of all who intend to benefit fully from this new and stimulating Course.

Betty Parr

Author's Preface

As has already been made clear in the Series Editor's preface, this book is intended for adults and older teenagers with some knowledge of written and spoken German, and a wish to practise and improve their command of the language to a standard sufficient for a good grade in the GCSE examination.

Although the primary aim of the book, with its accompanying cassette, is to provide the student with a complete revision programme for the examination, which may be used by the student alone or with a teacher, it is also intended that language should be presented in a real context, and not in the isolated and artificial sentences which often serve as the basis of examination preparation. In addition to a 'real' language context, the subject matter of the chapters is also authentic, and offers reading and listening materials which are concerned with issues in the societies where German is spoken. In this way the book seeks to assist the achievement of a high level of language skills, and, at the same time, inform readers about aspects of life in German-speaking societies, and give some of the flavour of reading authentic texts and hearing real conversations.

Because of national criteria and the syllabuses of the various Examination Groups, the types of test in the examination show more uniformity than was the case with the old GCE 'O'-level examination. Even so, it would be difficult for any one book to claim that it offered specific preparation for all the Boards. What can be claimed, however, is that this book offers a sound basis in all the language skills, and will help to bring the students up to a level of performance where they may confidently tackle the tests offered by the examination, the requirements of which are set out in Part III of the book, together with some sample materials. In addition, many of the exercises in each chapter are modelled on common forms of tests, using comprehension questions, multiple choice questions, letter-writing, etc.

In the ways explained above, it is hoped that the twin aims of language improvement based on the living language and on practice in specific examination skills will both be met. The following section gives more detail about the organisation of the book and suggests ways of working with it.

Organisation of the Book

The book has 14 chapters, of which Chapter 14 contains three reading passages with associated exercises. All the other chapters are divided into two parts — Reading Materials and Listening Materials. Within each section, there are a number of texts offering the chance to practise reading and listening skills at several levels. These include the Basic or General Level, which is the common core to be taken by all candidates in the new examination, and the Higher or Extended Level, which will be taken by candidates aiming at the higher grades. Reading and listening texts at the Basic Level are usually followed by exercises which test recognition and comprehension. The more extended written texts are followed by two sorts of exercises — Section A, concerned with comprehension and recognition, and

Section B, containing more formal exercises designed to practise certain key grammatical points, of which the text contains examples. For the information necessary to understand the grammar and carry out the exercises, reference is made to the detailed Grammar Summary in Part II of the book. Section B exercises also contain many opportunities to practise letter-writing, the most widespread examination test in the writing of the foreign language. The more extended dialogues in the section of Listening Materials are tested by comprehension exercises or multiple choice questions, and develop towards role play, important for the preparation of the Oral Examination.

Each of the texts in the sections of Reading and Listening Materials is followed by a select vocabulary and explanations of idioms and expressions. The texts themselves are all authentic, taken from German sources, or written by native speakers of German. In terms of difficulty, there is a general progression throughout the book, with Chapters 12–14 containing the most difficult texts.

After Part I, which contains the 14 teaching chapters, follows a Reference Section with a Key to Exercises, a Grammar Summary with all examples drawn from texts in the book, and a Guide to Pronunciation. Part III then gives information and guidance about the examinations, including sample materials. Accompanying the book is a cassette containing the Listening Materials from all the chapters and the Guide to Pronunciation.

Throughout the book, because of space limitations, the cases may be abbreviated N, A, G, D or Nom., Acc., Gen., Dat.

How to Use this Book

It is expected that students will normally work through the book, although it is quite possible for a chapter to be taken out of sequence if practice is needed in the vocabulary of a particular topic or on a specific point of grammar. Start first with the reading texts and try to understand as much as possible before turning to the explanations of vocabulary or grammar. Texts which at first sight seem difficult will appear less so if you consider the information given in the introductory English paragraph, and if you try to deduce the meaning of unknown words and phrases from the context of the passage. When first encountering an unknown text in a foreign language, you may be baffled by apparent difficulties which can disappear if the context is used to help understanding. Above all, do not be put off by one particular word which is unfamiliar, and do not feel that you should know every word in the passage before you have a fair understanding.

Having made your first effort to understand the text, try the exercises which are concerned with testing recognition and comprehension. Treat this whole process as one of detection and deduction. These are important skills to develop in any work with a foreign language. Check your answers with the ones given in the Key, and then study the lists of vocabulary and expressions. The vocabulary is selective and you may need to use a dictionary for unknown words which do not appear. Note in the lists of vocabulary that the plural of each noun is given in a shortened form after the word: for example, *der Ball (– e)* means that the plural in this case is *die Bälle*. Note also that the vowel changes of strong verbs are given in parentheses after the infinitive: for example, *schwimmen (a, o)* means that the Imperfect tense is *schwamm* and the past participle is *geschwommen*.

The Section B exercises are intended to provide intensive work on particular points of grammar. Of course, texts of an authentic kind, such as are used in this book, contain a wide range of grammatical features, and the technique here is to choose texts which highlight particular structures or parts of speech, and then help you to understand the use of that point of grammar in context. Reference is made to particular paragraphs of the Grammar Summary, which should be studied in conjunction with the text and the exercises. The detailed index following the Grammar Summary is an important aid to learning, as it provides cross-references between the texts and the reference section.

After dealing with the passages in the section of Reading Materials, turn to the passages for listening comprehension. It is important that the dialogues should be listened to on tape before the written version of the text is studied. The comprehension questions after the listening passages should be used, rather as in an examination, to test your powers of listening comprehension. The written text can then be used to confirm and consolidate your understanding. Besides offering practice in listening comprehension, the exercises move on to provide the chance to build up your own dialogues by participating in role play, thereby developing skills necessary for the Oral examination.

German has the particular advantage for learners, that it is a language spoken in four European societies – the Federal Republic of Germany, the German Democratic Republic, Austria and Switzerland. This offers not only a wide area for travel, but also a great cultural diversity. In the choice of texts this book tries to capture some of this diversity. It is hoped that, in this way, the book will not only help towards acquiring competence in the language, and towards success in the examination, but also help the student to find out more about contemporary German-speaking cultures.

Exeter, 1987   E. J. N.

Acknowledgements

My particular thanks for assistance in the preparation of materials for this book, and in the checking of the language content, are due to Mrs Anneli Ward and Mrs Gabriele Winter.

The author and publishers wish to thank the following who have kindly given permission for the use of copyright material:

Berliner Verlag for cartoons from *Für Dich*

Bundesminister für das Post- und Fernmeldewesen for extract from *Unsere Post 2*

Jugendscala for extracts from *Scala Jugendmagazin*

Niedersächsische Kultusminister for extract from *Von der Schule in die Arbeitswelt — aber wie?*

Pädagogischer Verlag Schwann-Bagel GmbH for extract from *Kleines Wörterbuch des DDR — Wortschatzes*

Southern Examining Group for material from draft examination questions. The material included on pages 239 to 245 is draft material from the Southern Examining Group's GCSE syllabus and taken on its own it will not provide an accurate indication of a typical Southern Group GCSE examination in German.

Umweltbundesamt for extract from *Auto und Umwelt*

Die Zeit for extract from *Zeitmagazin*, 36/81, by Norbert Klugman

The author and publishers also wish to acknowledge the following illustration sources:

J. Allan Cash Limited
Austrian National Tourist Office
Baden-Württemberg
Embassy of the Federal Republic of Germany
German National Tourist Office
Presse-und Informationsamt der Bundesregierung
Swiss National Tourist Office

Groups Responsible for GCSE Examinations

In the United Kingdom, examinations are administered by the following organisations. Syllabuses and examination papers can be ordered from the addresses given here.

Northern Examining Association (NEA)

Joint Matriculation Board (JMB)
Publications available from:
John Sherratt & Son Ltd
78 Park Road
Altrincham, Cheshire WA14 5QQ

North Regional Examinations Board
Wheatfield Road
Westerhope
Newcastle upon Tyne NE5 5JZ

Yorkshire and Humberside Regional Examinations Board (YREB)
Scarsdale House
136 Derbyside Lane
Sheffield S8 8SE

Associated Lancashire Schools Examining Board
12 Harter Street
Manchester M1 6HL

North West Regional Examinations Board (NWREB)
Orbit House, Albert Street
Eccles, Manchester M30 0WL

Midland Examining Group (MEG)

University of Cambridge Local Examinations Syndicate (UCLES)
Syndicate Buildings
Hills Road, Cambridge CB1 2EU

Oxford and Cambridge Schools Examination Board (O & C)
10 Trumpington Street
Cambridge CB2 1QB

Southern Universities' Joint Board (SUJB)
Cotham Road
Bristol BS6 6DD

East Midland Regional Examinations Board (EMREB)
Robins Wood House, Robins Wood Road
Aspley, Nottingham NG8 3NR

West Midlands Examinations Board (WMEB)
Norfolk House, Smallbrook
Queensway, Birmingham B5 4NJ

London and East Anglian Group (LEAG)

University of London School Examinations Board (L)
University of London Publications Office
52 Gordon Square
London WC1E 6EE

London Regional Examining Board (LREB)
Lyon House
104 Wandsworth High Street
London SW18 4LF

East Anglian Examinations Board (EAEB)
The Lindens, Lexden Road
Colchester, Essex CO3 3RL

Southern Examining Group (SEG)

The Associated Examining Board (AEB)
Stag Hill House
Guildford
Surrey GU2 5XJ

**University of Oxford Delegacy of
   Local Examinations** (OLE)
Ewert Place, Banbury Road
Summertown, Oxford OX2 7BZ

Southern Regional Examinations Board
   (SREB)
Avondale House
33 Carlton Crescent
Southampton
Hants SO9 4YL

**South-East Regional Examinations
   Board** (SEREB)
Beloe House
2–10 Mount Ephraim Road
Royal Tunbridge Wells
Kent TN1 1EU

South-Western Examinations Board
   (SWExB)
23–29 Marsh Street
Bristol BS1 4BP

Scottish Examination Board (SEB)

Publications available from:
Robert Gibson and Sons (Glasgow) Ltd
17 Fitzroy Place
Glasgow G3 7SF

Welsh Joint Education Committee (WJEC)

245 Western Avenue
Cardiff CF5 2YX

**Northern Ireland Schools Examinations
   Council** (NISEC)

Examinations Office
Beechill House, Beechill Road
Belfast BT8 4RS

Part I

TEACHING UNITS

1 Familie und Zuhause

1.1 Reading Materials

Talking about your family and asking other people about their families is an important part of everyday conversation. The family tree (*Stammbaum*) of Karl Schmidt, below, introduces you to the German for some of the members of the family. Perhaps not everyone is lucky enough to have such a wealth of relations, and the second text gives one solution to the problem of mothers who have to go out to work to help the family budget. If they need help in finding someone to look after their families, a scheme such as the Osnabrück *Tagesfamilien* could be of help. In the third passage a German girl writes to her English pen-friend about growing up in the family home in Munich.

1.1.1 Karl Schmidts Stammbaum

Karls Großvater	Karls Großmutter	Karls Großvater und Großmutter	
Wilhelm Schmidt	Luise Schmidt	Karl Schröder	Ottilie Schröder
72 Jahre alt	(geborene Müller)	68 Jahre alt	(geborene Stett)
	70 Jahre alt		69 Jahre alt

Karls Vater —————————————————— Karls Mutter
Heinrich Schmidt   Sophie Schmidt
48 Jahre alt   (geborene Schröder)
                                      42 Jahre alt

Karls Bruder Rolf	Karl Schmidt	Karls Schwester
— seine Frau Renate.	17 Jahre alt.	Gabi, 12 Jahre alt.
Beide 20 Jahre alt.	Sohn von Heinrich	Tochter von Heinrich
Renate ist Karls	und Sophie. Enkel	und Sophie. Enkelin
Schwägerin.	von Wilhelm, Luise,	von Wilhelm, Luise,
Rolf and Renate haben	Karl und Ottilie. Onkel	Ottilie und Karl. Tante
ein kleines Baby, Anna,	von der kleinen Anna.	der kleinen Anna.
nur 6 Monate alt. Anna		
ist die Nichte von Karl		
und Gabi.		

(i) *Comprehension Questions*

1. Look at the family tree and then decide how the following words would be translated into English: (a) Nichte; (b) Enkel; (c) Tante; (d) Schwägerin; (e) Großmutter.
2. The word *geborene* occurs with several of the women's names. What do you think it means?
3. If an English friend who knows no German asks you for some information, try to tell him or her: (a) all that you know about Karl's brother Rolf; (b) anything you can find out about both sets of grandparents?

3

1. If Karl was talking to you about the names and ages of the members of his family, he might say, for example: *mein Bruder heißt Rolf; er ist zwanzig Jahre alt*. What would he say to you if he was telling you about (a) his sister; (b) his mother; (c) his sister-in-law?
2. Now make similar statements in German (a) about yourself; (b) about members of your family. In each case, state names and ages.

1.1.2 Osnabrück braucht Tagesfamilien

Tagesfamilie — was ist das?
Eine Familie, die tagsüber Kinder anderer Eltern **in ihrem Haushalt** regelmäßig betreut und eine Genehmigung hat. Die Familie hat Zeit für Kinder. Sie bietet Spielmöglichkeiten und arbeitet mit den Eltern des Tageskindes eng zusammen.

Tagesfamilie — welche Kinder sind auf sie angewiesen?
Zumeist Säuglinge und Kleinkinder, aber auch Schulkinder.

Tagesfamilie — wie viele Kinder betreut sie?
In der Regel höchstens vier bis fünf Kinder. Die eigenen Kinder sind in dieser Zahl eingeschlossen.

Tagesfamilie — wie wird sie bezahlt?
Nach privater Vereinbarung mit den Eltern.

Es gibt viele Familien, die es sich im Umgang mit dem Vater nicht leicht machen
© Loriot, Diogenes Verlag, Zürich

(i) *Comprehension Questions*

Tagesfamilie is a made-up word which is applied to foster families where children whose parents are both out at work can be looked after during the working day. Four questions are asked above. You may not understand every word in the questions and answers, but see how much you can guess from the context and attempt the following questions:

1. What is offered by the foster families to the children who visit them?
2. What, roughly, is the age of the children who are fostered?
3. What is usually the maximum number of children placed with each family? Does this number depend on the number of children already in the family?

4. Are the families paid? If so, how is payment arranged?
5. Look again at the whole passage and find the German for the following: (a) all day long; (b) regularly; (c) mostly; (d) as a rule; (e) paid.

(ii) *Asking Questions*

1. From your reading of the passage, write out the German for the following questions: (a) how many children? (b) what is that? (c) how? (d) which children?
2. Here are some questions based on the same words. Translate these questions into English.

(a) Was ist eine Tagesfamilie?
(b) Wie viele Mütter und Väter sind berufstätig?
(c) Wie viele Kinder sind in einer Tagesfamilie?
(d) Welche Eltern betreuen die Kinder?
(e) Wie bezahlen die Eltern?
(f) Was spielen die Kinder?
(g) Was für Kinder bleiben in einer Tagesfamilie?

(iii) *Explanations*

Select Vocabulary

tagsüber — all day long
regelmäßig — regularly
betreuen — to look after
die Genehmigung — authorisation
bieten (o, o) — to offer
die Spielmöglichkeiten — opportunities for play

angewiesen (auf) — assigned (to)
der Säugling — baby
höchstens — at the most
eingeschlossen (in) — included (in)
bezahlen, zahlen — to pay
die Vereinbarung — arrangement, agreement

Grammar

Asking questions. See Grammar Summary, section 15(a)2.

1.1.3 Gabi schreibt einen Brief

München,
den 4. März 1986

Liebe Helen!

Was Du mir von Deiner Familie und Eurem Haus geschrieben hast, war sehr interessant. Ich kann mir gar nicht vorstellen, daß Ihr schon immer in einem Haus gewohnt habt. In Deutschland können sich nur die reicheren Leute ein Haus leisten. Die meisten Familien wohnen in einer Eigentums- oder Mietswohnung.

Meine Eltern, mein Bruder und ich haben auch 12 Jahre in einer Wohnung gelebt. Erst dann hatten meine Eltern genug Geld für ein Haus gespart.

Ich war auch verblüfft, als ich las, wie oft Ihr umgezogen seid. Ich bin nur zweimal umgezogen. Das erste Mal bin ich mit meiner Familie von unserer Wohnung in unser neues Haus umgezogen. In diesem Haus habe ich dann gewohnt, bis ich von zuhause fortgezogen bin.

Als ich noch bei meiner Familie wohnte, habe ich wie Du am Stadtrand gewohnt. So bin ich immer schnell sowohl im Grünen als auch in der Stadtmitte gewesen. In unserem Stadtviertel gab es sehr viele Einfamilienhäuser mit Gärten und fast keine Hochhäuser. Das habe ich immer sehr schön gefunden. Man hat meine Heimatstadt, München, schon immer die Großstadt mit Kleinstadtatmosphäre genannt.

In unsrem Viertel hat man nie etwas von der Anonymität der Großstadt gespürt. In der Schule oder im Sportverein haben sich die Jugendlichen der Gegend kennengelernt und Freundschaft geschlossen. Wenn ich Dir das alles schreibe, finde ich es fast schade, daß ich von diesem Zuhause fortgezogen bin.

Viele liebe Grüße,

Deine Gabi

(i) *Exercises – Section A*

The exercises in this section are concerned with comprehension and recognition, and they should be attempted before you look up explanations of vocabulary and grammar.

1. Comprehension questions
(a) Why does Gabi seem surprised to learn that Helen has always lived in a house?
(b) Where do most German families live, according to Gabi, if not in a house?
(c) How long did it take Gabi's parents to save up for a house?
(d) Something else surprises her about Helen's home life. What is this?
(e) What part of the town did Gabi live in?
(f) What does she think is special about Munich, where she lives?
(g) Gabi has left school and moved away from her parents' house now, but what does she feel as she looks back?

2. Word recognition Look through the letter and find the German words and phrases for the following:

    (a) I just cannot imagine.
    (b) Most families.
    (c) I was amazed.
    (d) District (of a town).
    (e) Home town.
    (f) Sports club.

(ii) *Explanations*

Select Vocabulary

sich vorstellen — to imagine
sich etwas leisten — to afford something
sparen — to save
verblüffen — to amaze
umziehen (o, o) — to move house
fortziehen (o, o) — to move away

das Stadtviertel (—) — district of a town
nennen (nannte, genannt) — to name
spüren — to feel
der Sportverein (—e) — sports club
(sich) kennenlernen — to get to know (one another)
das Zuhause — home

Note particularly vocabulary for places where you live:

die Wohnung (—en) — flat; apartment
die Eigentumswohnung (—en) — flat owned by the occupants
die Mietswohnung (—en) — rented flat

das Einfamilienhaus (¨er) — detached, one-family house
das Hochhaus (¨er) — high-rise block

Expressions and Idioms

ich kann mir gar nicht vorstellen — I just cannot imagine.
. . . können sich nur die reicheren Leute ein Haus leisten — only the richer people can afford a house

München — die Großstadt mit Kleinstadtatmosphäre

erst dann hatten meine Eltern genug Geld gespart — not until then had my parents saved enough money

bis ich von zuhause fortgezogen bin — until I moved away from home

sowohl im Grünen als auch in der Stadtmitte — out in the fields as well as in the town centre

(sie) haben Freundschaft geschlossen — (they) made friends

... finde ich es fast schade — I almost feel that it is a pity

Grammar

The following are the items of grammar of which there are examples in the text, and for which the Section B exercises provide practice. The references in parentheses give the section of the Grammar Summary where the particular points of grammar are explained.

(a) Letter writing (see section 6.4 of Part III).
(b) Perfect tense of weak and strong verbs (including Perfect of separable verbs) (12.6; 12.8(d)).
(c) Dative case after *in, bei, von, mit* (14.1).
(d) *als* and *wenn* clauses (13.2(a)).
(e) Possessive adjectives *mein, dein, unser, euer* (4(i)).

(iii) *Exercises – Section B*

1. The following sentences are in the Present tense. Rewrite them using the Perfect tense, remembering to choose the correct auxiliary verb, *haben* or *sein*.

   (a) Gabi schreibt von ihrer Familie und ihrem Haus.
   (b) Gabis Eltern sparen Geld für ein Haus.
   (c) Helen zieht sehr oft um.
   (d) Gabi zieht endlich von zuhause fort.
   (e) Sie ist immer schnell sowohl im Grünen als auch in der Stadtmitte.
   (f) Ich finde es schön in München.
   (g) Man nennt München die Großstadt mit Kleinstadtatmosphäre.
   (h) Die Jugendlichen der Gegend lernen sich kennen.

2. Rewrite each of the pairs of sentences below so that each becomes a single sentence, consisting of main clause + *als* or *wenn* clause as appropriate.

   Model 1: Wir wohnten in unserer ersten Wohnung. Wir hatten nur drei Zimmer.
   Response: Als wir in unserer ersten Wohnung wohnten, hatten wir nur drei Zimmer.
   Model 2: Die Familie hat genug Geld. Sie kauft ein neues Haus.
   Response: Wenn eine Familie genug Geld hat, kauft sie ein neues Haus.

   (a) Ich bin von unserer Wohnung fortgezogen. Wir haben ein neues Haus gekauft.
   (b) Ich wohnte bei meiner Familie. Ich habe am Stadtrand gewohnt.
   (c) Ich bin in München. Ich wohne bei meinen Eltern.
   (d) Ich habe in München gewohnt. Unser Haus war am Stadtrand.
   (e) Man wohnt in einem freundlichen Stadtviertel. Man spürt nichts von der Anonymität der Großstadt.
   (f) Ich schreibe Dir von meiner Kindheit. Ich finde es fast schade, daß ich von diesem Zuhause fortgezogen bin.

3. Write out the following sentences, inserting the correct Dative endings onto the possessive adjective (*mein, dein, unser, euer*).

   (a) Ich schreibe von mein — Haus und mein — Familie.
   (b) Wir haben schon immer in unser — Haus gewohnt.
   (c) Wohnst du noch bei dein — Eltern?
   (d) Ich bin mit mein — Familie umgezogen.
   (e) In unser — Viertel hat man nie etwas von der Anonymität der Großstadt gespürt.
   (f) Ich bin von mein — Zuhause fortgezogen.
   (g) Ihr habt mir von Eur — Haus geschrieben.

4. Write a letter to a German friend telling him or her about your family and the house where you live. Use some of the sentences in Gabi's letter to help you, and ask your German friend some questions also. Some of the following items may help you.

   Ich wohne in . . . . . . mit meiner Familie . . . . . . Ich habe dort . . . . . . Jahre gewohnt . . . . . . Als ich . . . . . . Jahre alt war, sind wir umgezogen . . . . . . Mein

Haus ist in der Stadtmitte/ im Grünen/ am Stadtrand . . . . . . Das Haus ist groß/ klein . . . . . . mit . . . . . . Zimmern . . . . . . Wie ist Dein Haus? . . . . . . Was . . . . . .? Wie viele . . . . . .?

1.2 Listening Materials 📼

Both the listening passages give you the chance to hear how people introduce themselves and talk about their families. With all the listening materials, try the comprehension exercises before you look at the written text.

1.2.1 Junge Leute stellen sich vor

When staying in Germany with a friend, you visit a youth club and meet some of the young people there. Listen to the statements made by individuals about themselves and their families, and then fill in the table to record the information you have heard. Finally, listen again and then check your answer with the written text.

(i) Hallo, ich bin Rolf Schmidt. Ich bin 18 Jahre alt. Mein Vater heißt Heinrich und meine Mutter Sophie. Ich habe einen Bruder, Karl, und eine Schwester, Gabi.

(ii) Grüß Gott. Ich komme aus München, und ich bin ein Einzelkind. Ich bin 17 Jahre alt, und wohne bei meiner Mutter, die Karin heißt. Mein Vater wohnt nicht mehr bei uns. Ich heiße Johann Weiß.

(iii) Ich bin Hans Schwarz, und ich habe viele Brüder und Schwestern. Zwei Brüder und eine Schwester sind älter als ich, und ich habe noch zwei jüngere Schwestern. Ich bin 16 Jahre alt und wohne in Süddeutschland. Meine Eltern heißen Hermann und Brigitte.

(iv) Ich heiße Jürgen und komme aus der Schweiz. Meine Familie besteht aus vier Personen; mein Vater Simon ist 45 Jahre alt, meine Mutter Greta ist etwas jünger. Ich bin 16 und meine Schwester Ursula ist 14.

Name	Age	How many brothers?	How many sisters?	Name of father	Name of mother
	18	1	1	Heinrich	Sophi
	17			Joron	Karen
	16	2	1	Hermen	Brigitte
	16	1	1	Zemon	Greta

1.2.2 Kennenlernen während einer Bahnfahrt

Karin: Das ist vielleicht eine langweilige Bahnfahrt. Ich fahre nicht gern mit dem Zug.

Martina: Ich auch nicht, und ich habe nicht mal Lust zum Lesen. Wo kommst du denn her?

Karin: Aus Rostock. Ich bin schon drei Stunden mit diesem Zug gefahren. Übrigens, ich heiße Karin.

Martina: Ich bin Tina. Zum Glück bin ich erst in Berlin eingestiegen. Wohin fährst du denn?

Karin: Nach Leipzig. Mein Studium fängt morgen an.

Martina: Das ist ja lustig. Ich fahre auch aus demselben Grund dahin. Was studierst denn du?

Karin: Mathematik, und du?

Martina: Journalistik. Das habe ich mir immer gewünscht.

Karin: Wieso? Ist dein Vater etwa ein Journalist?

Martina: Ja, und ich habe schon selbst ein bißchen für die Zeitung gearbeitet. Das macht mir wirklich Spaß. Was sind denn deine Eltern von Beruf?

Karin: Lehrer, das will ich auf keinen Fall werden.

Martina: Kann ich verstehen. Meine Mutter ist auch Lehrerin an einer Berufsschule. Da habe ich den Streß immer miterlebt.

Karin: Wo wohnst du denn in Berlin? Ich bin schon öfter mal dort gewesen.

Martina: Wir wohnen am Stadtrand. Wir haben eine Altbauwohnung in Friedrichshagen. Die Gegend ist ganz schön, nicht so überfüllt.

Karin: Das glaube ich. Wir wohnen in Evershagen. Das ist ein riesiges Neubauviertel bei Rostock. Da sieht ein Haus aus wie das andere. Aber wir haben eine schöne, große Vierzimmerwohnung. Ich habe nämlich noch drei Geschwister.

Martina: Oh, wie schön. Ich habe mir immer Geschwister gewünscht, aber meine Eltern haben es nie zu mehr Kindern außer mir gebracht. Bist du die Älteste?

Karin: Ja, wir sind wie die Orgelpfeifen, immer zwei Jahre auseinander. Meine Schwester und meine beiden Brüder gehen noch zur Schule. Das macht schon Spaß mit so einer großen Familie, aber manchmal habe ich mir auch gewünscht, ein Einzelkind zu sein. Da hast du wenigstens mal deine Ruhe und brauchst nicht immer alles zu teilen.

(i) *Comprehension — multiple choice* When you have listened to the conversation between Karin and Martina, select the correct answer from the four possibilities in each of the statements below:

1. Karin   (a) likes travelling by train.
         (b) never travels by train.
         (c) does not like train journeys.
         (d) does not read on train journeys.

2. Karin   (a) has already been on the train for three hours.
         (b) has still got three hours of her journey to go.
         (c) has had to wait three hours for her train.
         (d) is three hours late.

3. Martina (a) does not know what sort of work she wants to do.
         (b) has already done some work for the newspaper.
         (c) is reading a newspaper during the journey.
         (d) has a few newspapers with her.

4. Martina (a) lives in a nice district on the edge of Berlin.
         (b) lives in a nice district in the centre of Berlin.
         (c) lives in the old part of the town.
         (d) lives in a lovely country area.

5. Karin lives in a new development where
         (a) you can see houses all around.
         (b) you can look into your neighbours' houses.
         (c) one house looks very much like another.
         (d) there are very few other houses.

(ii) Listen to the tape again and write down the German expressions which are equivalent to the English given in parentheses below:

1. Ich fahre nicht gern mit dem Zug. (Nor do I).
2. Wo kommst du denn her? (From Rostock).
3. Wohin fährst du denn? (To Leipzig).

4. (What are you studying then?) Mathematik, und du?
5. Was sind deine Eltern von Beruf? (Teachers. I don't want to become one whatever happens.)
6. Die Gegend ist ganz schön. (I can just imagine).
7. Ich habe nämlich drei Geschwister. (Oh, that is nice!)

(iii) One of the characteristics of German conversations is the use of particles, words like *mal, doch, denn*, which can give a particular meaning to a question or statement. Read the section of the Grammar Summary (10) where the use of particles is explained; then try to find a good idiomatic English translation of the following sentences.

1. Wo kommst du denn her?
2. Übrigens, ich heiße Karin.
3. Wohin fährst du denn?
4. Das ist ja lustig.
5. Ist dein Vater etwa ein Journalist?
6. Ich bin schon öfter mal dort gewesen.
7. Ich habe nämlich noch drei Geschwister.
8. Das macht schon Spaß.
9. Da hast du wenigstens mal deine Ruhe.

(iv) *Role play*   Imagine yourself in a similar situation to the one in the dialogue and take your part in the following role play, asking questions and giving information about yourself.

Mitreisender: Ich fahre nicht gern mit dem Zug.
Sie: (Say nor do you. Ask where he comes from.)
Mitreisender: Aus Hamburg. Übrigens, ich heiße Rolf.
Sie: (Say what your name is, and say you are travelling to Munich.)
Mitreisender: Ich auch. Ich bin Student.
Sie: (Say so are you. You are English and learning German.)
Mitreisender: Sie sprechen schon gut Deutsch. Wo kommen Sie denn her?
Sie: (Say where you are from. Say you have already been on the train for three hours.)
Mitreisender: Bis München wird es noch eine weitere Stunde Fahrt sein. Ich war noch nie in England. Was ist das für eine Stadt, wo Sie wohnen?
Sie: (Say something about your town. Say that you live in the centre or at the edge of the town. Ask where he lives in Hamburg.)
Mitreisender: Am Stadtrand, in einer schönen Gegend. Haben Sie Geschwister?
Sie: (Say a little about your family.)
Mitreisender: Wie lange bleiben Sie in Deutschland?
Sie: (Say three weeks, with your pen-friend in Munich.)
Mitreisender: Also, viel Spaß!

1.2.3 Explanations

ich fahre nicht gern mit dem Zug — I do not like travelling by train
ich bin schon drei Stunden mit diesem Zug gefahren — I have already been travelling for three hours with this train
aus demselben Grund — for the same reason
das macht mir wirklich Spaß — I find that real fun
auf keinen Fall — under no circumstances
da sieht ein Haus wie das andere aus — one house looks like another there

... haben es nie zu mehr Kindern außer mir gebracht — ... never managed to
  have any children except me
wir sind wie die Orgelpfeifen — we are like the pipes of an organ
da hast du wenigstens mal deine Ruhe — at least, then, you have some peace and
  quiet

2 Transport und Reisen

2.1 Reading Materials

Learning foreign languages obviously involves travelling about quite a bit, using timetables, asking prices, and so on. The first of the reading passages suggests some of the things you would need to think about if you were travelling abroad by car. And what about Germans planning to come to Great Britain? The second passage shows you some of the information they can find out if they are planning a trip in this direction. The third passage tells about travelling by tram, a form of public transport which is still very popular in both the Federal Republic and the GDR, although trams are now very rare in Great Britain. The particular interest in the journey described in 2.1.3 is that it is the longest tram journey in the world.

2.1.1 Reisevorbereitung

Das sollten Sie Frühzeitig prüfen:

- Ist der Wagen in Ordnung?
- Sind Päße noch gültig?
- Haben Sie Reiseausweise für Kinder?
- Sind Impfungen erforderlich?
- Brauchen Sie einen internationalen Führerschein?
- Ist die grüne Versicherungskarte nötig?
- Haben Sie Straßenkarten und Reiseführer?

(i) *Comprehension Questions*

The first sentence in the above passage means: 'these are things you should check in plenty of time'. Bearing this in mind, and remembering that all these items

„Selbstverständlich sind alle unsere Modelle jederzeit fahrbereit"

© Loriot, Diogenes Verlag, Zürich

refer to a car journey which is being planned, see whether you can answer the following questions.

1. What is being asked about the car?
2. What do you think the word *Päße* means?
3. *Reiseausweise* are travel documents. Whose travel documents are referred to in the passage?
4. What are the words which mean 'driving licence' and 'insurance card'?
5. What other items of information are needed for the journey besides the ones mentioned already in these questions?
6. *Impfungen* are 'jabs' or 'inoculations'. What do you think might be the meaning of *sind Impfungen erforderlich*?

(ii) *Say it in German*

The short passage contains seven examples of questions where the verb comes first, as is also often the case in English. For example, *sind Päße noch gültig?* can be rendered directly as 'are passports still valid?' Another common way of making questions in English is to use the verb 'do', as in the question, 'do you need an international driving licence?' German does not have an equivalent to this construction, and simply inverts the verb and subject, as in the other examples: *brauchen Sie einen internationalen Führerschein?* Here are some statements using some of the same vocabulary as in the passage. Rewrite these statements as questions.

1. Der Wagen ist nicht in Ordnung.
2. Päße sind erforderlich.
3. Die Reiseausweise für die Kinder sind noch gültig.
4. Sie brauchen eine grüne Versicherungskarte.
5. Straßenkarten sind nötig.
6. Sie haben schon einen internationalen Führerschein.
7. Reiseausweise und Impfungen sind erforderlich.

2.1.2 Der schnelle Weg nach Großbritannien

Sie haben als Ihr Urlaubsziel Großbritannien ausgewählt. Oder dort einen Gesprächstermin abgestimmt. Oder Sie wollen einfach zum Shopping nach London fahren. Nur Ihr Reiseweg steht noch nicht fest. Wir helfen Ihnen dabei. Wählen Sie den schnellen, bequemen und preiswerten Weg mit Bahn und Schiff über Oostende nach Dover. Von vielen deutschen Großstädten kommen Sie ohne umzusteigen an den Kanal, mit allen Annehmlichkeiten, die eine Bahnreise bieten kann.

Fahrpreisbeispiele nach London (Victoria) über Aachen-Süd — Oostende — Dover

VON	einfach 2. Klasse	1. Klasse	Hin- und Rückfahrt 2. Klasse	1. Klasse
Berlin	DM 195,80	DM 272,50	DM 361,00	DM 499,00
Bonn	116,60	154,70	230,60	305,60
Düsseldorf	118,60	156,70	234,60	309,60
Frankfurt	145,60	196,70	274,60	369,60
Hamburg	176,60	243,70	328,60	449,60
Hannover	156,60	213,70	294,60	399,60

In London fahren Sie am besten mit London Transport. London, eine der eindrucksvollsten und faszinierendsten Städte, lernt man am besten mit London Transport kennen. Unser U-Bahn und Busnetz wird täglich von Millionen Londonern benutzt und ist das praktischste, billigste, sicherste und schnellste Verkehrsmittel in der englischen Hauptstadt.

Egal, was für Pläne Sie haben — denken Sie daran, daß Sie in London am besten mit London Transport fahren.

(i) *Comprehension Questions*

1. Give three reasons mentioned at the beginning of the passage to suggest why a German visitor might want to visit London.
2. What methods of transport are suggested to get to London?
3. Is it always necessary to change trains before reaching the Channel?
4. What is the best way of getting to know London, according to the passage?
5. What are four good reasons given for using London Transport?

(ii) *Using Sie, Ihr, Ihnen*

In the previous passage there were examples of how to put questions using the polite form *Sie*. In this passage there are further examples of *Sie*, and associated parts of speech, such as the Dative form *Ihnen* and the possessive adjective *Ihr* ('your'). Note particularly how to use the Imperative form of *Sie* — that is to say, the form used for giving commands. For example, *wählen Sie* = 'choose!'

In the sentences listed on the left below, someone is asking for information. The answers to the various requests are given in the Imperative, but they have been jumbled up. Write out the request and choose from the list the command which best suits the request. For example, the answer to the request *wie fahre ich am besten in London?* would be *fahren Sie mit London Transport*.

1. Welches Urlaubsziel soll ich wählen?	Fahren Sie mit London Transport.
2. Mein Reiseweg steht nicht fest. Wie soll ich fahren?	Lernen Sie nur London kennen.
3. Soll ich mit dem Flugzeug fahren?	Wählen Sie Großbritannien.
4. Ich habe Großstädte nicht gern.	Nein, fahren Sie mit der Bahn.
5. Wie fahre ich am besten in London?	Fahren Sie über Oostende nach Dover.

(iii) *Explanations*

Select Vocabulary

das Urlaubsziel (—e) — holiday goal/destination
der Gesprächstermin (—e) — business appointment for a talk
bequem — comfortable
preiswert — good value
die Annehmlichkeit (—en) — amenity

die Bahnreise (—n) — train journey
U-Bahn und Busnetz — underground and bus network
benutzen — to use
das Verkehrsmittel (—) — means of transport

Expressions and Idioms

Sie haben einen Gesprächstermin abgestimmt — you have arranged a business appointment
wir helfen Ihnen dabei — we shall help you (with your arrangements)
ohne umzusteigen — without changing

eine der eindrucksvollsten und faszinierendsten Städte — one of the most impressive and most fascinating towns

unser U-Bahn und Busnetz wird täglich . . . benutzt — our underground and bus network is used daily

egal, was für Pläne Sie haben — it does not matter what your plans are

Grammar

Imperative and other forms of *Sie*. See Grammar Summary, section 7.2(a).

2.1.3 Umsteigen, bitte!

Unsere Reporter träumten einen Kindertraum. Sie wollten mit der längsten Straßenbahnlinie der Welt fahren. Und sie fuhren 115 Kilometer kreuz und quer durch das Ruhrgebiet von Düsseldorf bis nach Dortmund. Hier ist ihr Bericht.

Unsere Fahrt begann in Düsseldorf. Wir parkten unser Auto in der Tiefgarage unter dem Jan-Wellem-Platz. Oben wartete die Linie 79 Richtung Duisburg. Laut und schwankend fuhr die Bahn in Richtung Norden. Die Fahrt über die alten Gleise erinnerte an die ersten Trambahnen in den Städten vor 80 Jahren.

Hinter Lohausen, zwischen Düsseldorf und Duisburg, wurde es leiser. Der Zug fuhr neben der Straße mitten durch Äcker und Wiesen. Duisburg begann für uns dort, wo die Linie 79 zur Hochbahn wird, und alle Straßen auf Pfeilern und Brücken überquert. Von hier aus ist es nicht mehr weit zum Hauptbahnhof.

Schräg gegenüber hielt die Linie 901. Sie war vorher an Europas größtem Binnenhafen vorbeigefahren, an den mächtigen Stahlwerken am Rhein und an Wohngebieten in den Stadtteilen Hamborn und Ruhrort. Die Bahn fuhr über die Ruhr. Noch vor zehn Jahren war der Fluß sehr verschmutzt. Heute wachsen Seerosen darauf. Wir stiegen wieder um in die Bahn nach Essen. Sie fuhr in der

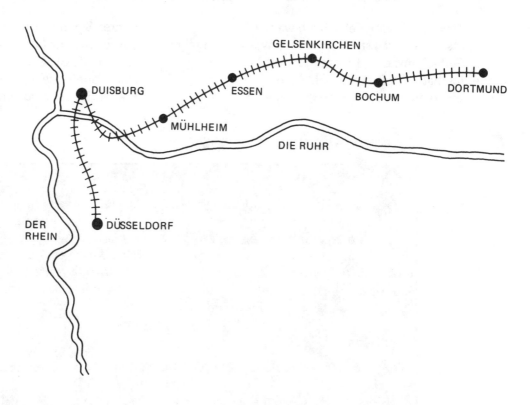

Die längste Straßenbahnlinie der Welt

16

Schnell und sicher durch den Verkehr — mit der Straßenbahn

Mitte der breiten Bundesstraße 1. Essen war einmal die größte Bergbaustadt des europäischen Kontinents. Noch um 1800 lebten hier kaum 3000 Einwohner. In wenigen Jahrzehnten wurde aus Essen eine qualmende, lärmende Industriestadt, beherrscht von Kohle und Stahl. Heute ändert sich Essen wieder, diesmal zur Gartenstadt.

Zehn Kilometer waren es bis Gelsenkirchen. Wieder wurde es grau. Die Linie 127 fuhr endlos durch die monotone Industrievorstadt. Draußen regnete es. In der 302 von Gelsenkirchen nach Bochum waren die Wagen überfüllt. Und so ging es weiter, bis die Linie 409 uns bis zum Endpunkt unserer Reise brachte, zum Stadtrand von Dortmund. Sechs Stunden dauerte unsere Fahrt über 115 Kilometer und mehr als 200 Haltestellen. Die Schnellbahn von Dortmund nach Düsseldorf brachte uns in etwa einer Stunde zurück. Unter dem Jan-Wellem-Platz wartete unser Auto.

© *Scala Jugendmagazin*, Dezember 1980

(i) *Exercises – Section A*

The exercises in this section are concerned with comprehension and recognition, and they should be attempted before you look at explanations of grammar or vocabulary.

1. *Comprehension questions*
   (a) What did the reporters want to do?
   (b) When they had parked their car, what did they do?
   (c) What was it like travelling in the first tram?
   (d) What happened to the tramlines as they arrived on the outskirts of Duisburg?
   (e) Where did they catch tram number 901?
   (f) Where had this tram travelled, before getting to the place where they caught it?
   (g) What difference is there between the river Ruhr ten years ago and now?
   (h) How is Essen different now from what it used to be?
   (i) What sort of impression do they have of the outskirts of Gelsenkirchen?
   (j) Where, exactly, is the end of their journey?
   (k) How did they get back to their car, and how long did it take them to return?

2. *Word recognition*   Look through the passage and find the German words and phrases equivalent to the following:

   (a) all over the Ruhrgebiet.
   (b) diagonally opposite.
   (c) Europe's biggest inland harbour.
   (d) very polluted.
   (e) and so it went on.
   (f) in approximately an hour.

   (ii)   **Explanations**

Select Vocabulary

träumen — to dream
der Bericht (—e) — report
schwankend — swaying
das Gleis (—e) — rail, tramline
erinnern (an + Acc.) — to remind
fahren (u, a) — to travel
der Pfeiler (—) — pillar; pier (of a bridge)

überqueren — to cross over
verschmutzt — polluted
die Seerose (—n) — water-lily
qualmend — smoking
lärmend — noisy
sich ändern — to change

Expressions and Idioms

kreuz und quer durch das Ruhrgebiet — all over the Ruhrgebiet
in Richtung Norden — towards the north
von hier aus — from here; from this point
schräg gegenüber — diagonally opposite
sie war vorher an Europas größtem Binnenhafen vorbeigefahren — previously, it had travelled past Europe's biggest inland port
noch vor zehn Jahren — ten years ago . . . was still . . .
und so ging es weiter — and so it went on
in etwa einer Stunde — in approximately one hour

Grammar

The following are the items of grammar of which there are examples in the text, and for which the Section B exercises provide practice. The references in parentheses give the section of the Grammar Summary where the particular points of grammar are explained.

> (a) Imperfect tense (12.8(c)).
> (b) Use of prepositions with Accusative and Dative cases (14.1; 14.2).
> (c) Superlative of adjectives and adverbs. See also examples in text 2.1.2 (6(b), (c)).

(iii) *Exercises – Section B*

1. The following passage is taken from the original text, but has been rewritten in the Present tense. Without looking back at the text, write this passage out, using the Imperfect tense for all verbs underlined, and then check your version with the original.

   Hinter Lohausen <u>wird</u> es leiser. Der Zug <u>fährt</u> neben der Straße mitten durch Äcker und Wiesen. . . Die Bahn <u>fährt</u> über die Ruhr. Wir <u>steigen</u> wieder um in die Bahn nach Essen. Sie <u>fährt</u> in der Mitte der breiten Bundesstraße 1. Wieder <u>wird</u> es grau. Draußen <u>regnet</u> es. Von Gelsenkirchen nach Bochum <u>sind</u> die Wagen überfüllt. Und so <u>geht</u> es weiter, bis die Linie 409 uns zum Endpunkt unserer Reise <u>bringt</u>.

2. In the following two passages, one taken from text 2.1.2 and the other from text 2.1.3, the prepositions have been omitted. In the first passage you are required to rewrite the passage, including the appropriate prepositions chosen from the list given below the passage. In the second passage you are required to choose the correct prepositions in the same way, and also to put the correct endings on the following words, according to whether they are in the Dative or the Accusative case.

   (a) Sie wollen zum Shopping . . . . . . London fahren. Wählen Sie den schnellen Weg . . . . . . Bahn und Schiff . . . . . . Oostende . . . . . . Dover. In London fahren Sie am besten . . . . . . London Transport. Unser U-Bahn and Busnetz ist das billigste Verkehrsmittel . . . . . . der englischen Hauptstadt. Denken Sie daran, daß Sie . . . . . . London am besten . . . . . . London Transport fahren.

   > Choose from the following prepositions: *in; nach; mit; über.*

   (b) Unsere Reporter wollten . . . . . . d— längst— Straßenbahnlinie der Welt fahren. Sie fuhren kreuz und quer . . . . . . d— Ruhrgebiet . . . . . . Düsseldorf . . . . Dortmund. Die Fahrt . . . . . . d— alt— Gleise erinnerte . . . . . . d— erst— Trambahnen . . . . . . d— Städten . . . . . . 80 Jahren.

   > . . . . . . Düsseldorf und Duisburg wurde es leiser. Der Zug fuhr . . . . . . d— Straße . . . . . . Äcker und Wiesen. Von hier . . . . . . ist es nicht mehr weit . . . . . . Hauptbahnhof. Schräg . . . . . . hielt die Linie 901. Sie war vorher . . . . . . Europas größt— Binnenhafen vorbeigefahren. Die Bahn fuhr über d— Ruhr.

   > Choose from the following prepositions: von; zwischen; über; mit; vor; neben; aus; zum; an; durch; gegenüber; bis nach; in; mitten durch.

3. *Comparative and superlative of adjectives and adverbs* Look again at the table of fare prices from German towns to London, which is given on page 14. Make up sentences on the basis of the information given in that table to say which journeys are cheaper or more expensive than others, or which are the cheapest and the most expensive journeys. You should use the adjectives *billig* ('cheap') or *preiswert* ('good value') and *teuer* ('expensive') in their comparative and superlative forms. For example: *die einfache Fahrt von Hamburg nach London ist billiger als die einfache Fahrt von Frankfurt nach London. Die Hin- und Rückfahrt von Berlin nach London ist teurer als von Bonn nach London. Die teuerste Fahrt ist erster Klasse hin und zurück von Berlin nach London.* Now make up similar sentences with the following suggestions:

(a) Die billigste Fahrt ist . . . . . .

(b) Die einfache Fahrt von Düsseldorf nach London ist . . . . . . Frankfurt . . . . . .

(c) Die Hin- und Rückfahrt von Hannover nach London ist . . . . . . Bonn . . . . . .

(d) Die Hin- und Rückfahrt erster Klasse von Berlin nach London ist . . . . . .

Practise making further comparisons of this kind.

4. The approximate distances in kilometres between the German towns mentioned and London are as follows:

Berlin 1093 km; Bonn 540 km; Düsseldorf 600 km; Frankfurt 782 km; Hamburg 985 km; Hannover 900 km.

Using this extra information, use the comparative and superlative of the adjectives *lang, kurz* to make statements modelled on the following: *die längste Fahrt ist die Fahrt von . . . . . . nach London; von . . . . . . nach London ist kürzer als von . . . . . .*

5. Look through texts 2.1.2 and 2.1.3 and make a list of all superlatives you can find. Then make short sentences using the adjective and an appropriate noun from the list below. For example: *Die Straßenbahnlinie von Düsseldorf nach Dortmund ist die längste der Welt.*

Weg; Stadt; Verkehrsmittel; Hafen; Straßenbahnlinie; Hauptstadt; Bergbaustadt.

6. Below are two lists. On the left is a list of adverbs or adjectives; they have the same form, but for the purpose of this exercise we are thinking of their adverbial use. On the right are various forms of transport. Make up sentences using the superlative of the adverb and the verb *fahren*. For example: *am billigsten fährt man mit der Straßenbahn.*

schnell   Flugzeug
bequem   Zug
preiswert   D-Zug
praktisch   Fahrrad
sicher   Taxi
teuer   Autobus
langsam   Straßenbahn

2.2   Listening Materials 📼

In the reading materials you have already read about several forms of travel. In the listening materials we shall concentrate on travelling by rail. In the first passage you will hear a series of station announcements; the dialogues which follow are concerned with booking tickets and getting information about a journey.

2.2.1 Bahnhofsansagen

— Achtung auf Gleis 3! Der Orientexpress von München nach Belgrad fährt ein.

— Achtung auf Gleis 2! Die Türen schließen! Der Zug fährt ab.

— Achtung, Reisende! Der Schnellzug von München nach Mailand hat voraussichtlich 25 Minuten Verspätung.

— Achtung, Reisende! Wir bitten Sie die Fahrplanänderungen, die an Schalter 1 aushängen, zu beachten.

— Achtung, Reisende! Wegen Bauarbeiten entlang der Bahnlinie wird der Schnellzug von Ulm nach Karlsruhe voraussichtlich 10 Minuten länger Aufenthalt haben.

(i) *Comprehension Questions*

1. What is happening on platform 3? *leaving*
2. Why must travellers on platform 2 close the doors? *train is leaving*
3. What do you think the word *Achtung!* means? *attention*
4. Which train is 25 minutes late?
5. There have been some changes to the timetable. Where can passengers read the notice that gives them this information?
6. The express from Karlsruhe to Ulm has to stay ten minutes longer in the station. Why is this?

2.2.2 Auf dem Bahnhof

Christa: Guten Tag!

Beamter: Guten Tag!

Christa: Können Sie mir bitte den nächsten Zug nach Köln sagen?

Beamter: Der nächste Zug nach Köln fährt um elf Uhr fünfundzwanzig.

Christa: Naja, und muß ich umsteigen oder fährt der direkt?

Beamter: Das ist ein D-Zug. Er fährt direkt über Bonn nach Köln. Sie brauchen nicht umzusteigen.

Christa: Ich möchte später heute nachmittag zurückkommen. Fährt ein Zug so um siebzehn Uhr zurück?

Beamter: Also, ab Köln fährt ein Zug um siebzehn Uhr zwanzig, aber dann müssen Sie in Bonn umsteigen. Am besten wäre der Zug um siebzehn Uhr vierundvierzig. Der fährt direkt.

Christa: Und wann kommt er an?

Beamter: Um neunzehn Uhr zehn.

Christa: Vielen Dank. Könnten Sie vielleicht das alles aufschreiben?

Beamter: Ja. Also, ab Koblenz um elf Uhr fünfundzwanzig. Der Zug fährt auf Gleis vier. Ankunft in Köln um zwölf Uhr siebenundvierzig. Rückfahrt ab Köln entweder mit dem Zug um siebzehn Uhr zwanzig, oder siebzehn Uhr vierundvierzig.

Christa: Gibt es vielleicht eine Tagesrückfahrkarte?

Beamter: Ja. Wenn man am gleichen Tag zurückkommt, kostet das fünf Mark weniger.

Christa: Vielen Dank. Kann ich hier die Fahrkarte lösen?

Beamter: Nein, hier ist nur Auskunft. Für die Fahrkarte müssen Sie zum Fahrkartenschalter gehen.

Christa: Vielen Dank. Auf Wiedersehen.

Beamter: Bitte schön. Auf Wiedersehen.

(i) *Multiple Choice*

When you have listened to the conversation between Christa and the station official, select the correct answer from the four possibilities in each of the statements below.

1. Christa wants to know (a) the time of the next train to Cologne. *11.25*
                         (b) the next train due from Cologne.
                         (c) the nearest station to Cologne.
                         (d) the time her train arrives in Cologne.
2. If she takes the 11.25 (a) she will have to change at Bonn.
                         (b) she will travel direct to Bonn.

(c) she will not need to change. ✓

(d) she can change if she wishes.

3. Christa is planning

(a) to come back later that day.

(b) to come back the following day.

(c) to be back by the early afternoon.

(d) to catch a train at about seven.

Auf dem Bahnhof

(ii) *Comprehension Questions*

1. Why would the 17.20 train from Cologne not be so good as the later train for the return journey?
2. When he has given her the information, what does Christa then ask the official to do?
3. What are the advantages of a day-return ticket?
4. What does the official reply when she asks whether she can buy her ticket there?

(iii) *Role Play*

You are staying in Hameln, and decide to take a day trip by train to Braunschweig. You go to the information desk to find out about times of trains.

You: (Ask when the next train leaves for Braunschweig.)

Beamter: Der nächste Zug fährt um zehn Uhr fünfzehn.

You: (Ask whether it is direct or whether you must change.)

Beamter: Der Zug fährt direkt nach Braunschweig.

You: (Ask whether there is a train back at about 5.0 p.m.)

Beamter: Ab Braunschweig fährt ein Zug um siebzehn Uhr zwanzig.

You: (Ask what time it arrives in Braunschweig.)

Beamter: Um achtzehn Uhr achtundfünfzig.

You: (Ask whether he could please write down the details for you.)

Beamter: Ja, hier haben Sie es aufgeschrieben.

You: (Thank him and say goodbye.)

2.2.3 Explanations (Listening Texts 2.2.1 and 2.2.2)

... hat voraussichtlich 25 Minuten Verspätung — is expected to be 25 minutes late

wegen Bauarbeiten — because of building work

... wird der Schnellzug voraussichtlich 10 Minuten länger Aufenthalt haben — the
    express is expected to remain in the station for ten more minutes

Sie brauchen nicht umzusteigen — you don't need to change

am besten wäre der Zug um siebzehn Uhr vierundvierzig — the best train would be
    the 17.44

könnten Sie das alles aufschreiben? — could you write it all down?

kann ich hier die Fahrkarte lösen? — can I buy the ticket here?

3 Ferien

3.1 Reading Materials

With no fewer than four German-speaking countries to choose from, there is every possibility you can imagine for a holiday. The first passage below is a post-card from someone on holiday in Austria. Then there is an extract from a brochure persuading you to visit Ulm in the southern part of the Bundesrepublik. The report from the GDR is about a different sort of holiday. It is quite popular in the GDR for families to spend their holiday at a holiday home run by a trade union. The last passage is a letter from someone wanting to book at a hotel in Switzerland — holidays in all four German-speaking countries are represented here.

3.1.1 Eine Postkarte aus Innsbruck

Wir haben schönes Wetter in Innsbruck. Gestern sind wir in den Bergen gewandert. Gestern Abend waren wir in der Altstadt. Unser Programm heute: Stadtbummel, Einkäufe, abends Theater. Und morgen ist unser schönes Wochenende schon vorbei.
 	
  Viele Grüße
   Caroline und Heinz
	Familie John Brown,
	5 School Road,
	Chudleigh,
	Devon,
	England.

(i) *Comprehension Questions*

1. Where are Caroline and Heinz spending their holiday break?
2. How long are they there for?
3. Are they lucky with the weather?
4. What are they doing on the day they write their card?
5. Where will they be going that evening?

(ii) *Say it in German*

1. Find the German words or phrases for the following: yesterday; yesterday evening; today; tomorrow; fine weather.
2. Write a post-card in German to a friend, using not more than 20 words. Use some of the ideas from the one above, or make it up completely. You can use short phrases, as in the Innsbruck post-card; not all that you say has to be in complete sentences.

3.1.2 Fahr mit nach Ulm!

Ja, kommen Sie mal auf ein Wochenende nach Ulm an die Donau. Sie werden überrascht sein, was diese Stadt Ihnen bietet. Schon von weitem begrüßt Sie das weltbekannte Münster mit dem höchsten Kirchturm der Erde. Willkommen in Ulm!

Ob Sie nun mit der Bahn, mit dem Reisebus oder im eigenen Auto kommen, am Münsterplatz treffen sich unsere Gäste aus allen Himmelsrichtungen, um Ulmer Spezialitäten kennenzulernen.

Zum Beispiel unsere romantische Altstadt mit prächtigen Bauten und hübschen Brunnen. Daneben das malerische Fischerviertel mit reizvollen, engen Gassen, Brücken und Plätzen.

Spazieren Sie mal auf der Stadtmauer, oder erleben Sie den Ulmer Wochenmarkt: jeden Samstag auf dem Münsterplatz. Machen Sie einen Einkaufsbummel durch die Stadt — über 1000 Geschäfte lassen keinen Wunsch unerfüllt.

Danach eine Pause? Am besten bei Köstlichkeiten der schwäbischen Küche in unseren gemütlichen Wirtshäusern. Und am Abend? Ob Sie gerne tanzen oder lieber ins Theater gehen, gibt es hier zahlreiche Tanzlokale und zwei Theater.

Sie sehen, ein Wochenende in Ulm lohnt sich.
WILLKOMMEN IN ULM!

(i) *Comprehension Questions*

1. Which river does Ulm stand on?
2. Why is the minster church world-famous?
3. What can one see in the old town?
4. When and where does the weekly market take place?
5. What sort of things are served in the inns?
6. What sort of things are there if you want an evening out?

(ii) *Practice with Prepositions*

Read the passage again and also section 14 in the Grammar Summary. Then, without looking back at the text, see whether you can fill in the correct prepositions in the gaps below, choosing from the list of prepositions given.

1. *Places*
   (a) Kommen Sie . . . . . . Ulm.
   (b) Willkommen . . . . . . Ulm.
   (c) . . . . . . Münsterplatz treffen sich unsere Gäste.
   (d) Spazieren Sie mal . . . . . . der Stadtmauer.
   (e) Machen Sie einen Einkaufsbummel . . . . . . die Stadt.
   (f) Ob Sie gerne tanzen oder lieber . . . . . . Theater gehen.

   in; ins; auf; durch; nach; am.

2. *Transport*
   Ob Sie nun . . . . . . der Bahn, ... dem Reisebus, oder . . . . . . eigenen Auto kommen.

   mit; im.

3. *Time*
   (a) Kommen Sie mal . . . . . . ein Wochenende nach Ulm.
   (b) Und . . . . . . Abend?

   auf; am.

Schon von weitem begrüßt Sie das weltbekannte Ulmer Münster

4. Read the section in the Grammar Summary (7.2(d)) explaining the formation of forms like *danach* and *daneben*. Then attempt the following exercise.
   Model: Hier ist die Altstadt, und neben der Altstadt ist das Fischerviertel.
   Response: Hier ist die Altstadt, und daneben ist das Fischerviertel.

(a) Wir machen einen Einkaufsbummel, und nach dem Einkaufsbummel machen wir eine Pause.
(b) Am Münsterplatz ist ein Schild aufgestellt, und auf dem Schild steht: ,,jeden Samstag Wochenmarkt''.
(c) Ich habe ein Päckchen bekommen, und in dem Päckchen war ein Reiseführer von Ulm.

(iii) *Explanations*

kommen Sie mal auf ein Wochenende nach Ulm — just come for a week-end to Ulm

ob Sie nun mit der Bahn fahren, oder . . . — whether you travel by train, or . . .

aus allen Himmelsrichtungen — from all points of the compass

jeden Samstag — every Saturday

ob Sie gerne tanzen oder lieber ins Theater gehen — whether you like dancing or prefer to go to the theatre

ein Wochenende in Ulm lohnt sich — a week-end in Ulm is worth it

3.1.3 Fünf zogen aus, Ferien zu machen

Ein Bericht aus dem FDGB Erholungsheim „August Bebel", Friedrichroda, in dem sich große Familien besonders wohl fühlen.

Sonne und Schnee konnten noch so sehr locken, als erstes eroberten die fünf Roggenbucks im Feriendomizil die Schwimmhalle. „Als wir die Nachricht erhielten, daß Badesachen mitzubringen sind, war vor allem bei unseren Kindern das Hallo groß," erzählt der Berliner Elektro-Monteur Jörg Roggenbuck. Schwimmen wird in seiner Familie das ganze Jahr über großgeschrieben. Und die Aussicht darauf verdoppelte ihre Vorfreude auf den Winterurlaub. Bis zur Abfahrt waren die neunjährige Nicolle, der sechsjährige Raik und vor allem das vierjährige Kraftbündel Denny kaum noch zu bremsen.

Das Ehepaar empfindet es als besonders wohltuend, wie ihnen das Heim entgegenkommt. Zwei Zimmer, verbunden durch eine Tür, stehen Roggenbucks zur Verfügung. „Die Kinder sind ungestörter, wir auch. Zu fünft in einem Zimmer verlangt große Rücksichtnahme. Das wissen wir von anderen Ferienaufenthalten aus eigener Erfahrung."

Erfreulich, daß man bereits beim Bau neuer Heime sehr familienfreundlich plant und denkt. Im „August-Bebel" Heim, einem der größten in unserem Land, sind von den rund 1500 Gästen, die es in jedem Durchgang beherbergt, ungefähr 500 Kinder. Das quirlt, schwätzt, hopst und kichert, das schwirrt durch die Gänge und Räume. Betrieb wie in einem Bienenhaus.

Seit Eröffnung des Hauses 1980 haben sich hier schon 120 000 Werktätige erholt, und sicher ebenso geschwärmt, wie die Roggenbucks: „Es ist wie im Interhotel, nur viel billiger."

Ferien in Familie — Roggenbucks geniessen sie und können es sich schöner nicht vorstellen. Dann werden andere Gäste die Annehmlichkeiten des Heims geniessen. Denn für große Familien ist durchgehend Saison.

Angelika Hassler

© *Für Dich*, 11/85

(i) *Exercises — Section A*

The exercises in this section are concerned with comprehension and recognition, and they should be attempted before you look at explanations of grammar or vocabulary.

1. *Falsch oder Richtig*   Decide which of the following statements are true or false, according to the text.
   (a) Die Familie Roggenbuck ging zuerst schwimmen.
   (b) Die Kinder waren besonders froh, weil sie schwimmen konnten.
   (c) Die Roggenbucks gingen im Sommer in Urlaub.
   (d) Herr und Frau Roggenbuck haben drei Kinder im Alter von vier bis neun Jahren.

(e) Die Familie hat ein Familienzimmer im Erholungsheim.

(f) Ein Drittel aller Gäste im Heim sind Kinder.

(g) Das Haus ist 1980 eröffnet worden.

(h) Die Roggenbucks möchten ihre Ferien lieber anderswo verbringen.

2. *Synonyms and definitions* Find words in the text corresponding to the following definitions:

(a) Im Krieg nehmen; gewinnen.

(b) Verlangsamen; zurückhalten.

(c) Angenehm.

(d) Günstig.

(e) Nachtlager geben.

(f) Wieder zu Kräften kommen.

(g) Bequemlichkeit.

(ii) **Explanations**

Select Vocabulary

der Bericht (—e) — report

das Erholungsheim (—e) — rest home; holiday home

FDGB (Freier Deutscher Gewerkschaftsbund) — GDR trade union organisation

locken — to entice

erobern — to conquer

die Aussicht (—en) — prospect

die Vorfreude (—n) — pleasurable anticipation

bremsen — to brake

die Rücksichtnahme — consideration

die Erfahrung (—en) — experience

beherbergen — to accommodate

quirlen — to twirl

schwatzen — to chatter

hopsen — to hop

kichern — to giggle

schwirren — to buzz

der Betrieb (—e) — activity; bustle

der Werktätige (—n) — working person

schwärmen (für) — to be enthusiastic (about)

geniessen (o, o) — to enjoy

die Annehmlichkeit (—en) — amenity; comfort

Expressions and Idioms

Sonne und Schnee konnten noch so sehr locken — sun and snow could be as enticing as they liked

. . . war bei unseren Kindern das Hallo groß — there was a terrific hullabaloo from the children

Schwimmen wird . . . großgeschrieben — swimming is regarded as very important

sie waren kaum noch zu bremsen — they could hardly be kept in check

zwei Zimmer stehen Roggenbucks zur Verfügung — two rooms are at the disposal of the Roggenbucks

zu fünft in einem Zimmer — five of us together in a room

sie können es sich schöner nicht vorstellen — they cannot imagine it any nicer

für große Familien ist durchgehend Saison — the holiday season is continuous for big families

Grammar

The following are the items of grammar of which there are examples in the text, and for which the Section B exercises provide practice. The references in parentheses give the section of the Grammar Summary where the particular points are explained.

(a) Subordinate clause construction after *als; daß* (13.2(a); 15(b) 2).
(b) Some uses of the Genitive case (1.5(c)).
(c) Reflexive verbs (7.2(e)).

(iii)   *Exercises — Section B*

1. Following the model below, rewrite the sentences so that they make use of a subordinate clause introduced by *als:*

Model: Wir erhielten die Nachricht, und das Hallo war groß.
Response: Als wir die Nachricht erhielten, war des Hallo groß.

(a) Wir kamen an das Erholungsheim, und wir eroberten als erstes die Schwimmhalle.
(b) Man plante das Heim familienfreundlich und baute Zimmer für die Kinder.
(c) Das Haus wurde 1980 eröffnet, und viele Gäste kamen sofort.

2. Here are some statements about the holiday home where the Roggenbuck family spent their holiday:

Badesachen sind mitzubringen.
Schwimmen wird großgeschrieben.
Man plant und denkt familienfreundlich.
120 000 Werktätige haben sich hier erholt.

Now make sentences from these statements, introduced by one of the phrases given below. Remember to change the word order after *daß.*

Model: Ich weiß, daß Badesachen mitzubringen sind.

(a) Erfreulich, daß . . . . . .
(b) Wir erhielten die Nachricht, daß . . . . . .
(c) Wir wissen, daß . . . . . .
(d) Wir freuen uns, daß . . . . . .

3. There are two phrases in the text which use the Genitive case, *beim Bau neuer Heime* and *die Annehmlichkeiten des Heims.* Using these as a pattern to follow, make up further short phrases of the same kind by linking an item from the left-hand column below with an item from the right-hand column, remembering that the latter must be put into the Genitive.

(a) beim Bau   moderne Wohnblocks
                                    neue Heime
                                    schöne, neue Wohnungen
                                    familienfreundliche Ferienheime
(b) die Annehmlichkeiten   das neue Heim
                                    der schöne Ort
                                    das moderne Hotel
                                    die malerische Stadt

4. Answer the following questions in German, using a reflexive verb chosen from the following three verbs: *sich erholen; sich vorstellen; sich wohl fühlen.*

(a) Wie fühlen sich die Roggenbucks im Heim?
(b) Was machen Werktätige hier im Heim?
(c) Was für schönere Ferien möchten die Roggenbucks haben?

29

3.1.4 Brief an ein Hotel

Sehr geehrte Damen und Herren,

ich habe Ihre Adresse einem Hotelverzeichnis entnommen, in dem alle Hotels in der Nähe des Vierwaldstättersees aufgelistet sind. Ich würde gerne im Sommer nächsten Jahres zwei Wochen bei Ihnen verbringen und möchte Sie deshalb fragen, ob Sie vom 10. Juli bis zum 24. Juli noch ein Doppelzimmer mit Bad und WC freihaben. Es ist mir sehr wichtig, daß das Zimmer eine ruhige Lage hat. Wenn möglich hätte ich auch gern ein Zimmer mit Balkon und Blick auf den See.

Könnten Sie mir bitte den Preis für eine Übernachtung mit Frühstück pro Person und Nacht mitteilen? Besteht in Ihrem Hotel auch die Möglichkeit, Zimmer mit Halb- oder Vollpension zu buchen? Oder ist Ihrem Hotel ein Restaurant angeschlossen, in dem Hotelgäste ihr Menü frei zusammenstellen können?

Ich möchte Sie bitten, mir einen Prospekt von Ihrem Hotel zu schicken, dem ich die genaue Lage und Größe des Hotels, die Art der Ausstattung von Zimmern und Aufenthaltsräumen und eine Beschreibung der Anfahrtswege entnehmen kann.

Da ich mit dem Wagen ankommen werde, wäre es für mich auch wichtig, zu wissen, ob Sie einen bewachten Hotelparkplatz haben, oder ob es zumindest Parkmöglichkeiten in der Nähe Ihres Hauses gibt.

Der Vierwaldstättersee in der Zentralschweiz

Ferner möchte ich Sie bitten, mir Informationen über das Gebiet zu schicken. Gibt es viele Sehenswürdigkeiten? Was für Sport- und Wandermöglichkeiten gibt es? Besteht die Möglichkeit, am See Segelboote auszuleihen? Bieten die Orte Unterhaltung am Abend, und welcher Art ist diese Unterhaltung?

Vielen Dank für Ihre Mühe,

Gabriele Münzer

(i) *Exercises – Section A*

The exercises in this section are concerned with comprehension and recognition, and they should be attempted before you look at explanations of grammar or vocabulary.

1. *Comprehension questions*
    (a) How did Gabriele find the name of the hotel she is writing to?
    (b) What sort of room does she want to book, and for how long?
    (c) What is particularly important for her?
    (d) What does she ask the price for?
    (e) What reasons does she give for wanting a prospectus of the hotel?
    (f) How will she make the journey to the hotel?
    (g) What sort of information does she want to have about the area?

2. Here are some jottings which Gabriele made before writing her letter, to remind her of the points she wanted to ask. For each item noted, write out a complete sentence as you might actually write it if you were composing a letter.

    Model: Wichtig – Zimmer – ruhige Lage.
    Response: Es ist mir sehr wichtig, daß das Zimmer eine ruhige Lage hat.

    (a) gern – Zimmer – Blick auf den See.
    (b) Preis – Übernachtung mit Frühstück – pro Person und Nacht.
    (c) Prospekt schicken – Lage und Größe – Ausstattung von Zimmern.
    (d) bewachter Hotelparkplatz oder Parkmöglichkeiten in der Nähe?
    (e) Sehenswürdigkeiten im Gebiet? Segelboote ausleihen? Unterhaltung am Abend?

(ii) **Explanations**

Select Vocabulary

das Verzeichnis (–se) – list; index
die Lage (–n) – position
mitteilen – to inform
angeschlossen – attached to; associated with
zusammenstellen – to put together; to compile
die Ausstattung – furnishings
der Aufenthaltsraum (⸚e) – recreation room

der Anfahrtsweg (–e) – journey; route
bewacht – supervised
das Gebiet (–e) – region
die Sehenswürdigkeiten (plural) – sights; places worth a visit
ausleihen (ie, ie) – to hire
die Unterhaltung (–en) – entertainment
die Mühe (–n) – trouble

(iii)   *Exercises — Section B*

1. The letter has a number of examples of different ways of expressing wishes and requests in a polite way. For example:

   ich würde gern . . .
   ich möchte gern . . .
   ich hätte gern . . .
   könnten Sie bitte . . .
   ich möchte Sie bitten . . .
   es wäre für mich wichtig . . .

   The following items represent a list of things you want to mention when writing a letter to book a holiday at a hotel. Write out each one as a full sentence, choosing one of the above phrases to make it a polite request. For example: *ich würde gern zwei Wochen in der Schweiz verbringen.*
   (a) ein Zimmer mit einer ruhigen Lage.
   (b) ein Zimmer mit Blick auf den See.
   (c) der Preis für eine Übernachtung mit Frühstück.
   (d) ein Zimmer mit Vollpension buchen.
   (e) einen Prospekt schicken.
   (f) Informationen über das Gebiet haben.
   (g) zwei Wochen in der Schweiz verbringen.

2. Below is a list of questions you might ask someone if you were talking to them directly. In a formal letter you might decide to use a construction like *ich möchte Sie fragen, ob . . .* or *ich möchte wissen, ob . . . .* Rewrite the following questions, using these two possibilities. For example, the question *Haben Sie ein Doppelzimmer* will become: *Ich möchte Sie fragen, ob Sie ein Doppelzimmer haben.*
   (a) Haben Sie einen bewachten Hotelparkplatz?
   (b) Gibt es zumindest Parkmöglichkeiten in der Nähe?
   (c) Haben Sie ein Doppelzimmer mit Bad und WC?
   (d) Kann man ein Zimmer mit Vollpension buchen?
   (e) Können Sie mir Informationen über das Gebiet schicken?
   (f) Bieten die Orte Unterhaltung am Abend?

3. In the following passage prepositions and the articles following them have been omitted. Rewrite the passage, choosing prepositions from the list given below the text, and make sure you use the correct form of the article. Attempt the exercises from memory, and then check with the original letter to see whether you have the right cases.

Ich habe Ihre Adresse dem Hotelverzeichnis entnommen. Ich suche ein Hotel . . . . Nähe des Vierwaldstättersees. Ich möchte gerne . . . . . . Sommer nächsten Jahres zwei Wochen dort verbringen. Ich hätte gern ein Zimmer mit Blick . . . . See. Ich fahre . . . . Wagen, und ich möchte deshalb wissen, ob Sie einen bewachten Parkplatz haben. Können Sie mir bitte Informationen . . . . Gebiet schicken? Besteht die Moglichkeit . . . . . . See Segelboote auszuleihen? Bieten die Orte Unterhaltung . . . . Abend?

auf; an; über; mit; aus; in.

4. In the letter to the hotel the Dative pronoun *mir* is used with verbs such as *schicken, mitteilen*. For example, *ich möchte Sie bitten mir Informationen über das Gebiet zu schicken* — 'I would like to ask you to send me information about the area.' *mir* is also used in the expression *es ist mir wichtig* — 'it is important for me'. This may also be expressed *es ist für mich wichtig*. Using this information, and other details in Grammar Summary section 7.1, translate the following sentences into German.

(a) It is important for me to have a room in a quiet position.
(b) Could you please let me know the price for a room with breakfast?
(c) I should like to ask you to send me a prospectus of your hotel.
(d) It is important for me to know whether you have a supervised car-park.
(e) Would you please send me information about the area?

5. In Chapter 1 you were given an example of an informal letter from a friend. In this chapter you have an example of a more formal letter, of the kind you would write to a hotel, or to get information from a tourist office. Make a list of the sort of information you wish to have from a regional tourist office, and then write a letter of about 150 words asking for the information you require and using the polite ways of putting such requests which you have already practised in previous exercises. Your letter should be addressed to the *Städtisches Verkehrsamt* of the town you want to go to, and should begin: *Sehr geehrte Damen und Herren*. It can finish *Mit freundlichen Grüßen*.

3.2 Listening Materials 📼

3.2.1 Im Reisebüro

While queuing to collect some rail tickets in a travel agent's in Germany, you hear some announcements made, advertising various holiday possibilities to the waiting customers. Listen to the announcements on tape before reading the text, and try to answer the comprehension questions.

— Amerika bietet die große Freiheit für eine Handvoll Dollar.
— Buchen Sie Flugreisen für bessere Urlaubsqualität!
— Genießen Sie den magischen Strand der magischen Stadt Venedig!
— In Spanien finden Sie alte Tradition verbunden mit moderner Leistungsfähigkeit.
— Erleben Sie die Faszination der mexikanischen Kultur!

1. What might the freedom of America cost you? *a handfull of $*
2. How might you travel to get the best quality on your holidays? *plane*
3. What is especially magic about the magic town of Venice? *streets*
4. Name one reason why you are encouraged to visit Spain. *old tradition*
5. Where might you find a fascinating culture? *mexico*

3.2.2 Telefongespräch mit einem Hotel

Herr Lamm: Hallo, ist dort das Gasthaus „zum Goldenen Adler"?
Empfangsdame: Ja, Gasthaus „zum Goldenen Adler". Was kann ich für Sie tun?
Lamm: Hätten Sie vielleicht ein Doppelzimmer und ein Einzelzimmer frei, für heute nacht?
Dame: Für heute nacht . . . ja, wir haben noch Zimmer frei. Möchten Sie Zimmer mit Bad oder Dusche?
Lamm: Beide mit Dusche, wenn es geht.
Dame: Wir haben ein Doppelzimmer mit Dusche zu DM 46, aber Einzelzimmer mit Dusche haben wir leider nicht. Ich kann Ihnen nur ein kleines Zimmer ohne Dusche für DM 26 anbieten.
Lamm: Gut, dann nehmen wir das Einzelzimmer auch ohne Dusche. Und ist Frühstück im Preis eingeschlossen?
Dame: Ja, Frühstück und Bedienung sind inbegriffen.
Lamm: Gut, wir nehmen die zwei Zimmer. Aber wir sind noch unterwegs, und werden wahrscheinlich erst spät ankommen. Wahrscheinlich erst gegen neun Uhr.
Dame: In Ordnung. Wir erwarten Sie also gegen neun Uhr. Auf Wiederhören!
Lamm: Auf Wiederhören!

1. The questions are given in the same order as they were asked by Herr Lamm, but the answers below have been jumbled. Listen to the tape and then write out the answers so that they match the questions they refer to.

   (a) Ist dort das Gasthaus „zum Goldenen Adler"?
   (b) Hätten Sie vielleicht ein Doppelzimmer und ein Einzelzimmer frei?
   (c) Was kosten die Zimmer?
   (d) Ist Frühstück im Preis eingeschlossen?

   Wir haben ein Doppelzimmer mit Dusche zu DM 46 . . . Ich kann Ihnen nur ein kleines Zimmer ohne Dusche für DM 26 anbieten.
   Ja, Gasthaus „zum Goldenen Adler".
   Ja, Frühstück und Bedienung sind inbegriffen.
   Ja, wir haben noch Zimmer frei.

2. You are travelling through Germany, but unexpectedly you get held up on the way, and find that you will have to spend the night at a hotel before getting to your final destination. From a service station on the Autobahn you telephone a hotel in the nearest town to see whether they have room for you. Work out your part of the telephone conversation on the basis of the following information:

   (a) There are four in your family: your parents, you and your sister.
   (b) Your parents want a double room and you and your sister either a single room each, or a twin-bedded room (*ein Zweibettzimmer*) if you are also a girl.

(c) Your parents would like a room with bath or shower, but you and your sister do not mind either way. The important thing is to make sure you can get a room of some kind.

(d) You should ask the price of the rooms, but you do not want to pay more than DM 40 for each room, so be ready to ask for something a little less expensive if it should be necessary.

(e) When given a price, you will want to ask whether breakfast is included and also service.

(f) Say what time you expect to arrive and ask whether it will still be possible to have an evening meal on your arrival.

(g) Thank the person and say goodbye.

3.2.3 Anmeldung am Campingplatz

Herr Brown: Guten Abend. Ich bin der Leiter dieser englischen Schülergruppe hier, und wollte Sie fragen, ob wir unsere Zelte hier aufschlagen können.

Mann: Wieviel Schüler haben Sie?

Herr Brown: 7 Schüler auf drei Zelte verteilt, und ich habe ein Ein-Mann-Zelt.

Mann: Sie brauchen also vier Plätze. Das geht in Ordnung. Ist das Ihr Minibus?

Herr Brown: Ja.

Mann: Das kostet 6 DM pro Tag extra. Sie zahlen für jede erwachsene Person 4 DM und für ein Zelt 3 DM pro Tag. Ihre Schüler gelten als Erwachsene. Für wie lange wollen Sie hier bleiben?

Herr Brown: Wahrscheinlich für fünf Tage.

Mann: Kein Problem. Ihre Zelte können Sie aufschlagen, wo Sie wollen, beziehungsweise, wo Sie Platz finden. Hier sind Ihre 4 Nummern. Hängen Sie sie bitte an Ihre Zelte.

Herr Brown: Und wo sind bitte die Toiletten und Waschräume?

Mann: Hier hinten links. Für heiße Duschen müssen Sie sich an der Rezeption Münzen besorgen.

Herr Brown: Gut, das werden wir später erledigen. Vielen Dank!

1. *Comprehension questions*
   (a) What is Mr Brown's position in the group? *Englishman*
   (b) How many are there in the group and how many tents have they? *7 1,1m*
   (c) What is the extra cost of the minibus?
   (d) How long does the group wish to stay? *5 days*
   (e) Why does the man at camp reception give them numbers?
   (f) What must they do if they want hot showers?

2. You are travelling in Germany with your family and you stop to book in at a camp site. You have to act as interpreter, as you are the only member of your family to speak German. How would you reply to the following questions?

   (a) Wieviel Personen sind Sie?
   (b) Haben Sie Ihre eigenen Zelte?
   (c) Was für ein Fahrzeug haben Sie?
   (d) Für wie lange wollen Sie hier bleiben?
   Now decide how you would ask the following questions:
   (e) Have you still got room left?
   (f) How much does it cost?
   (g) Where are the toilets and wash-rooms?

(i) *Explanations for Conversations 3.2.2 and 3.2.3*

ist Frühstück im Preis eingeschlossen? — is breakfast included in the price?

. . . sind inbegriffen — . . . are included

erst gegen neun Uhr — not until nine o'clock

ein Zelt aufschlagen — to pitch a tent

auf drei Zelte verteilt — divided between three tents

Ihre Schüler gelten als Erwachsene — your pupils count as adults

beziehungsweise — or

hier hinten links — behind here on the left

. . . müssen Sie Münzen besorgen — . . . you must obtain tokens

das werden wir später erledigen — we shall deal with that later

4 Städte der Bundesrepublik

4.1 Reading Materials

Because of the strong regional traditions in Germany, the big cities often seem more like capitals than just provincial towns. This is not really surprising when one thinks that a number of these towns – for example, Stuttgart, Frankfurt, Munich and Hamburg, which are all mentioned in this chapter – were all state capitals in the days when Germany consisted of a number of separate and largely independent states. So let us imagine that you have the chance to go sight-seeing in these towns, and you want to find out a little more about them. But first of all you want to check on the weather forecast, so read the forecast below first, and see whether you can answer the comprehension questions.

4.1.1 Deutscher Wetterdienst

Vorhersage für den 6. Juli 1986.

Lage: Die Kaltfront eines Tiefs bei Island überquert Deutschland unter Abschwächung ostwärts. Von Westen setzt sich rasch wieder Hochdruck—einfluß durch.

Vorhersage: Am Samstag in der Osthälfte sonnig und sehr warm mit Höchstwerten bis 28 Grad. In der Westhälfte teils heiter, teils stark bewölkt und einzelne Schauer oder Gewitter. Höchstwerte hier 23 bis 26 Grad. Tiefsttemperaturen in der Nacht zum Sonntag bei 13 Grad. Am Samstag in der Osthälfte sonnig und sehr warm mit Höchstwerten bis 28 Grad. In der Westhälfte teils heiter, teils stark bewölkt. Wind, anfangs aus Ost bis Süd, später auf westliche Richtung drehend.

Aussichten: Freundlich und warm.

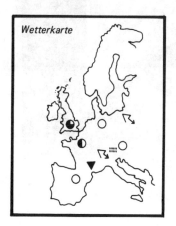

Wetterkarte

Zeichenerklärung	
wolkenlos	○
heiter	◐
teils bedeckt	◑
wolkig	◕
bedeckt	●
Regen	|||||
Schauer	▼
Gewitter	⬎

Wetter und Temperaturen in Grad Celsius		
Hamburg	wolkenlos	21
Berlin	heiter	20
Frankfurt	wolkenlos	23
München	heiter	18
Konstanz	bedeckt	18
Oberstdorf	Regen	16
Zugspitze	in Wolken	4

(i) *Comprehension Questions*

From your reading of the text and the other information provided answer the following questions.

1. What is the weather like in the eastern half of Germany?
2. Where might you expect to have showers and thunderstorms?
3. What sort of weather will you expect on Sunday in the north-east?
4. What will be the direction of the wind at first?
5. What will the weather be like in Frankfurt and Hamburg, the two towns mentioned in the following passages?
6. Why do you think it is so cloudy and cold on the Zugspitze?

Einkaufsbummel in einer Frankfurter Fußgängerzone

4.1.2 Impressionen von Frankfurt

Frankfurt ist für mich die Stadt der Autofahrer und Verkehrsampeln. An die Fußgänger denkt kaum einer. Sie „leben" in kleinen „Fußgängerzonen". Die wenigen Menschen die hier bei Grün eine Straße überqueren können, wären Weltmeister beim 100-Meter-Lauf. Alle anderen riskieren in Frankfurt ihr Leben. Aber die Autofahrer haben es gut: sie stellen ihren Wagen ab, wo sie ihn loswerden können.

Aber die Frankfurter haben mich auch positiv überrascht. In anderen Ländern hält man die Großstädter für arrogant und hochnäsig. Die Leute hier waren hilfsbereit und freundlich. Es fiel uns also leicht, vierzehn Tage in dieser „Großstadt mit Herz" zu verbringen. Wer hätte das vorher gedacht?

Walter Daems

In München und Düsseldorf sitzt man gerne im Straßencafé, um Leute zu sehen und von Leuten gesehen zu werden. Ein typisches Großstadtverhältnis. Ganz anders die Frankfurter. Sie haben nicht das Selbstbewußtsein der Großstadtmenschen. Sie möchten nicht mit der neuesten Mode imponieren. Sie lieben mehr die gemütlichen Innenhöfe der Apfelweinkneipen. Da sind sie auch meistens unter sich. Fremden gegenüber sind sie trotzdem offen und freundlich.

Hermann Peters
adapted from Scala Jugendmagazin © Jan./Feb. 1985

(i) *Falsch/Richtig*

When you have read the two extracts above, which both relate impressions of Frankfurt, decide whether the following statements are true or false.
1. Pedestrians are more important than cars in Frankfurt.
2. To cross the road you need to be a world champion sprinter.
3. The people who live there are friendly and helpful.
4. The people of Frankfurt are fond of sitting in street cafés, just like the people in Munich and Düsseldorf.
5. They do not like trying to impress you with the latest fashion.
6. They are open and friendly with strangers.

(ii) *Sentence Matching*

Make sentences by linking a phrase from the left-hand column with an appropriate phrase from the right-hand column. For example: *die Frankfurter haben mich auch positiv überrascht.*

1. An die Fußgänger	haben mich auch positiv überrascht.
2. Die Autofahrer	die Großstädter für arrogant.
3. Die Frankfurter	mit der neuesten Mode imponieren.
4. In anderen Ländern hält man	denkt kaum einer.
5. Es fiel uns also leicht	sind sie trotzdem offen.
6. Sie möchten nicht	haben es gut.
7. Sie lieben mehr	vierzehn Tage hier zu verbringen.
8. Fremden gegenüber	die gemütlichen Innenhöfe.

(iii) *Explanations*

Select Vocabulary

die Verkehrsampel (—n) — traffic lights   das Verhältnis (—se) — relationship
die Fußgängerzone (—n) — pedestrian precinct   das Selbstbewußtsein — self-confidence

überqueren — to cross over
der Weltmeister (—) — world champion
abstellen — to park (a car)
loswerden — to get rid of
überraschen — to surprise

imponieren — to impress
der Innenhof (¨e) — inner courtyard
die Kneipe (—n) — bar; pub
trotzdem — nevertheless

Expressions and Idioms

an die Fußgänger denkt kaum einer — hardly anyone thinks of the pedestrians
die Autofahrer haben es gut — the car-drivers are onto a good thing
in anderen Ländern hält man die Großstädter für arrogant — in other countries
    city dwellers are thought to be arrogant
es fiel uns also leicht . . . — so we found it easy . . .
wer hätte das vorher gedacht? — who would have thought it previously?
um Leute zu sehen und von Leuten gesehen zu werden — to see people and to be
    seen by them
da sind sie meistens unter sich — there they are mostly among friends
Fremden gegenüber — towards foreigners

4.1.3 Hamburg

Das Bundesland „Freie und Hansestadt Hamburg" hat 1,6 Millionen Einwohner.
Es liegt an der Elbe, etwa 100 Kilometer von der Nordsee entfernt. Nord- und
Ostsee bestimmen das Klima: im Winter mild, im Sommer oft mit frischen Winden.

Hamburg hat den größten und wichtigsten Hafen Deutschlands. Etwa 16 000
Schiffe fahren in jedem Jahr nach Hamburg. Es gibt Linienverbindungen (regelmäßige Schiffe) zu 1100 Häfen der Erde. Hamburg ist ein Universalhafen: für
Container, flüssige Güter (Gas, Öl) und feste Waren (Autos, Kaffee, Holz) und auch
für den Transithandel (Waren kommen zollfrei in das Freihafengebiet und gehen
wieder hinaus in ein anderes Land).

Der Fischmarkt im Stadtteil Altona ist eine Hamburger Kuriosität. Am Sonntagmorgen um fünf Uhr kann man hier schon einkaufen. Es gibt nicht nur frische
Fische aus der Nordsee. Es gibt auch alte Schallplatten, Bananen, rostige Schrauben,
Teller aus Porzellan, lebende Hühner, heiße Würste, Uhren und viele, viele interessante Leute.

Blankenese ist ein Vorort von Hamburg. Es liegt an der Elbe und auf einem
Berg. Der Süllberg ist 85 Meter hoch. Von oben hat man eine schöne Aussicht auf
die Elbe und in das flache Land hinter den Elbdeichen. Blankenese ist eine
Mischung aus Dorf und Stadt, Strand und Berg. Hier wohnen alte Seemänner und
Fischer neben Politikern und Filmstars. Man lebt in der Großstadt und doch im
Grünen — wenn man genug Geld hat oder wenn man schon lange hier wohnt.

© *Jugendscala*, März 1983

(i) *Exercises — Section A*

The exercises in this section are concerned with comprehension and recognition,
and should be attempted before you look at explanations of grammar or vocabulary.

1. *Comprehension*
    (a) Does the port of Hamburg lie at the mouth of the river Elbe?
    (b) Why is Hamburg particularly important?
    (c) Give some examples of the sort of trade which Hamburg is involved in.

(d) At what sort of unusual time can you start shopping in Altona?

(e) Can you describe where Blankenese lies?

(f) What sort of people live in Blankenese?

2. The following sentences have been taken from the text about Hamburg but the words have been jumbled up. Without looking back at the original text, rewrite the sentences correctly.

(a) größten Hafen wichtigsten hat den und Deutschlands Hamburg.

(b) fünf um schon man kann am hier Sonntagmorgen Uhr einkaufen.

(c) hat schöne flache das Elbdeichen von man oben eine Aussicht auf in den die Land Elbe hinter und.

(d) man Geld oder wenn genug hat wohnt lange wenn hier man schon.

Hamburg — Blick von Altona auf den Hafen

(ii) *Explanations*

flüssig – liquid
die Güter (plural) – goods; freight
zollfrei – duty free
einkaufen – to do one's shopping
der Teller (–) – plate

das Huhn (¨er) – chicken; hen
der Vorort – suburb
der Deich (–e) – dyke
die Mischung (–en) – mixture

Expressions and Idioms

Das Bundesland „Freie und Hansestadt Hamburg" – The full title of Hamburg reminds one that it is both city and a Federal State (Land) of the Bundesrepublik.

etwa 100 Kilometer von der Nordsee entfernt – some 100 km distant from the North Sea

von oben hat man eine schöne Aussicht auf die Elbe – from above one has a lovely view over the Elbe

man lebt in der Großstadt und doch im Grünen – you live in the city and yet in the country as well

Grammar

The following are the items of grammar of which there are examples in the text, and for which the Section B exercises provide practice.
(a) Use of *es gibt* (12.10(d)(1)).
(b) Practice with adjectival endings (4(b)).

(iii) *Exercises – Section B*

1. The passage about Hamburg gives a number of expressions for describing the position of a town, and the things that can be seen and visited. *Es gibt* is used a good deal, and expressions such as *es liegt*, and statements about distance, weather and shopping. Write a letter to a German pen-friend describing the town or village where you live, and using as many of the phrases you can find in the text as possible. You can use the outline below to help you:

Meine Heimatstadt heißt . . . Es liegt . . . im Norden/Süden/Osten/Westen von England/Schottland/Wales, in Nordirland. Das Klima ist hier . . . im Sommer, und im Winter . . . Meine Stadt hat . . . Einwohner . . . viele arbeiten . . . Meine Stadt hat einen Markt jeden . . . tag. Da kann man . . . kaufen. In der Stadt gibt es . . . es gibt auch.

2. In the following extracts from the passage about Hamburg the adjectival endings are missing. Rewrite the passage with the correct endings.

In Hamburg ist das Klima im Winter mild und im Sommer oft mit frisch– Winden. Hamburg hat den größt– und wichtigst– Hafen Deutschlands. Est gibt regelmäßig– Schiffsverbindungen zu 1100 Häfen der Erde. Hamburg is ein Universalhafen für flüssig– Güter und für fest– Waren. Ferner ist es ein Hafen für den Transithandel. Da kommen zollfrei– Waren in das Freihafengebiet und gehen wieder hinaus in ein ander– Land. Im Fischmarket des Stadtteils Altona kann man alles einkaufen: frisch– Fische aus der Nordsee, alt– Schallplatten, lebend– Hühner, heiß– Würste. Man kann auch viele Interessant– Leute kennenlernen. Blankenese ist ein Vorort und liegt auf dem 85 hoh– Süllberg. Von oben hat man eine schön– Aussicht in das flach– Land hinter den Elbdeichen. In Blankenese wohnen alt– Seemänner neben berühmt– Politikern.

42

4.2 Listening Materials 📼

Having read something about German towns, you need to know how to find your way around in a strange town, and also how you might make arrangements to meet a friend.

4.2.1 Wie komme ich zum . . .?

You are standing in the *Kohlmarkt* in Braunschweig, of which there is a simplified town plan below. You ask the way to a number of places and the answers you might receive are given on the tape. To show that you are able to understand the directions, find the place on the map that you want to go to and write down your answers.

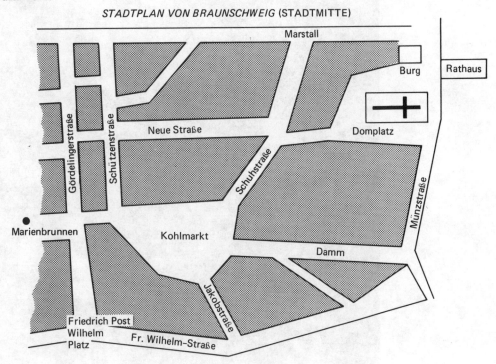

STADTPLAN VON BRAUNSCHWEIG (STADTMITTE)

(i) Listen to the instructions and decide where they lead to.
1. Nehmen Sie die Schuhstraße. Biegen Sie dann rechts ab, und Sie kommen zum . . . . . .
2. Gehen Sie die Jakobstraße entlang, dann rechts, und dann befinden Sie sich in der . . . . . . straße.
3. Gehen Sie den Damm entlang, dann kommen Sie zur Münzstraße. Gehen Sie dann links, und Sie finden es rechts, gegenüber vom Dom.
4. Das ist nicht weit von hier. Gehen Sie die Schuhstraße entlang. Gehen Sie dann rechts, und nach ein paar Metern befinden Sie sich auf dem Domplatz. Gehen Sie über den Domplatz, und dann sehen Sie . . . . . . schon.

4.2.2 Telefongespräch — Wo treffen wir uns?

Claudia:	Hallo, Sabine! Hier ist Claudia. Hast du heute abend schon etwas vor?
Sabine:	Nein, warum?
Claudia:	Ich habe heute den ganzen Tag nur für die Schule gelernt. Jetzt brauche ich unbedingt eine Abwechslung. Ich dachte, daß wir vielleicht etwas zusammen unternehmen könnten, wenn du Lust hast.

Sabine:	Gern, ja. Hast du etwas Bestimmtes vor?
Claudia:	Eigentlich nicht, nein. Wir könnten Eis essen und dann ins Kino gehen. Aber ich weiß nicht, ob momentan gute Filme laufen.
Sabine:	Ich auch nicht. Aber ich kann unterwegs eine Zeitung mit dem Kinoprogramm kaufen. Ich bringe sie mit ins Café, und dann können wir beim Eis Essen diskutieren, welchen Film wir anschauen wollen.
Claudia:	Gut. Treffen wir uns im Café oder soll ich erst zu dir kommen?
Sabine:	Ich glaube, wir treffen uns am besten gleich im Café. In welches Café wollen wir gehen? Ins Café am Dom? Dann sind wir auch gleich beim Kino.

„Wir treffen uns am besten gleich im Café"

Claudia:	Das Café am Dom kenne ich nicht.
Sabine:	Stell dir vor, es ist am Dom!
Claudia:	Okay, gehen wir ins Café am Dom. Um wieviel Uhr?
Sabine:	Das ist mir gleich.
Claudia:	Um 16.30 Uhr? Dann haben wir anderthalb Stunden Zeit bis zur ersten Abendvorstellung.
Sabine:	Und wir können auch noch die letzten Sonnenstrahlen genießen, während wir unser Eis essen. Wie kommst du zum Café? Per Bus?
Claudia:	Der Bus ist so teuer. Ich glaube, ich komme mit dem Fahrrad. Muß ich am Dom rechts oder links abbiegen, wenn ich zum Café will?
Sabine:	Links, und dann bist du auch schon da.
Claudia:	Gut, das ist einfach. Also bis dann!
Sabine:	Bis dann!

(i) *Comprehension Questions*

1. Why is Claudia so keen to have an evening off? she has no h/wk
2. What does Claudia suggest that she and Sabine might do together?
3. How does Sabine suggest she might find out what is on at the cinema?
4. Where do they decide to meet?
5. Is their meeting place far from the cinema?
6. What time will the evening cinema performance start?
7. How will Claudia come into town for the meeting?

(ii) *Say it in German*

Listen again to the text and write down the German expressions which are equivalent to the English expressions below.
1. Have you already got anything on this evening?
2. I've just got to have a change.
3. Shall we meet in a café?
4. Right next to the cinema.
5. I don't mind.
6. Should I turn left or right?
7. See you soon.

(iii) *Role Play*

While staying in Germany, a friend asks you whether you'd like to go out for an evening. Play your part in the role play given in outline below.

Peter Schmidt:	Guten Tag, Michael. Hast du heute abend schon etwas vor?
You:	(Say no, this evening you are free.)
Peter:	Wir könnten vielleicht etwas zusammen unternehmen, wenn du Lust hast.
You:	(Say with pleasure. Ask whether he has any definite plans.)
Peter:	Eigentlich nicht, nein. Wir könnten vielleicht zuerst etwas essen und dann ins Kino gehen.
You:	(Say fine, you'd like that. Ask whether he knows what films are on at the moment.)
Peter:	Ich weiß nicht genau, aber ich kann ja die Zeitung mit dem Kinoprogramm kaufen. Wir könnten uns im Café treffen. Kennst du das Café am Dom?
You:	(Say you do not know the café, but you know where the cathedral is.)

Peter: Gut, das Café ist also gleich beim Dom. Treffen wir uns um circa fünf Uhr?

You: (Say yes, five o'clock is fine. Cheerio for now.)

Peter: Bis dann!

(iv) *Explanations*

Select Vocabulary

die Abwechslung (—en) — change; diversion

unternehmen (unternahm; unternommen) — to do; to undertake

momentan — at the moment

anderthalb — one and a half

die Abendvorstellung (—en) — evening performance

der Sonnenstrahl (—en) — ray of sunshine

abbiegen (o, o) — to turn

Expressions and Idioms

hast du heute abend schon etwas vor? — have you already got anything on this evening?

ich brauche unbedingt eine Abwechslung — I've just got to have a change

wenn du Lust hast — if you would like to

beim Eis Essen — while we are eating our ices

gleich beim Kino — right next to the cinema

bis dann! — see you soon!

---

5 Essen und Trinken

5.1 Reading Materials

Food and drink are a never-ending subject for anyone interested in a foreign culture, and this is especially the case when dealing with the several cultures where German is spoken. In the space of one chapter we can give only a brief idea of some of the pleasures of eating and drinking in German-speaking countries. First, a menu gives you some ideas for a meal. Then follows a recipe for gingerbread men — a traditional German children's delicacy. Then follows a letter from Gabi to her English pen-friend, telling her about German food.

5.1.1 Speisekarte

	DM
Kalte Vorspeisen	
Käseteller mit Butter und Brot	8,20
Schinken, Bauernbrot und Butter	9,90
Warme Vorspeisen	
Ochsenschwanzsuppe	3,80
Französische Zwiebelsuppe	4,30
Hauptgerichte	
Kalbsrahmbraten mit Spätzle und Salatteller	15,60
Schweinebraten mit Kartoffeln und Salat	13,40
Dessert	
Vanilleeis mit Schlagsahne	6,20
Gemischter Eisbecher	4,80
Getränke	
Apfelsaft	1,80
Mineralwasser	1,80
Exportbier (0,5 L)	3,10
Moselwein (0,25 L)	4,80

(i) *Comprehension Questions*

1. How do you think you might translate the headings in *italics* on the menu (for example, *Hauptgerichte*)?
2. What sort of dishes are offered as hot starters?
3. Without necessarily knowing what the main meat dishes are, can you say what sort of meat is on offer?
4. What can you have for dessert?
5. How much wine do you get for DM 4.80?

(ii) *Role Play*

While staying in Germany with a pen-friend, you receive money from your parents to take your hosts out for a meal. When the waiter comes to take the order, they tell him what they want and leave you to order your own meal. Using the menu, order the meal you would like (money no object!).

"Putzi ißt uns nichts weg. Er pickt nur die Rosinen"

© *Für Dich*, Berlin (DDR)

5.1.2 Backrezept: Lebkuchenfiguren

Der Teig:

zuerst die Honigmasse: 300 g Honig

150 g Zucker

50 g Butter

1 Prise Salz

$\frac{1}{8}$ Liter Kaffee

Erwärmen, bis Honig und Butter flüssig sind. Abkühlen lassen (nicht im Kühlschrank.)

500 g Mehl

3 gehäufte Teelöffel Backpulver

1 Ei

4–6 Tropfen Bittermandelöl

2 Eßlöffel Rum

1 gestrichener Teelöffel Zimt

$\frac{1}{4}$ Teelöffel Nelkenpfeffer

und die Honigmasse

In die Schüssel geben und verrühren.

Der Teig muß leicht vom Löffel abreißen. Der Teig wird mit einem Teigschaber, den man häufig in Wasser taucht, gut 1 cm dick auf ein gefettetes Backblech gestrichen.

Backzeit 20 Minuten bei starker Hitze. Gut abkühlen lassen.

Der Zuckerguß   1 Eßlöffel Backfett

100 g Puderzucker

Wasser

Wasser in eine Bratpfanne gießen. Einen Topf hineinstellen. Wasser kochen und auf ganz kleine Flamme schalten. Fett im Topf schmelzen. Puderzucker hinzugeben.

Heißes Wasser vorsichtig hinzugeben und rühren. Der Zuckerguß darf nicht zu dünn werden!

(i) *Comprehension Questions*

There will be a number of technical words which you probably do not know, but, remembering that it is a recipe for gingerbread men, try to guess at the meanings of words you do not know and answer the following questions.

1. What are the main ingredients for the honey mixture?
2. How long should you warm the honey and butter?
3. What should you *not* do to cool off the mixture?
4. What do you think *in die Schüssel geben und verrühren* means?
5. How long must the mixture cook, and how hot must the oven be?
6. *Zuckerguß* is icing. What does it tell you to be careful of when making the icing? (See the last sentence of the recipe.)

„Aber da sagt man doch Achtung, Torte! Oder so"

(ii) *Translation*

Recipes often use the Infinitive form of the verb for telling you what to do. For example, *erwärmen* means 'heat up'. Use the vocabulary which follows this exercise, and translate into English the last paragraph of the recipe, beginning: *Wasser in eine Bratpfanne gießen.*

(iii) *Explanations*

Select Vocabulary

der Lebkuchen — gingerbread	der Zimt (—e) — cinnamon
der Honig (no plural) — honey	der Nelkenpfeffer — ground cloves
die Masse (—n) — mass; mixture (in cooking)	die Schüssel (—n) — bowl; dish
der Zucker (no plural) — sugar	verrühren — to stir
die Butter (no plural) — butter	der Teig (—e) — dough
das Salz (—e) — salt	abreißen (i, i) — to break off; to come off
erwärmen — to heat up	der Teigschaber (—) — dough scraper
abkühlen — to cool	häufig — frequently
flüssig — liquid	tauchen — to dip
der Kühlschrank (¨e) — refrigerator	das Backblech (—e) — baking tray

das Mehl (—e) — flour	streichen (i, i) — to spread
gehäuft — heaped	die Bratpfanne (—n) — frying pan
der Teelöffel (—) — teaspoon	gießen (o, o) — to pour
das Backpulver (—) — baking powder	kochen — to boil
das Ei (—er) — egg	schalten — to switch
das Öl (—e) — oil	schmelzen (o, o) — to melt
die Bittermandel (—n) — bitter almond	dünn — thin

Expressions and Idioms

abkühlen lassen — allow to cool
1 gestrichener Teelöffel — one level teaspoon
bei starker Hitze — at a high temperature
heißes Wasser vorsichtig hinzugeben — add hot water carefully
. . . darf nicht zu dünn werden — . . . must not become too thin

5.1.3 Essen in Deutschland

Liebe Karen!

Vielen Dank für Deinen langen Brief. Es hat mich sehr gefreut, zu hören, wie es Dir geht und was Du so machst.

Du mußt also einen Aufsatz über Essen und Trinken in Deutschland schreiben. Nun, ich will Dir einige Tips für diesen Aufsatz geben.

Ich werde gleich mit dem Frühstück anfangen. Es gibt Deutsche, vor allem deutsche Kinder, die zum Frühstück Kornflakes oder Müsli essen. Aber die meisten Deutschen beginnen den Tag mit Schwarzbrot oder Semmeln, Butter und Marmelade oder Honig. Dazu gibt es Tee oder Kaffee. Am Wochenende, wenn man sich zum Frühstück mehr Zeit lassen kann, gibt es oft auch ein weiches Ei, Käse und Wurst. Am Sonntag frühstücken viele Familien Kaffee, Kuchen und Schlagrahm.

Die Hauptmahlzeit in Deutschland ist das Mittagessen. Da die Schule in Deutschland bereits mittags aus ist, kommen die Kinder zum Mittagessen nach Hause. Es gibt Fleisch mit Beilagen, wie beispielsweise Kartoffeln, Reis oder Nudeln und Gemüse oder Salat. Ein typisch deutsches Gericht gibt es nicht. Jede Gegend in Deutschland hat ihre eigenen Spezialitäten. Eine bayerische Spezialität ist der Schweinebraten mit Knödeln und Blaukraut.

Nachmittags gibt es dann Kaffee und Kuchen. Die berühmte Schwarzwälderkirschtorte gibt es aber leider nur an Festtagen. Unter der Woche gibt es einfachere Kuchen wie beispielsweise Apfelkuchen.

Die meisten Väter kommen erst zum Abendessen nach Hause. Zum Abendessen gibt es bei uns Schwarzbrot und Vollkornbrot, Butter, verschiedene Käsesorten und Aufschnitt. Dazu trinken wir Tee, Limonade oder auch Bier.

Hast Du Lust bekommen, Deinen englishen „tea" oder Dein englisches „supper" gegen unser leichtes, deutsches Abendessen einzutauschen?

Viele liebe Grüße,

Deine Gabi

(i) *Exercises — Section A*

The exercises in this section are concerned with comprehension and recognition, and they should be attempted before you look at explanations of grammar or vocabulary.

1. *Comprehension questions*
   (a) What do most Germans eat for breakfast?
   (b) Why do the Germans sometimes have a bigger breakfast at the week-end?
   (c) Give examples of the extra things they might eat for a week-end breakfast.
   (d) Why do children usually have their mid-day meal at home?
   (e) What might you eat with your meat for the mid-day meal?
   (f) Why is there not a dish which can be considered typical for the whole of Germany?
   (g) Do the Germans have anything similar to English afternoon tea?
   (h) Make a list of the things which you might find on the table for the evening meal.

2. Without referring back to the text, write out the following passage, filling in the gaps:

   Es gibt Deutsche, die zum . . . . . . Kornflakes essen. Aber die meisten . . . . . . beginnen den Tag mit Semmeln, Butter und . . . . . . oder Honig. Dazu gibt es Tee oder . . . . . . Am Wochenende gibt es oft ein weiches . . . . . ., Käse und . . . . . . Die Hauptmahlzeit ist das . . . . . . Es gibt Fleisch mit . . . . . ., wie beispielsweise Kartoffeln, ... oder Nudeln. Nachmittags gibt es dann Kaffee und . . . . . . Zum . . . . . . gibt es bei uns Schwarzbrot, Butter und verschiedene . . . . . . Dazu trinken wir . . . . . ., Limonade oder Bier.

   Choose from the following words: Beilagen; Mittagessen; Marmelade; Kaffee; Kuchen; Tee; Käsesorten; Frühstück; Ei; Deutschen; Wurstsorten; Reis; Abendessen.

   (ii) **Explanations**

   Select Vocabulary

   das Frühstück (—e) — breakfast
   die Semmel (—n) — bread roll (also das Brötchen (—))
   die Marmelade (no plural) — jam
   die Wurst (⁻e) — sausage
   der Käse (die Käsesorten) — cheese
   der Schlagrahm (no plural) — whipped cream
   die Mahlzeit (—en) — meal
   die Hauptmahlzeit — main meal
   das Mittagessen (—) — mid-day meal
   die Beilage (—n) — side dish
   beispielsweise — for example

   der Reis (—e) — rice
   die Nudel (—n) — noodle
   das Gemüse (no plural) — vegetables
   das Gericht (—e) — dish
   der Schweinebraten (—) — roast pork
   der Knödel (—) — dumpling
   das Blaukraut — red cabbage
   die Schwarzwälderkirschtorte — Black Forest gâteau
   das Vollkornbrot (—e) — wholemeal bread
   der Aufschnitt (no plural) — plate of assorted cold meats
   eintauschen — to exchange

   Expressions and Idioms

   es hat mich sehr gefreut, zu hören . . . — I was very pleased to hear . . .
   ich will Dir einige Tips geben — I'd like to give you a few tips
   wenn man sich . . . mehr Zeit lassen kann — when one can allow oneself more time
   die Schule ist bereits mittags aus — schools have already finished by mid-day
   unter der Woche — during the week
   . . . kommen erst zum Abendessen nach Hause — do not come home until it is time for the evening meal
   hast Du Lust bekommen . . .? — do you feel that you would like . . .?

(iii) *Exercises – Section B*

1. On the right-hand side of the page is a list of things you enjoyed doing in Germany. Write out each item in a complete sentence beginning *es hat mich sehr gefreut*. For example, if you are given *in einer deutschen Familie essen*, you will write the sentence: *es hat mich sehr gefreut, in einer deutschen Familie zu essen.*

   (a)   den Tag mit Semmeln beginnen.
   (b)   am Sonntag Kuchen und Schlagrahm frühstücken.
   (c)   eine bayerische Spezialität probieren.
   (d)   nachmittags Kaffee und Kuchen essen.
   (e)   Bier zum Abendessen trinken.

2. Rewrite each of the following sentences so that they make use of a subordinate clause beginning with *da*. For example:

   Model: Die Schule ist bereits mittags aus, also kommen die Kinder zum Mittagessen nach Hause.
   Response: Da die Schule bereits mittags aus ist, kommen die Kinder zum Mittagessen nach Hause.

   (a) Du mußt einen Aufsatz schreiben, also gebe ich Dir einige Tips.
   (b) Man kann sich mehr Zeit lassen, also ißt man Käse und Wurst.
   (c) Jede Gegend in Deutschland hat ihre eigenen Spezialitäten, also gibt es kein typisch deutsches Gericht.
   (d) Die Schwarzwälderkirschtorte gibt es nur an Festtagen, also ißt man unter der Woche einfachere Kuchen.
   (e) Die Hauptmahlzeit ist normalerweise das Mittagessen, also essen wir abends kalt.

3. Each of the following sentences should be rewritten, using the correct form of *müssen* or *wollen* as shown in parentheses. For example:

   Model: Du schreibst einen Aufsatz über Essen und Trinken. (müssen)
   Response: Du mußt einen Aufsatz über Essen und Trinken schreiben.

   (a) Ich fange gleich mit dem Frühstück an. (wollen)
   (b) Die meisten Deutschen beginnen den Tag mit Semmeln. (wollen)
   (c) Die Kinder kommen zum Mittagessen nach Hause. (müssen)
   (d) Nachmittags esse ich Kuchen und trinke Kaffee. (wollen)
   (e) Am Sonntag frühstücken viele Familien Kaffee, Kuchen und Schlagrahm. (wollen)

4. Without referring back to the text, rewrite the following sentences, inserting the correct forms of the adjectival endings.

(a) Es gibt Deutsch— , vor allem deutsch— Kinder, die zum Frühstück Kornflakes essen.

(b) Am Wochenende gibt es oft ein weich— Ei.

(c) Ein typisch deutsch— Gericht gibt es nicht. Jede Gegend hat ihre eigen— Spezialitäten.

(d) Unter der Woche gibt es einfacher— Kuchen.

(e) Die meist— Väter kommen erst zum Abendessen nach Hause.

(f) Zum Abendessen gibt es verschieden— Käsesorten.

(g) Hast du Lust bekommen, deinen englisch— 'tea' gegen unser leicht— deutsch— Abendessen einzutauschen?

5.2 Listening Materials 🔊

5.2.1 Was essen Sie?

(i) Several people are interviewed here about their meals during a normal day. Listen to the tape, and then attempt the exercise to check comprehension. Attempt the exercises before looking at the written version of the text.

1. Also, Herr Lange, Sie arbeiten in einer Fabrik, das heißt, Sie müssen früh zur Arbeit gehen. Was essen Sie normalerweise zum Frühstück?

   Normalerweise stehe ich, wie gesagt, früh auf, und habe nicht viel Zeit zum Frühstücken. Ich trinke viel Kaffee, das ist mir am Morgen sehr wichtig. Ich esse vielleicht ein Brötchen mit Butter und Marmelade, aber sonst nichts.

2. Peter, Sie sind Student, Sie essen also mittags in der Mensa?

   Ja, ich esse in der Mensa. Da ist das Essen viel billiger als im Restaurant. Das Mittagessen ist meine Hauptmahlzeit. Ich esse vielleicht ein Kotelett mit Kartoffeln oder Pommes frites. Dazu nehme ich einen Salatteller, und trinke vielleicht ein Bier.

3. Frau Stett, essen Sie gern Kuchen am Nachmittag?

   Als Rentnerin ist es für mich wichtig nachmittags auszugehen, um Freunde zu treffen und ein bißchen zu plaudern. Wir treffen uns im Café und essen Kuchen mit Tee oder Kaffee dazu. Ich persönlich trinke am liebsten Tee.

4. Also, Bruno, was ißt du gern am Abend, wenn du zu Hause bist?

   Am Abend esse ich gern Aufschnitt, das heißt, eine kalte Platte mit Wurst, Käse und so weiter. Ich trinke normalerweise Limonade dazu, aber meine Eltern trinken Tee.

(ii) After listening to the tape, make a list of the things that each person likes to eat and drink, setting out the information in a table, like the following:

   Herr Lange: Breakfast
   Peter: Lunch
   Frau Stett: Afternoon tea
   Bruno: Supper

(iii) Make your own statements about what you eat for meals, basing them on the sentences used by the speakers you have heard on tape. For example:

   zum Frühstück esse ich . . . . . . und trinke . . . . . . Mittags esse ich . . . . . . am Abend . . . . . .

5.2.2 Partypläne

Karin: Du, Tina, wir haben schon so lange nichts Verrücktes mehr gemacht. Wollen wir wieder mal 'ne Party geben?

Martina: Mensch, das ist eine tolle Idee. Die letzte Party ist schon ewig her.

Karin: Wollen wir nicht diesmal vielleicht etwas kochen zur Abwechslung? Das macht doch Spaß.

Martina: Wieviel Leute wollen wir denn einladen?

Karin: Keine Ahnung, sagen wir zehn.

Martina: Ja, das reicht. Sonst sind die Töpfe zu klein.

Karin: Wir könnten doch eine Riesenpizza backen. Dann brauchen wir keine Töpfe. Und dazu gibt es Rotwein.

Martina: Ach, Pizzas machen jetzt alle. Das ist nichts Besonderes mehr, und ich esse sie sowieso nicht so gern.

Karin: Na, dann mach du mal einen Vorschlag.

Martina: Wie wäre es mit etwas Orientalischem, indischem Curry und dazu Bier für den Durst.

Karin: Das ist zu kompliziert. Außerdem bekommst du hier nicht die richtigen Gewürze und Zutaten dafür, oder es wird alles zu teuer.

Martina: Ja, du hast recht. Aber wer will schon Kartoffelsuppe mit Bockwurst essen? Das kann man doch jeden Tag haben.

Karin: Und mir hängt das zum Halse 'raus. Es muß schon etwas Extrafeines sein.

Martina: Hast du schon mal chinesisch gegessen?

Karin: Nein, wo kann man denn das?

Martina: Na, in Berlin kann man alles. Ich war vor einem Monat mit meinen Eltern im China-Restaurant. Das war einfach Klasse, und das Essen dort hat ausgezeichnet geschmeckt.

Karin: Aber die Chinesen verwenden doch sicher auch besondere Gemüsearten und Soßen. Wo willst du die denn herbekommen?

Martina: Meine Mutter hat mal versucht, zu Hause chinesisch zu kochen. Das hat eigentlich ganz gut geklappt, auch mit deutschen Zutaten.

Karin: Was war denn das, und was braucht man dazu?

Martina: Ich weiß nicht mehr genau, wie das Gericht hieß, aber alles, was wir brauchen, ist ein Weißkohl, Zwiebeln, Schweinefilet, Soyasoße, Reis und natürlich Reisstäbchen.

Karin: Das klingt nicht so kompliziert und wird bestimmt lustig. Wollen wir das probieren? Laß uns mal ausrechnen, wieviel wir brauchen. Und was gibt es übrigens zu trinken?

Martina: Was die Gäste mitbringen.

(i) *Comprehension Questions*

1. What does Karin suggest to her friend Tina?
2. Have they had a party recently?
3. How many people do they suggest inviting?
4. What is the first suggestion that Karin makes?
5. Why does Tina turn down this first suggestion?
6. What is the next proposal, made by Tina this time?
7. Why does Karin not like this second suggestion?
8. What are they fed up with eating?
9. What has given Tina the idea of a Chinese meal?
10. Does Karin have doubts? What are they?
11. What do they decide to do in the end?
12. Where will the drink for their party come from?

„Wollen wir wieder mal eine Party geben?"

(ii) *Role Play*

Listen again to the tape and note ways in which suggestions can be made. Make a list of the phrases you hear — for example: *wollen wir nicht . . .? ; wir könnten doch . . .; wie wäre es mit . . .?* Note also ways of responding to suggestions — for example: *das ist eine tolle Idee; ja, du hast recht; das klingt nicht so kompliziert.* Now, with this information and the knowledge you already have about putting questions, play your part in the two role plays below, in the first one of which you are telephoning a friend to suggest having a party, and in the second one of which you are replying to a friend who has called round to ask you out for a meal. Various other phrases from the text are included in the role plays. If you do not know these phrases, listen again to the conversation, or turn to the explanation of vocabulary.

1. (Say hallo to your friend, and say what about having a party.)

Freund: Das ist eine tolle Idee. Was machen wir?

You: (Say what about cooking something for a change.) was uber kuchen fur ein wechslen

Freund: Ja, schön. Wie viele Leute wollen wir denn einladen?

You: (How about ten?)

Freund: Ja, das reicht. Und was essen wir, meinst du?

You: (How about a pizza? And say that you could drink beer or wine.)

Freund: Gut, machen wir 's so. Das ist nicht zu kompliziert.

You: (Say yes, he is right. It is best to suggest something simple. Shall we try that? Suggest that you should both meet up next day to make plans.)

Freund: Gut, also morgen um II Uhr im Domcafé. Also, tschüß.

2. (Say hallo to your friend and ask her in.)

Freund: Tag, Peter. Hast du schon für heute abend etwas vor? Wollen wir vielleicht im Restaurant essen?

You: (Say that is a very good idea. It is a long time since you both had a meal together in a restaurant. What does she suggest?)

Freund: Wie wäre es mit etwas Orientalischem? Ein indischer Curry wäre doch schön, nicht?

You: (Say you are not too keen on curry. Ask her whether she has ever had a Chinese meal.)

Freund: Chinesisch? Ja aber das ist schon lange her. Weißt du, das ist keine schlechte Idee. Wo kann man denn das?

You: (Say there is a new Chinese restaurant in the *Marktstraße.* You could both give it a try.)

Freund: OK, ich hole dich also um 8 Uhr ab. Bis dann, tschüß.

You: (Say see you soon.)

(iii) **Explanations**

Select Vocabulary

die **Abwechslung** (—en) — change; diversion; variety
einladen (u, a) — to invite
sonst . . . — otherwise . . .
der **Topf** (¨e) — pot; pan
backen — to bake
der **Vorschlag** (¨e) — suggestion
außerdem — besides
das **Gewürz** (—) — spice

die **Zutaten** (plural) — ingredients
ausgezeichnet — excellent
verwenden — to use
die **Soße** (—n) — sauce
der **Weißkohl** — white cabbage
die **Zwiebel** (—n) — onion
das **Reisstäbchen** (—) — chop-stick
der **Gast** (¨e) — guest

Expressions and Idioms

wollen wir . . .? — shall we . . .
das ist eine tolle Idee — that is a great idea
das macht doch Spaß — that's terrific fun
zur Abwechslung — as a change
keine Ahnung — I've no idea
das reicht — that's enough
ich esse sie sowieso nicht gern — anyway, I don't like them much
wie wäre es mit . . .? — what about . . .?
für den Durst — to quench one's thirst
du hast recht — you are right
mir hängt das zum Halse 'raus — I've had as much of that as I can take
das war einfach Klasse — that was simply fantastic
wollen wir das probieren? — shall we try it?

Grammar

Note a number of examples in the text where *nichts* or *etwas* are used with a following adjectival noun. For example:

nichts Verrücktes — nothing crazy

nichts Besonderes — nothing special

etwas Extrafeines — something really delicious

Note that, when necessary, the adjective used as a noun takes adjectival endings — for example: wie wäre es mit etwas Orientalischem? (See also explanation in Grammar Summary sections (4e); 8.5(p).)

6 Einkaufen und Post

6.1 Reading Materials

The first reading passage below, taken from a publicity hand-out in a large store, shows that the consumer society is as much a feature of the Federal Republic as of other Western European countries. The passage also shows the extent to which English (or American) words are used in such promotions. Then follows a guide to the departments of a big store, and the helpful instructions of the *Deutsche Bundespost* on how to address letters.

6.1.1 Besondere Angebote zu besonderen Preisen!

Alle diese tollen Angebote können Sie in Ihrem Kaufhaus gleich mitnehmen oder im Service-Center bestellen.

Wer schnell ist, hat den Vorteil!!

Darum — gleich kommen oder in die Verkaufsstelle anrufen!	
Besonders leiser Haartrockner	DM 20
Car-Stereo	DM 229
Quarzuhr — Sensationell im Preis!	DM 45
Kleinbildkamera — auto-Focus — jederzeit scharfe Bilder	DM 298
Für den richtigen Urlaubssound! — Stereo-Radio-Recorder	DM 199
Touren Sporträder	ab DM 199
Haus- und Gartenarbeit leicht gemacht Black and Decker Rasentrimmer	DM 76
Waschvollautomat zum Super-Sparpreis	DM 648

Das ist Service! Das ist Leistung! Schnell und problemlos in Ihrem Kaufhaus.

(i) *Comprehension Questions*

1. Do you have to visit the store in person to buy these things?
2. What is special about the hair-dryer?
3. What do they claim you always get when you use the camera on offer?
4. Do they suggest that you use the stereo radio and recorder at work or on holiday?
5. What is the cheapest price for a touring cycle?
6. What is claimed for the Black and Decker tool on offer?
7. What is the most expensive item offered in this list?

Kaufhäuser an der Hauptgeschäftsstraße, Frankfurt am Main

(ii) *Role Play*

At the beginning of the list of items it says that you can order by telephone if you wish. Decide what you would like to order, and then prepare what you might say on the telephone, using the following list of points to help you plan your part of the conversation.

1. Ask whether that is the Kaufhaus Hertie.
2. Say you would like to buy a quartz clock.
3. Ask whether the price is still DM 45.

4. Ask whether you must come to the store or whether they can send it to you by post.

5. Ask whether you can pay by cheque or is cash better.

You can practise this role play by asking about other articles you might be interested in.

6.1.2 Im Kaufhaus

Below is set out the complete guide to the departments of a big store, just as you might see them near the lift or escalator. This will help you with vocabulary for things you might want to mention in role plays. There are probably quite a few words you do not know, but see whether you can guess at some of the meanings.

1. What do you think is the German for the following items: poultry; fruit and vegetables; children's furniture; presents; gloves; ladies' hats; lost property office; bed-linen; sweets.

2. On which floor will you find the following: children's department; aprons; sports articles; umbrellas; jewellery; curtains; kitchen furniture?

3. Make up short sentences to ask politely where you can find: the cafeteria; the tea-room; men's wear; handkerchiefs.

6. Stock	Brot/Backwaren	Geflügel	Tiefkühlkost
	Cafeteria	Lebensmittel	Weine
	Delikatessen	Obst und Gemüse	Wild
	Fisch	Spirituosen	
	Fleisch		
5. Stock	Auslegeware	Kleinmöbel	Silberterrasse
	Betten	Lampen	Teppiche
	Federbetten	Möbelstoffe	Wachstücher
	Deko-Stoffe	Orient	Bilder
	Gardinen	Plastik	
4. Stock	Bestecke	Haushaltswaren	Schlüsselbar
	Elektro-Artikel	Hobby	Stahlwaren
	Geschenkartikel	Keramik	Wirtschaftsartikel
	Glas	Küchenmöbel	
		Porzellan	
3. Stock	Bücher	Kunstgewerbe	Spielwaren
	Erfrischungsraum	Musikinstrumente	Tabakwaren
	Fernsehen	Rundfunk	Teeraum
	Kindermöbel	Schallplatten	Zeitschriften
	Kinderwagen	Schreibwaren	Zeitungen
2. Stock	Alles für das Kind	Herrenoberbekleidung	Mädchenbekleidung
	Damenoberbekleidung	Knabenbekleidung	Sammelkasse
	Damenhüte	Kundendienst	
	Fundbüro	Künstliche Blumen	
1. Stock	Autozubehör	Handarbeiten	Schürzen
	Badeartikel	Schuhe	Sportartikel
	Bettwäsche	Strickwaren	Taschentücher
Erdgeschoß	Foto-Optik	Lederwaren	Stoffe
	Handschuhe	Parfümerie	Strümpfe
	Herrenartikel	Schirme	Süßwaren
	Herrenhüte	Schmuck	Uhren

6.1.3 Nachrichten übermitteln

Wer schriftliche Nachrichten versenden will, hat zum Beispiel folgende Möglichkeiten:

Kurze Mitteilung auf einer Ansichtskarte ⟶ Postkarte
Längeres Schreiben im Umschlag ⟶ Brief
Gedruckter Glückwunsch mit Unterschrift ⟶ Drucksache
Gedruckte Einladung mit handschriftlichen Zusätzen ⟶ Briefdrucksache

Eine vollständige Übersicht der Sendungsarten, Gebühren, Maße und Gewichtsstufen enthält das Postgebührenheft, einen Auszug davon das amtliche Fernsprechbuch.

Damit die Sendung schnell zum richtigen Empfänger kommt, braucht sie eine vollständige Anschrift.

Was steht auf einer Briefsendung?

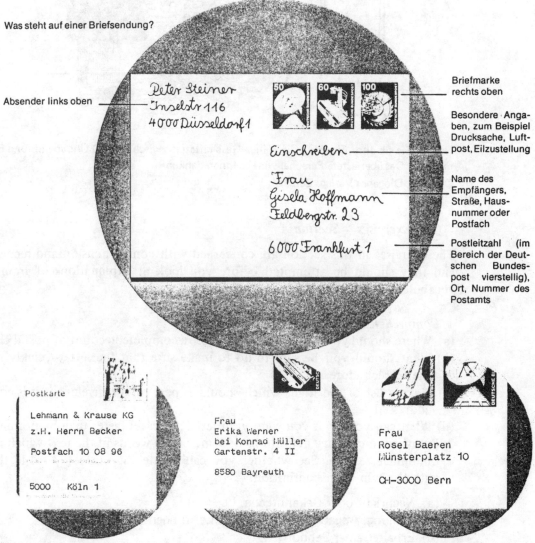

Absender links oben

Peter Steiner
Inselstr 116
4000 Düsseldorf 1

Einschreiben

Frau
Gisela Hoffmann
Feldbergstr. 23

6000 Frankfurt 1

Briefmarke rechts oben

Besondere Angaben, zum Beispiel Drucksache, Luftpost, Eilzustellung

Name des Empfängers, Straße, Hausnummer oder Postfach

Postleitzahl (im Bereich der Deutschen Bundespost vierstellig), Ort, Nummer des Postamts

Postkarte

Lehmann & Krause KG
z.H. Herrn Becker

Postfach 10 08 96

5000   Köln 1

Frau
Erika Werner
bei Konrad Müller
Gartenstr. 4 II

8580 Bayreuth

Frau
Rosel Baeren
Münsterplatz 10

CH-3000 Bern

Gegen besondere Gebühr werden eilige Briefe und Postkarten mit Luftpost befördert oder von Eilboten zugestellt. Besondere Klebezettel kennzeichnen zum Beispiel:

Luftpostsendung   Eilsendung   Einschreibsendung   Wertsendung

Stand 06/79

Informationsmappe UNSERE POST 2

61

Nutzen Sie für Ihre Einkäufe die ruhige Geschäftszeit zwischen 8.00 Uhr abends und 5.00 Uhr morgens. Das überlastete Personal wird es Ihnen danken
© Loriot, Diogenes Verlag, Zürich

(i) *Exercises – Section A*

The exercises in this section are concerned with comprehension and recognition, and they should be attempted before you look at explanations of grammar or vocabulary.

1. *Comprehension questions*
(a) Where should you look if you want to see a complete account of postal charges?
(b) What should you be sure to do to make sure that the letter quickly reaches the correct addressee?
(c) Make a list of the items which should appear on an envelope if it is correctly addressed.
(d) What can you do if you want your letter to travel faster than by normal mail?
2. Below are dictionary definitions of some of the words in the text which may be unfamiliar to you. See whether you can locate the correct word in the text with the help of this definition.

(a) Nachricht oder Bekanntgabe.
(b) Zahlung; Abgabe für behördliche Leistungen.
(c) Erhalter einer Sendung.
(d) fortbringen; transportieren.
(e) Dienstmann, der Gänge besorgt (meist zu Rad oder Motorad).

(ii) *Explanations*

Select Vocabulary

die Nachricht (–n) – news	der Absender (–) – sender
die Mitteilung (–en) – communication	der Empfänger (–) – addressee; recipient
der Umschlag (¨e) – envelope	die Briefmarke (–n) – postage stamp
gedruckt – printed	die Angabe (–n) – statement; instruction

Guter Briefstil will erarbeitet sein. Nur durch regelmäßige Lektüre verschiedener Privat- und Geschäftskorrespondenzen gelingt die Vervollkommnung der eigenen schriftlichen Ausdrucksform.

© Loriot, Diogenes Verlag, Zürich

der Glückwunsch (⸚e) — congratulations
der Zusatz (⸚e) — additional remark
die Übersicht (—en) — overview
die Gebühr (—en) — charge; postage; fee
das Maß (—e) — measurement
das Gewicht (—e) — weight
die Gewichtsstufe (—n) — weight
  categories
vollständig — complete
die Anschrift (—en) — address

die Drucksache (—n) — printed material
die Luftpost — airmail
die Eilzustellung (—en) — special delivery
das Einschreiben — recorded delivery
die Postleitzahl (—en) — postal code
befördern — to send by post; to transport
der Eilbote (—n) — messenger
zustellen — to deliver
der Klebezettel (—) — sticky label

Expressions and Idioms

wer schriftliche Nachrichten versenden will . . . — whoever wants to send a written
  message
damit die Sendung schnell zum richtigen Empfänger kommt . . . — in order that
  the item (letter) quickly reaches the right addressee

links oben . . . rechts oben – top left . . . top right
gegen besondere Gebühr – for a special fee

Grammar

The following are the items of grammar of which there are examples in the text, and for which the Section B exercises provide practice. The references in parentheses give the sections of the Grammar Summary where the particular points are explained.

(a) Use of *wer* as subordinating conjunction (8.2(4)).
(b) *damit* clauses (12(14)(c)).

(iii) *Exercises – Section B*

1. In the text the opening sentence uses *wer* as a subordinating conjunction meaning 'whoever' or 'a person who . . .'. Take each of the four short statements that follow the opening sentence and make a similar *wer* clause. For example:

Model: Kurze Mitteilung auf einer Ansichtskarte ⟶ *Postkarte*
Response: Wer eine kurze Mitteilung auf einer Ansichtskarte versenden will muß eine Postkarte schicken.

(a) Längeres Schreiben im Umschlag ⟶ Brief
(b) Gedruckter Glückwunsch mit Unterschrift ⟶ Drucksache
(c) Gedruckte Einladung mit handschriftlichen Zusätzen ⟶ Briefdrucksache

2. Take as your model the sentence: *Damit die Sendung schnell zum richtigen Empfänger kommt, braucht sie eine vollständige Anschrift.* Using this sentence and introducing the verb *müssen*, make similar sentences from the following items. For example:

Model: Absender links oben.
Response: Damit die Sendung schnell zum richtigen Empfänger kommt, muß der Absender links oben stehen.

(a) Briefmarke rechts oben.
(b) Besondere Angaben unter den Briefmarken, rechts oben.
(c) Der Name des Empfängers in der Mitte des Umschlags.
(d) Die Postleitzahl vor dem Namen der Stadt.
(e) Die Nummer des Postamts nach dem Namen des Orts.

3. Write a formal letter to the German Post Office expressing interest in German postage stamps and asking whether it is possible to have sets of stamps sent to collectors. Use the outline below to help you. This is only a short letter, but set it out carefully, as explained for formal letters on page 247, and also prepare the envelope you would send, making sure you follow the recommendations of the German Post Office for the correct addressing of envelopes. The address for the envelope is: der Bundesminister für das Post- und Fernmeldewesen, Dienstgebäude, Adenauerallee 81, 5300 Bonn 1.

Ich interessiere mich für; ich sammle gern . . .; ich habe eine große Briefmarkensammlung; ich interessiere mich besonders für . . .; eine vollständige Reihe (a full set); ich möchte sehr gern . . .; Darf ich fragen, ob . . .; Könnten Sie mir vielleicht . . .; wäre es vielleicht möglich . . .?

6.2 Listening Materials 🖭

In the section of reading materials you worked on a text giving a series of offers at a big store. The first listening text is rather similar. This time you actually visit the store, and over the loudspeakers you hear announcements about the bargains you will find in certain departments. Then follows a conversation between a woman shopping and a young woman carrying out a consumer survey about shopping preferences.

6.2.1 Im Kaufhaus

— Verehrte Kunden! Beachten Sie unsere Schmuckabteilung im ersten Stock!
— Heute gibt es wieder preiswerte Sonderangebote im Untergeschoß. Greifen Sie zu, solange der Vorrat reicht.
— Vergessen Sie nicht, einen Blick in unsere Lederabteilung im Erdgeschoß mit ihren Superangeboten zu werfen!
— Unsere Parfümerieabteilung bietet heute französische Parfüms zu stark reduzierten Preisen an. Lassen Sie sich diese Chance nicht entgehen!
— Lassen Sie sich die Sonderangebote der Damenabteilung nicht entgehen! Schicke Damenröcke in sommerlichen Farben sind von 98 DM auf 49 DM reduziert.

(i) *Comprehension Questions*

1. On which floor is the jewellery department?
2. What is on offer in the basement?
3. What is on special offer on the ground floor?
4. The perfume department has something to offer. What is it?
5. What do they tell you about the ladies' skirts which are on offer?
6. What is the reduction in price of the skirts?

(ii) *Say it in German*

Listen again to the text and see whether you can find the German expressions for the following:

1. As long as the stock lasts.
2. Do not forget.
3. Do not miss this chance.
4. At considerably reduced prices.
5. In summer colours.

(iii) *Explanations*

> *Select Vocabulary*
>
> | | |
> |---|---|
> | verehren — to honour | zugreifen (i, i) — to act fast; to get in quickly |
> | der Kunde (—n) — customer | der Vorrat ($\ddot{}$e) — supply; stock |
> | beachten — to pay attention to; to take heed of | das Leder (—) — leather |
> | der Schmuck (plural unusual) — jewellery; decorations | das Erdgeschoß (—sse) — ground floor |
> | die Abteilung (—en) — department | anbieten (o, o) — to offer |
> | preiswert — cheap; of good value | entgehen (entging, entgangen) — to escape |
> | das Sonderangebot (—e) — special offer | schick — smart; chic |
> | das Untergeschoß (—sse) — basement | |

6.2.2 Meinungsumfrage

Karin Schröder: Guten Tag. Mein Name ist Karin Schröder. Ich mache eine
                  Umfrage für das Verbraucherinformationsbüro. Wären Sie bereit,
                  ein paar Fragen für uns zu beantworten?

Frau Kienzel: Ja, wenn es denn sein muß, aber ich habe nicht viel Zeit. Ich muß
                  noch einkaufen.

K S: Keine Sorge. Das dauert nur ein paar Minuten, und hier ist gleich die erste
       Frage. Wie oft gehen Sie in der Woche einkaufen?

„Am Wochenmarkt ist alles so frisch"

F K: Tja, das ist unterschiedlich. Kleinigkeiten kaufe ich fast jeden Tag, aber Großeinkauf mache ich nur einmal in der Woche, am Freitag.

K S: Und wo machen Sie Ihre Einkäufe?

F K: Am Freitag fahren mein Mann und ich zum Aldi Supermarkt, wo wir alle wichtigen Lebensmittel und Hausartikel für die kommende Woche einkaufen. Brot und Brötchen holen wir jedoch immer frisch vom Bäcker, und Fleisch und Wurst schmecken bei unserem Fleischer besser. Obst und Gemüse kaufe ich am Sonnabend und Mittwoch auf dem Bauernmarkt ein.

K S: Und wie sieht es mit den Kleinigkeiten aus, die Sie vielleicht vergessen haben?

F K: Die kaufe ich im Laden um die Ecke bei uns oder wenn ich zufällig in die Stadt fahre.

K S: Ziehen Sie also den Supermarkt dem Tante Emma Laden vor?

F K: Nein, das möchte ich eigentlich nicht sagen. Ich finde die Supermärkte sehr unpersönlich und nervenaufreibend, aber dort ist es eben billiger, und man sieht oft günstige Sonderangebote.

K S: Und was gefällt Ihnen am Tante Emma Laden?

F K: Oh, man kennt einander und hat beim Einkaufen auch Zeit für einen kleinen Plausch. Nur ist eben alles teurer.

K S: Was schätzen Sie dann am Wochenmarkt?

F K: In erster Linie die große Auswahl und daß alles so frisch ist, ohne Konservierungsstoffe. Man kann da auch sehr preisgünstig einkaufen.

K S: Was für Verbesserungen würden Sie sich für den Einkauf wünschen?

F K: Vielleicht die Einführung einer Bestellung per Telefon und die Lieferung der Lebensmittel durch den Supermarkt. Das wäre besonders nützlich für Kranke und Behinderte.

K S: Vielen Dank, ich habe keine weiteren Fragen.

F K: Gern geschehen.

(i) *Comprehension Questions*

1. Why is Frau Kienzel a little unwilling to answer questions at first?
2. How long does Karin say that the questions will last?
3. How often does Frau Kienzel do a big shopping expedition?
4. Where do the Kienzels do their main shopping expedition of the week?
5. What sort of things does Frau Kienzel prefer to buy from small traders?
6. What do you think is meant by the expression *Tante Emma Laden*?
7. What are the advantages and disadvantages of shopping at the supermarket?
8. Give three reasons why Frau Kienzel likes shopping at the weekly market.
9. What two changes does Frau Kienzel think would improve shopping?
10. Who would receive the greatest assistance if supermarkets had a delivery service?

(ii) *Fill the Gap*

Listen carefully to the tape, and then fill in the gaps in the following statements, without reference to the written text.

1. Ich mache eine . . . . . . für das Verbraucherinformationsbüro. Wo machen Sie Ihre . . . . . .?
2. Am Freitag fahren mein Mann und ich zum Aldi Supermarkt, wo wir alle wichtigen . . . . . . und . . . . . . für die kommende Woche einkaufen. Obst und Gemüse kaufe ich am Sonnabend und Mittwoch auf dem . . . . . . ein.
3. Ich finde den Supermarkt sehr . . . . . . und . . . . . . aber dort ist es eben billiger.

4. In erster Linie die große . . . . . . und daß alles so frisch ist. Man kann da auch sehr . . . . . . kaufen.
5. Vielleicht die Einführung einer . . . . . . per Telefon und . . . . . . der Lebensmittel durch den Supermarkt.

(iii) *Role Play*

Play your part in the following short shopping scenes:
1. *Beim Bäcker*

   Verkäuferin: Guten Morgen. Was darf es sein?
   You: (Say you would like four bread rolls and a wholemeal loaf.)
   Verkäuferin: Ja, sicher. Sonst noch etwas?
   You: (Say you would like something special for a friend's birthday. Has she got a Black Forest gâteau?)
   Verkäuferin: Leider nicht. Aber einfachere Kuchen haben wir.
   You: (Ask what sort of cakes she has.)
   Verkäuferin: Wir haben Apfelkuchen, Kirschkuchen, Nußtorte.
   You: (Say a Nußtorte would be nice.)
   Verkäuferin: Also, eine Nußtorte. Sonst noch etwas?
   You: (Say no, thank you, that is all. What does that come to?)
   Verkäuferin: Das macht zusammen DM 17.50 bitte.
   You: (Say here is 17.50. Thank you and goodbye.)
   Verkäuferin: Danke schön. Auf Wiedersehen.

2. You visit the department of a store which sells *Geschenkartikel*, so that you can buy a present for your German hosts, before returning home. In the left-hand column below is a list of the sort of expressions you need when shopping. In the right-hand column are the sort of things which the sales person might say. Afterwards there follows a list of possible presents, although you can add anything to this list which you think you might personally want to buy. Try to put together a complete conversation, such as might take place in the circumstances described:

ich möchte bitte . . .	was darf es sein?
ich hätte gern . . .	was für ein . . . möchten Sie?
geben Sie mir bitte . . .	leider nicht, aber hier haben wir . . .
ich hätte lieber . . .	haben Sie außerdem noch einen Wunsch?
könnten Sie mir bitte . . . zeigen?	Ist das alles?
was kostet . . .?	das macht zusammen . . .
Was macht das zusammen?	

Schallplatten	Vase
Parfüm	Ziergegenstand (aus Porzellan)
Schmuck	Gemälde
Holzschnitt	Gläser

(iv) *Explanations*

vorziehen (like ziehen, zog, gezogen) — to prefer
nervenaufreibend — nerve-racking
der Plausch (—e) — chat

der Ziergegenstand (¨e) — ornament
das Gemälde (—) — painting
das Glas (¨er) — glass

Expressions and Idioms

keine Sorge — don't worry
wenn ich zufällig in die Stadt fahre — if I happen to go into town
der Tante Emma Laden — the little shop on the corner
in erster Linie — above all
gern geschehen — you're welcome; don't mention it
tja . . . — well . . .

7 Schule und Erziehung

7.1 Reading Materials

There are some obvious differences between life at school in Great Britain and in the Federal Republic. Some of these differences emerge just by looking at a typical timetable, like the one below, or at a school report. In the passage where Leif talks about his school, other differences become clear, such as the earlier start in the morning, the afternoons without lessons, and so on. The passage from the German Democratic Republic tells about an earlier stage of education, a child's first experience of going to the crèche where working mothers can leave their children during the day.

7.1.1 Leifs Stundenplan

Zeit	Montag	Dienstag	Mittwoch	Donnerstag	Freitag	Samstag
8.10–8.55	Biologie	Englisch	Mathe	Biologie	Chemie	Englisch
9.0–9.45	Chemie	Französisch	Mathe	Musik	Französisch	Französisch
10.0–10.45	Musik	Mathe	Deutsch	Latein	Sozialkunde	Deutsch
10.50–11.35	Latein	Deutsch	Deutsch	Religion	Physik	
11.45–12.30	Physik	Geschichte	Religion	Englisch	Physik	
12.35–1.10	Englisch	Sozialkunde	Französisch	Mathe	Physik	

(i) *Comprehension Questions*

1. How many languages does Leif study (including German), and what are they all called? Latin, English, French, German (4)
2. Which subjects does he do which you do not do at school? Sozialkunde
3. Is there anything you do at school which does not appear on his timetable? Drama
4. How many periods per week of History does he do? 1
5. What do you think *Sozialkunde* means? social education

(ii) *Say it in German*

Write out your own school timetable as though you were sending it to a German pen-friend. Write out all the subjects, with their German names.

7.1.2 Reinhard Fischers Zeugnis

> *Städtische Grundschule am Adenauerplatz*
> # Zeugnis
> für Reinhard Fischer
> geboren am 18.7.76
> *Sozialverhalten und Arbeitsverhalten*
> Reinhard arbeitete gern mit den anderen Kindern am Gruppentisch zusammen. Über lange Zeit konnte er aufmerksam an seiner Arbeit bleiben. Seine Aufgaben erledigte er zuverlässig. Oft brachte er den Unterricht durch eigene Ideen weiter.
> *Hinweise zu Lernbereichen*
> Reinhard hat die grundlegenden Anforderungen im Lesen, Schreiben und in Mathematik erreicht. Kleine Texte aus der Klassenbücherei kann er schon selbständig lesen. Wenn Reinhard sich Zeit läßt, kann er sauber und fleißig schreiben. Wenn gemalt oder gesungen wird, ist Reinhard mit Begeisterung dabei.

(i) *Comprehension Questions*

1. What sort of school does Reinhard attend?
2. Does he like working in groups with other children?
3. Does he have ideas of his own?
4. What stage has Reinhard reached in his reading?
5. What is his writing like?
6. What is his attitude to painting and singing?

(ii) *Unjumble it*

In the following sentences words have been jumbled up. Without looking back at the original report, see whether you can unscramble the words and write the sentences in the correct order.

1. gemalt wird Begeisterung wenn Reinhard dabei gesungen oder ist mit.
2. gern anderen Kindern mit Reinhard arbeitete den zusammen Gruppentisch am.
3. Ideen durch weiter er oft brachte Unterricht den eigene.

(iii) *Summarise*

Can you summarise, in about 40 words of English, what you know about Reinhard's school performance.

(iv) *Explanations*

Select Vocabulary

die Grundschule (–n) — primary school	grundlegend — basic; fundamental
das Sozialverhalten — social attitude	die Anforderung (–en) — requirement; demand
das Arbeitsverhalten — attitude to work	selbständig — independent
aufmerksam — attentive	sauber — clean
erledigen — to complete	malen — to paint
zuverlässig — reliable	singen (a, u) — to sing
der Hinweis (–e) — comment	die Begeisterung — enthusiasm
der Lernbereich (–e) — area of study	

7.1.3 Mittags fängt das Leben an

Wie sieht der Tag eines Schülers in der Bundesrepublik Deutschland aus? Darauf gibt es viele Antworten, denn einen ,,Durchschnittsschüler'' gibt es nicht. Leif Stange beschreibt hier seinen Schulalltag, der mit dem Leben anderer Schüler doch vieles gemeinsam hat.

Hallo! Ich bin Leif, und ich bin 14 Jahre alt. Jeden Morgen fahre ich zur Schule nach Wiesbaden. Deshalb muß ich ziemlich früh aufstehen. Mein Wecker klingelt kurz nach 6 Uhr. Ich esse mein Frühstück, und um halb acht gehe ich aus dem Haus. Zur Bushaltestelle muß ich ungefähr 10 Minuten laufen. Am Bus stehen viele Leute, die zur Schule fahren. Die meisten sind in meinem Alter. Wir haben einen Schulbus, der uns direkt zur Schule bringt. Im Bus treffe ich viele von meinen Klassenkameraden. Die meisten arbeiten noch schnell an ihren Hausaufgaben. Einige unterhalten sich über Fußball. Der Bus fährt etwa 20 Minuten bis zur Schule.

Die erste Stunde beginnt um 8.10 Uhr. Heute ist Donnerstag. In der ersten Stunde haben wir Biologie. Der Unterricht ist manchmal richtig interessant, aber oft langweilen wir uns und machen Blödsinn. Fünf Minuten vor 9.00 Uhr ist die Stunde zu Ende. Wir haben jetzt eine kleine Pause. In der zweiten Stunde haben wir Musik. Nach 45 Minuten (so lange dauert bei uns eine Schulstunde) haben wir 15 Minuten ,,große Pause''. Dritte Stunde Latein und danach Religion. Die erste interessante Stunde heute. Dann kommt die zweite Pause, die 10 Minuten dauert, und dann die fünfte Stunde. Endlich haben wir Mathematik, und dann das langersehnte Schlußklingeln. Alle stürzen ins Freie. Jetzt beginnt das Leben! Ich fahre nach Hause, esse immer allein, weil ich so spät aus der Schule komme, dann lege ich mich hin. Ich bin mittags immer total erschöpft. Nach ungefähr einer Stunde fange ich mit den Hausaufgaben an.

© *Scala Jugendmagazin*, Dezember 1980

(i) *Exercises — Section A*

The exercises in this section are concerned with comprehension and recognition, and they should be attempted before you look at explanations of grammar or vocabulary.

1. *Falsch/Richtig* Read the following statements and decide which you think are true and which are false, according to the information contained in the passage above.

(a) Leif's alarm clock rings before 6.0 a.m.
(b) He has to run to catch a bus at ten past six.
(c) He meets up with his school friends on the bus.
(d) They think that football is very entertaining.
(e) The bus takes about 20 minutes to get to school.
(f) On a Thursday he has Biology first.
(g) Lessons last 45 minutes.
(h) He finds Religious Education the first interesting lesson of the day.
(i) He has his lunch at home alone.
(j) After eating, he starts immediately with his homework.

Jugendliche können auch ohne Abitur glücklich werden

© Loriot, Diogenes Verlag, Zürich

2. Below is an account of a day at school, similar to that described by Leif, but written in note form. Rewrite these notes in continuous German — if possible, without referring back to the text.

6 Uhr Wecker klingelt.
6.10 Uhr aufstehen.
7 Uhr Frühstück
7.30 Uhr das Haus verlassen.
Zehn Minuten zu Fuß. 7.45 Uhr Bus kommt, fährt 20 Minuten zur Schule.
8.10 Uhr erste Stunde — Mathematik.
9.45 Uhr große Pause.
6 Stunden am Morgen. 1.10 Uhr Schlußklingeln, Schule aus.
1.45 Uhr komme zu Hause an. Mittagessen, hinlegen.
2.30 Uhr Hausaufgaben.

(ii) *Explanations*

Select Vocabulary

der Durchschnittsschüler — average pupil
der Schulalltag — everyday school routine
der Wecker (—) — alarm clock
das Alter (—) — age
sich unterhalten (ie, a) — to chat; to converse

sich langweilen — to get bored
langersehnt — longed for
das Schlußklingeln — final bell
sich hinlegen — to lie down
erschöpft — exhausted

Expressions and Idioms

es hat mit dem Leben anderer Schüler vieles gemeinsam — it has a lot in common with the life of other pupils
in meinem Alter — the same age as me
wir machen Blödsinn — we act the fool; we play about
alle stürzen ins Freie — everyone rushes out into the open air

(iii) **Exercises — Section B**

1. In the following sentences the relative pronoun has been omitted. Rewrite the sentences, inserting the correct form of the relative pronoun.

   (a) Er beschreibt seinen Schulalltag, ... mit dem Leben anderer Schüler doch vieles gemeinsam hat.
   (b) Am Bus stehen viele Leute, ... zur Schule fahren.
   (c) Ich habe einige Freunde, ... sich über Fußball unterhalten.
   (d) Ich habe viele Klassenkameraden, ... noch schnell an ihren Hausaufgaben arbeiten.
   (e) Dann kommt die zweite Pause, ... 10 Minuten dauert.
   (f) Endlich kommt das Schlußklingeln, ... wir alle schon lange ersehnt haben.

2. On the basis of the model given below, rewrite the following sentences, using a clause beginning *weil*:

   Model: Jeden Morgen fahre ich nach Wiesbaden, deshalb muß ich früh aufstehen.
   Response: Ich muß früh aufstehen, weil ich jeden Morgen nach Wiesbaden fahre.

   (a) Der Bus fährt um dreiviertel acht, deshalb gehe ich um halb acht aus dem Haus.
   (b) Der Bus hat etwas Verspätung, deshalb stehen viele Leute da.
   (c) Der Unterricht ist nicht sehr interessant, deshalb langweilen wir uns.
   (d) Die Schule ist aus, deshalb stürzen alle ins Freie.
   (e) Ich bin mittags immer total erschöpft, deshalb lege ich mich hin.
   (f) Ich habe viel zu tun, deshalb fange ich mit den Hausaufgaben an.

3. Using the same sentences, rewrite them, using *denn*. For example:
   Ich muß früh aufstehen, denn ich fahre jeden Morgen nach Wiesbaden.

4. First, draw up your own weekly timetable in German, rather like the example of Leif's timetable given earlier. Then write a letter to a German friend describing a typical day. Use Leif's account of his school day as a model, and write out the times in full. For example: *Um sieben Uhr stehe ich auf, esse mein Frühstück, und um halb acht gehe ich aus dem Haus . . .*, etc.

7.1.4 Kinderkrippe in Cottbus (DDR)

Es ist Silkas erster Tag in der Krippe, ein erster Besuch für die Dauer von einer Stunde. Aber das Kind fühlt sich hier nicht fremd, denn es ist mit seiner Mutter gekommen, die aufgeregt im Hintergrund sitzt und voller Spannung beobachtet, wie sich ihr Töchterchen hier zurechtfindet. Ab und zu kommt Silka für einen Moment zu ihr gelaufen, und zeigt ihr, was sie gerade entdeckt hat — und ist schon wieder unterwegs.

Markus, ein Jahr und einen Monat alt, verhält sich zunächst ganz anders. Er ist erschrocken über die neuen Eindrücke, die fremden Menschen und die unbekannten Räumlichkeiten. Er weint, und hält sich an der Mutter fest. Doch schnell versiegen die Tränen. Er beginnt, seine Umgebung zu beobachten. Dann macht er sich los, als ihm die Tante ein großes Lastauto bringt, mit dem er durch das ganze Zimmer robbt, denn laufen kann er noch nicht.

Die schöne, helle Kinderkrippe im Cottbuser Neubauviertel Sachsendorf-Madlow ist im Dezember 1980 eröffnet worden. Insgesamt 40 Mitarbeiter sorgen hier dafür, daß 144 Kinder tagsüber ein zweites Zuhause haben. „Jedes Kind soll sich bei uns vom ersten Tag an wohlfühlen" sagt Leiterin Angelika Wetzel. „Und jede Erzieherin muß es so betreuen, als wäre es ihr eigenes. Gerade das Lebensalter von etwa einem Jahr, in dem die meisten zu uns kommen, ist für die Entwicklung des Kindes besonders wichtig."

Zunächst einmal soll die Erzieherin das Kind kennenlernen, noch ehe es zur Krippe kommt. Die verantwortliche Kollegin besucht jetzt gemeinsam mit der Leiterin erst einmal die Familie zu Hause. Und dann der erste Besuch. Die eine, erste Stunde ist für das Kind eine lange Zeit. Da muß die Mama einfach dabei sein. Nach der ersten Stunde wird gemeinsam besprochen, ob die Anwesenheit der Mutter auch weiterhin nötig ist.

In der Stadt Cottbus besuchen zur Zeit etwa 4400 Kinder eine Krippe, d.h. 88,8 Prozent aller Kinder in diesem Alter.

Helgard Behrendt

© *Neue Berliner Illustrierte*, 52/84

(i) *Exercises – Section A*

The exercises in this section are concerned with comprehension and recognition, and they should be attempted before you look at explanations of grammar or vocabulary.

1. *Comprehension questions*
   (a) How long does Silka's first visit to the crèche last?
   (b) Why does the child not feel worried about being in a strange place?
   (c) What does Silka do when she comes to find her mother?
   (d) Does Markus fit in as well as Silka to start with?
   (e) What helps him to leave his mother for the first time?
   (f) What is the main aim of the assistants in the crèche as far as the children in their care are concerned?
   (g) What is the first task of the nursery assistant?
   (h) How long does the child's first visit last?
   (i) Does the mother need to visit again after the first hour?

2. Fill in the gaps in the following passage by choosing words from the list below the text.

   Das Kind fühlt sich hier nicht . . . . . ., denn es ist mit seiner Mutter . . . . . ., die . . . . . . im Hintergrund sitzt. Ab und zu kommt Silka zu ihr . . . . . ., zeigt ihr, ... sie gerade entdeckt hat — und ist schon wieder . . . . . . Markus verhält sich . . . . . . ganz anders. Er ist erschrocken . . . . . . die neuen Eindrücke, die . . . . . . Menschen. Er weint, hält sich an der Mutter . . . . . . Doch schnell . . . . . . die Tränen. Er beginnt, seine Umgebung zu . . . . . . Dann macht er sich . . . . . ., als ihm die Tante ein großes Lastauto . . . . . ., mit dem er durch das ganze . . . . . . robbt.

   zunächst; fremd; beobachten; unterwegs; über; versiegen; Zimmer; gelaufen; fest; los; bringt; gekommen; was; fremden; aufgeregt.

Select Vocabulary

die **Dau**er (no plural) – duration	die **U**mgebung (–en) – surroundings
aufgeregt – excited	**r**obben – to crawl
be**o**bachten – to observe	er**ö**ffnen – to open
sich zu**r**echtfinden (a, u) – to find one's	die Erz**i**eherin (–nen) – nursery nurse;
way around	nursery assistant
sich ver**h**alten (ie, a) – to behave	be**tr**euen – to look after
er**schr**ocken – scared (er**schr**ecken	die Entwicklung (–en) – development
(a, o) = to scare)	ver**a**ntwortlich – responsible
der **Ei**ndruck (–e) – impression	die **A**nwesenheit – presence
die R**äu**mlichkeiten (plural) – premises	w**ei**terhin – on top of that
vers**i**egen – to dry up	

Expressions and Idioms

voller Spannung – full of excitement
ab und zu – from time to time
Silka kommt gelaufen – Silka comes running (see Grammar Summary 12.13(b)4)
dann macht er sich los – he breaks away
als wäre es ihr eigenes – as though it were her own
noch ehe es zur Krippe kommt – even before it comes to the crèche
da muß die Mama einfach dabei sein – Mummy has simply got to be there

Grammar

The following are the items of grammar of which there are examples in the text, and for which the Section B exercises provide practice. The references in parentheses give the sections of the Grammar Summary where the particular points are explained.

(a) More on relative clauses (8.4).
(b) *sollen* and *müssen* (12.11(b)).
(c) *als wäre* . . . (12.14(b)).
(d) Possessive adjectives *sein/ihr* (4(i)).
(d) Dative pronouns *ihr/ihm* (7.1).

(iii) *Exercises – Section B*

1. The text contains one example of *was* as a relative pronoun: *Silka zeigt ihr, was sie gerade entdeckt hat*. This could be translated 'Silka shows her what she has just discovered'. Following the same pattern, translate the following sentences into German:

   (a) Silka tells her what she has just done.
   (b) The assistant shows Markus what she has brought.
   (c) The director of the crèche explains what is done there.
   (d) The assistant must know what is especially important for the child.

2. Following the example of the model, form sentences using the Dative form of the relative pronoun.

   Model: Die Tante bringt ihm ein großes Lastauto. Er robbt damit durch das ganze Zimmer.

Die Erzieherin muß die Kinder gut kennenlernen

Response: Die Tante bringt ihm ein großes Lastauto, mit dem er durch das ganze Zimmer robbt.

(a) Heute ist Silkas erster Tag in der Krippe. Sie wird hier schöne Tage erleben.
(b) Er ist erschrocken über die fremden Menschen. Er findet sich mit ihnen zum ersten Mal zusammen.
(c) Die Kinder lieben die Erzieherinnen. Sie verbringen den ganzen Tag mit ihnen.
(d) Das Lebensalter von einem Jahr ist wichtig. Die meisten Kinder kommen in diesem Alter zur Krippe.

3. *Retranslation* The following sentences are English renderings of sentences from the German text containing either *soll* or *muß*. Attempt to translate them back into German without looking back at the text.

(a) Each child should feel happy with us from the very first day.
(b) Each assistant must look after it just as if it were her own.
(c) First of all the assistant should get to know the child.
(d) The mother simply must be present.

4. To practise using *als wäre* with a following clause, rewrite the sentences below, following the pattern of the model.

Model: Die Erzieherin betreut jedes Kind. Es ist wie ihr eigenes.
Response: Die Erzieherin betreut jedes Kind so, als wäre es ihr eigenes.

(a) Silka ist glücklich. Ist sie schon öfter hier in der Krippe gewesen?

(b) Markus ist schüchtern. Sind ihm alle Leute hier fremd?

(c) Markus·hält sich an der Mutter fest. Er ist wie erschrocken.

(d) Jedes Kind fühlt sich hier wohl. Es ist hier wie zu Hause.

5. In the following short extracts from the text there are gaps instead of possessive adjectives *sein/ihr* and instead of the Dative forms of the personal pronouns *ihm/ihr*. Rewrite these extracts without referring to the text, and insert the correct forms.

(a) Silka ist mit . . . . . . Mutter gekommen, die beobachtet, wie sich . . . . . . Töchterchen hier zurechtfindet.

(b) Ab und zu kommt Silka zu . . . . . . gelaufen und zeigt . . . . . ., was sie gerade entdeckt hat.

(c) Markus beginnt, ... Umgebung zu beobachten. Dann macht er sich los, als . . . . . . die Tante ein Lastauto bringt.

(d) Jede Erzieherin muß es so betreuen, als wäre es . . . . . . eigenes.

7.2 Listening Materials 🖭

7.2.1 In der Schule

(i) *Comprehension*

Here are some German pupils saying something about their schools, and their favourite subjects. Listen to the tape and then attempt the exercises.

1. Ich bin Paul. Ich gehe hier in München aufs Gymnasium. Ich bin in der sechsten Klasse und habe am liebsten Mathe und Physik. Fremdsprachen habe ich gar nicht gern. Später möchte ich vielleicht Mathe an der Uni studieren.

2. Ich heiße Petra. Ich gehe auf eine Realschule in München. Es ist eine Mädchenrealschule, aber ich wäre lieber in einer gemischten Schule mit Jungen. Ich bin in der achten Klasse und lerne sehr gern Englisch und auch Französisch. Physik und Chemie habe ich nicht gern. Das finde ich langweilig. Ich würde später gern Sprachlehrerin werden.

3. Ich komme aus Braunschweig, heiße Julia und gehe auf eine Gesamtschule. Eigentlich gibt es hier in der Stadt nur die eine Gesamtschule, aber es gefällt mir hier. Es ist gar nicht so schlimm, wie manche sagen. Ich bin jetzt in der zwölften Klasse und mache mein Abitur. Kunst ist mein Lieblingsfach, und ich möchte später auf die Kunsthochschule gehen. Sprachen habe ich auch gern, aber Mathe nicht so.

4. Also, ich bin Manfred, komme aus Singen, einer kleinen Stadt in Süddeutschland, und ich gehe hier in die Realschule. Ich bin in der neunten Klasse, und meine Lieblingsfächer sind Mathe und Englisch. Ich möchte nicht weiterstudieren. Ich würde lieber sofort arbeiten, vielleicht in einer Bank, wenn es geht.

After listening to the tape, fill in the information in the table below:

Name	Type of school	Class	Favourite Subjects	Subjects Disliked	Future Plans
Paul					
Petra					
Julia					
Manfred					

das Gymnasium (die Gymnasien) — Grammar School	die Gesamtschule (—n) — Comprehensive School
die Realschule (—n) — A secondary school for which there is no real British equivalent. In a selective system it provides a middle layer between the *Gymnasium*, taking the top layer of ability, and the *Hauptschule*, taking the rest	die Universität (—en) — (sometimes shortened to *Uni*)
	das Abitur — equivalent of 'A' level
	die Kunst ($\ddot{}$e) — art
	die Kunsthochschule (—n) — art college

The years of schooling in German schools start with year 1, when a child starts Primary School (*Grundschule*) at the age of 6. After 4 years of *Grundschule*, pupils therefore begin their secondary education in year 5, in one of the types of secondary school mentioned above, and depending on the area where they live. Full-time secondary education finishes at the age of 16, after completion of the tenth year of schooling. Pupils who wish to stay on at school for the *Abitur*, and possibly wish to go on to Higher Education at *Universität* or *Hochschule*, complete a total of 12 or 13 years of schooling.

This information about schools is true only of the Bundesrepublik. In the other German-speaking countries the education systems are different. The GDR, for example, has a completely comprehensive system of schooling, where the main type of school is the POS — that is, *Polytechnische Oberschule.*

7.2.2 Ganztags- oder Halbtagsschule?

Schüler in der Bundesrepublik Deutschland haben meistens von acht Uhr früh bis etwa ein oder zwei Uhr mittags Unterricht. Der Nachmittag ist frei. In anderen Ländern gibt es Ganztagsschulen. Was ist besser?

Matthias: Den ganzen Tag Schule — das ist ja wie ein Arbeitstag bei den Erwachsenen. Ich finde das zuviel.

Oliver: Ich war in einer Ganztagsschule in der Schweiz. Da hatte man nicht so viel Freiheit wie hier.

Matthias: Ich habe einen französischen Brieffreund — wenn der nach seiner Ganztagsschule nach Hause kommt, dann hat er zusätzlich noch Hausaufgaben. Die Ganztagsschule bringt nicht so viele Vorteile. Man lernt nämlich gar nicht so viel, denn so nach vier oder fünf Stunden läßt die Konzentration doch unheimlich nach. Und außerdem: man kann ja gar nichts Anderes mehr machen an dem Tag. Ich meine, ich habe ja auch noch andere Interessen außer Schule.

Oliver: Also da bin ich anderer Meinung. Für das Lernen finde ich die Ganztagsschule besser. Man hat mehr Zeit im Unterricht, und man lernt an einem Tag wahrscheinlich mehr als hier. Und trotzdem finde ich das deutsche System besser, weil man da einfach mehr Zeit hat für Sport, Musik — in der Gruppe oder auch ganz alleine.

Matthias: Das stimmt. Mein französischer Freund hat fast überhaupt keine Freizeit. Der findet unser System auch besser. Ich finde es nicht gut, wenn man den ganzen Tag lang in der Schule ist. Da steht man immer unter Aufsicht und wird immer beobachtet. Ich finde es besser, wenn man alleine arbeitet. Das muß man ja auch mal lernen.

Oliver: Ich meine, man muß auch mal an die Lehrer denken. Die brauchen auch
            mal Freizeit oder Zeit zum Vorbereiten.

adapted from Scala Jugendmagazin, © Dezember 1980

(i) *Comprehension Questions*

1. What does a whole day at school seem like to Matthias?
2. Oliver has experience of a whole-day school. Where did he get this experience?
3. Where does Matthias get his information about whole-day schools?
4. Why does Matthias think that one does not learn any more by going to school all day?
5. What is another reason he gives for not wanting to spend all day in school?
6. Oliver also prefers the German system. What reasons does he give for this preference?
7. Having the afternoons free teaches one something, according to Matthias. What does it teach one?
8. Oliver has another good reason for thinking mornings-only school is better. What is this last reason?

(ii) *Fill the Gap*

German conversation is full of little words such as *doch, mal, ja*. These 'particles', as they are called, give particular emphasis to what one has to say. Read section 10 in the Grammar Summary, which explains the meanings of the common particles. Then listen to the tape and write out the sentences given below, filling in the gaps with the particle which you hear used in the conversation.

1. Das ist . . . . . . wie ein Arbeitstag bei den Erwachsenen.
2. Man lernt . . . . . . gar nicht so viel, denn so nach vier oder fünf Stunden läßt die Konzentration . . . . . . unheimlich nach.
3. Und außerdem: man kann . . . . . . gar nichts Anderes mehr machen an dem Tag. Ich meine, ich habe . . . . . . noch andere Interessen außer Schule.
4. Das muß man . . . . . . auch . . . . . . lernen. Ich meine, man muß auch . . . . . . an die Lehrer denken. Die brauchen auch . . . . . . Freizeit.

(iii) *Translation*

When you have filled in the gaps and read the relevant section of the Grammar Summary, translate the above sentences into English, and try to catch the best idiomatic rendering of the German.

(iv) *Stating your Case*

This conversation has many of the phrases and expressions needed for expressing opinions, or for agreeing and disagreeing with the opinions of others. For example:

ich finde das zuviel.
ich finde das besser.
ich finde es nicht gut . . .
ich meine, . . .
da bin ich anderer Meinung.
und außerdem, . . .
das stimmt.

In addition to these expressions, there is the use of the particles mentioned above. For example, *nämlich*, which can be translated 'you see': *man lernt nämlich nicht so viel* — 'you see, one doesn't learn as much'. Using these expressions, and any other turns of phrase which come from the discussion between Matthias and Oliver, decide how you would state your own point of view on the subject of whole-day or mornings-only school, if you were faced with some of the opinions listed below, which might be put to you by a German friend.

Ganztagsschule — das ist ja wie ein Arbeitstag bei den Erwachsenen.
Da hat man nicht genug Freizeit.
Man lernt nämlich nicht so viel, denn nach vier oder fünf Stunden läßt die Konzentration doch unheimlich nach.
Man kann ja gar nichts Anderes mehr machen an dem Tag.
Man hat nicht genug Zeit für Sport, Musik und so weiter.
Man kann nicht alleine arbeiten.
Die Lehrer brauchen auch mehr Freizeit.

(v) *Explanations*

Select Vocabulary

der Erwachsene (—n) — adult; grown-up
zusätzlich — in addition
der Vorteil (—e) — advantage
die Meinung (—en) — opinion

trotzdem — nevertheless
das Vorbereiten — preparation (also: die Vorbereitung)

Expressions and Idioms

ich finde das zuviel — I think that's too much
. . . läßt die Konzentration doch unheimlich nach — there is certainly a fantastic loss of concentration
da bin ich anderer Meinung — I don't share that opinion; I have a different point of view
weil man da einfach mehr Zeit hat . . . — because one simply has more time . . .
den ganzen Tag lang — the whole day long
man wird immer beobachtet — you are always being observed

8 Von der Schule in die Arbeitswelt

8.1 Reading Materials

Leaving school and finding a job can be a worrying process, whether one lives in Great Britain or in one of the German-speaking countries. The first reading passage below presents a table showing the ten most popular jobs for which school-leavers, boys and girls, were training in 1981. Then follows an account of the choices facing four young West Germans, and finally a letter from one of the four, who is applying for an apprenticeship with a local firm.

8.1.1 Berufswahl

Jungen
Die zehn wichtigsten Ausbildungsberufe für Jungen (1981)

Tausend	100	80	60	40	20
Kraftfahrzeugmechaniker					
Elektroinstallateur					
Maschinenschlosser					
Tischler					
Maurer					
Lackierer					
Gas- und Wasserinstallateur					
Kaufmann im Großhandel					
Bäcker					
Werkzeugmacher					

Mädchen
Die wichtigsten Ausbildungsberufe für Mädchen (1981)

Tausend	100	80	60	40	20
Verkäuferin					
Friseurin					
Bürokauffrau					
Arzthelferin					
Industriekauffrau					
Einzelhandelskauffrau					
Zahnarzthelferin					
Bankkauffrau					

Sie arbeitet mit, weil das Einkommen ihres Mannes nicht ausreicht

© Loriot, Diogenes Verlag, Zürich

(i) *Word Study*

You may not know the English for some of these jobs, but you can probably have a good guess if you look at the ways the words are made up, and if you are given some help with the meanings. For example, *Kraftfahrzeugmechaniker* is made up of *Kraftfahrzeug*, meaning 'motor vehicle', and *Mechaniker*, meaning 'mechanic'. See whether you can work out other meanings from the following bits of information:

ein Schlosser is 'a fitter'.
der Tisch means 'the table'.
die Mauer is 'the wall'.
installieren means 'to install'.
ein Werkzeug means 'a tool'.
verkaufen is 'to sell'.
Friseursalon is a hairdresser's salon.
Kauffrau is a general word for a woman working in business.
Einzelhandel is 'retail trade' and Großhandel is 'wholesale trade'.
ein Zahnarzt is 'a dentist'.
eine Bank is 'a bank'.

(ii) *Comment*

Now that you have more idea of what the jobs are, write two or three sentences in English which sum up bits of information from the tables. For example, you could write: 'The most popular job for boys is vehicle mechanic. The second most popular job for girls is hairdresser.' You can also make any comments which strike you as different from the English situation. For example, would you expect baker to come so high up the list of boys' jobs in England?

(iii) *Explanations*

der Beruf (—e) — job; profession; trade   die Wahl (—en) — choice
die Ausbildung (—en) — training

8.1.2 Die Suche nach einer Arbeitsstelle

Die vier Freunde Beate, Petra, Uwe und Holger kennen sich schon seit einigen Jahren, da sie Nachbarn sind. Für die vier Freunde stehen wichtige Entscheidungen an. Sie werden bald ihre Schule verlassen und müssen sich daher entscheiden, wie es weitergehen soll. Sie haben bereits festgestellt, daß sie recht unterschiedliche Möglichkeiten haben. Beate, Petra, Uwe und Holger haben vier Möglichkeiten einmal zusammengestellt.

Eine Möglichkeit besteht darin, daß sie möglichst bald nach dem Verlassen der Schule eine Arbeitsstelle annehmen. Zum zweiten könnten sie eine betriebliche Ausbildung in einem anerkannten Ausbildungsberuf beginnen. Als dritte Möglichkeit können sie sich auch für eine berufliche Ausbildung in einer berufsbildenden Schule entscheiden. Schließlich bietet sich ihnen viertens der Weg, eine berufsbildende Schule zu besuchen, um einen bestimmten weiterführenden schulischen Abschluß zu erreichen.

Jugendliche, die möglichst bald arbeiten gehen, verdienen zunächst eigentlich ganz gut. Aber dieser Vorteil ist nicht von Dauer, und es gibt noch andere Gründe, weshalb sich Jugendliche mit einer Ausbildung besser stehen. Das wohl wichtigste Argument für eine Berufsausbildung ist die Tatsache, daß Ungelernte als Hilfsarbeiter in Zeiten schlechter Wirtschaftslage entweder gar nicht eingestellt oder als erste entlassen werden.

adapted from *Von der Schule in die Arbeitswelt — aber wie?*
© Niedersächsisches Kultusministerium 1983

(i) *Exercises – Section A*

The exercises in this section are concerned with comprehension and recognition, and they should be attempted before you look at explanations of grammar or vocabulary.

1. We are told that the four friends have four possible choices facing them when they leave school. Without going into detail, can you write down a brief idea of what each possibility is? To help you, the key sentences to look at are as follows: (a) Eine Möglichkeit besteht darin . . . . (b) Zum zweiten . . . . (c) Als dritte Möglichkeit . . . . (d) Schließlich . . . viertens.
2. *Comprehension questions*
   (a) How long have the four friends known each other?
   (b) What do they have to decide?
   (c) What is the advantage for a young person who leaves school and starts to work immediately?
   (d) What happens to unqualified workers at times when the economy is not functioning well?

(ii) *Explanations*

Select Vocabulary

der Nachbar (−n) — neighbour	sich bieten (o, o) — to offer itself
die Entscheidung (−en) — decision	erreichen — to reach; to attain
verlassen (ie, a) — to leave	verdienen — to earn
sich entscheiden (ie, ie) — to decide	die Tatsache (−n) — fact
feststellen — to establish; to ascertain	der Ungelernte (adjectival noun) — unqualified person
die Möglichkeit (−en) — possibility	die Wirtschaftslage (−n) — economic situation

zusammenstellen — to draw up; to compile   einstellen — to take on (for a job)
anerkannt — recognised   entlassen (ie, a) — to dismiss; to lay off (workers)
beruflich — vocational

Expressions and Idioms

sie kennen sich schon seit einigen Jahren — they have already known each other
    for a few years
für die 4 Freunde stehen wichtige Entscheidungen an — the 4 friends are facing up
    to important decisions
möglichst bald — as soon as possible
eine betriebliche Ausbildung — training in a firm
eine berufsbildende Schule — a technical/vocational school
ein weiterführender schulischer Abschluß — a further secondary school qualifica-
    tion
dieser Vorteil ist nicht von Dauer — this advantage does not last
es gibt noch andere Gründe, weshalb . . . — there are still further reasons, why . . .
entweder gar nicht eingestellt oder als erste entlassen werden — either do not get
    a job at all or are the first to be dismissed.

Grammar

The following are the items of grammar of which there are examples in the text
and for which the Section B exercises provide practice. The references in parentheses refer to the sections in the Grammar Summary where the particular points
are explained.

(a) Constructions with *seit* (13.2(a)).
(b) Future tense with *werden* (12.8(b)).
(c) *um . . . zu* followed by Infinitive (12.12(c)4).

(iii)   *Exercises — Section B*

1. Write out complete sentences in answer to the question: *wie lange?*
Follow the example given in the model.

   Model: Wie lange kennen sich schon die 4 Freunde? (einige Jahre)
   Response: Die vier Freunde kennen sich seit einigen Jahren.

   (a) Wie lange dauert schon deine Ausbildung als Mechaniker? (3 Jahre).
   (b) Wie lange besuchst du schon diese Schule? (4 Jahre).
   (c) Wie lange arbeitest du schon als Ungelernter? (1 Jahr).
   (d) Wie lange bist du schon bei dieser Firma eingestellt? (2 Jahre).

2. Form sentences using the Future tense, following the pattern of the model

   Model: die vier Freunde — bald — die Schule verlassen.
   Response: Die vier Freunde werden bald die Schule verlassen.

   (a) Beate — später — eine Arbeitsstelle annehmen.
   (b) Petra — nächstes Jahr — eine betriebliche Ausbildung beginnen.
   (c) Holger — zunächst — eine berufsbildende Schule besuchen.
   (d) Uwe — nächste Woche — sich um einen Ausbildungsplatz bewerben.

3. Write out the same sentences as in exercise 2, but, instead of using *werden* to
form the Future tense, use the modal verb *können*. For example: *Die vier
Freunde können bald die Schule verlassen.*

4. To practise the use of *um . . . zu* with following infinitive, complete the following sentences according to the model.

Model: Sie verlassen die Schule. Warum? (Sie nehmen eine Arbeitsstelle an).
Response: Um eine Arbeitsstelle anzunehmen.

(a) Sie entscheiden sich für eine betriebliche Ausbildung. Warum?
(Sie beginnen in einem anerkannten Ausbildungsberuf).

(b) Sie entscheiden sich für eine berufliche Ausbildung. Warum?
(Sie erreichen einen weiterführenden Abschluß).

(c) Einige gehen möglichst bald arbeiten. Warum?
(Sie verdienen zunächst besser).

(d) Die vier Freunde haben vier Möglichkeiten zusammengestellt.
Warum? (Sie können sich dann entscheiden).

8.1.3 Looking for a Training Place — Ausbildungsplatzsuche

Uwe bewirbt sich um einen Ausbildungsplatz mit dem Berufsziel Maschinenschlosser. Wie er dabei vorgegangen ist, zeigt der folgende Brief.

Uwe Schröder,
Kastanienallee 24   Emdover, den 11.01.1986

Firma Heinrich Meyer,
Maschinenfabrik,
Am Berge 14–18,
Emdover.

Betr: Bewerbung

Sehr geehrter Herr Meyer!
    Ich bewerbe mich bei Ihnen um eine Ausbildungsstelle als Maschinenschlosser
zum 01.08.1986.
    Ich besuche zur Zeit die Klasse 9 der Hauptschule und werde im Juni 1986 die
Schule verlassen.
    Mein Leistungsschwerpunkt liegt deutlich in den Fächern wie Mathematik und
Physik. Im Betriebspraktikum habe ich die Arbeit des Maschinenschlossers bereits
kennengelernt. Das Praktikum hat mich in meinem Berufswunsch bestärkt.
    Ich übersende Ihnen die Kopien meiner beiden letzten Zeugnisse, einen hand-
geschriebenen Lebenslauf und ein Lichtbild.
    Ich würde mich sehr freuen, wenn Sie mir bald Gelegenheit zu einer persön-
lichen Vorstellung geben würden.
    Mit freundlichen Grüßen,

Uwe Schröder

(i)   *Exercises — Section A*

The exercises in this section are concerned with comprehension and recognition,
and should be attempted before you look at the explanations of grammar or
vocabulary.

1. Search through the passage and find the German phrases meaning the following:

(a) I am applying to you for a training place.
(b) At the moment.
(c) I shall leave school in June 1986.
(d) Work experience.
(e) I am sending you . . . .
(f) I would be very pleased.

2. *Comprehension questions*
   (a) What sort of job is Uwe applying for?
   (b) When is he going to leave school?
   (c) What subjects does he feel are his strongest?
   (d) What strengthened his wish to take up this particular job?
   (e) What does he say would give him particular pleasure?

(ii) **Explanations**

Select Vocabulary

sich bewerben (a, o) um — to apply for

das Berufsziel (—e) — profession one is aiming for

Betr: = Betreff — Ref.: = with reference to

die Leistung (—en) — performance; achievement

der Schwerpunkt (—e) — main emphasis; main focus

das Betriebspraktikum (Betriebspraktika) — work experience

bestärken — to strengthen

übersenden (übersandte; übersandt) — to send

das Zeugnis (—se) — testimonial; report

der Lebenslauf — summary of career; curriculum vitae

das Lichtbild (—er) — photograph

die Gelegenheit (—en) — opportunity

die Vorstellung (—en) — introduction; presentation

Expressions and Idioms

ich bewerbe mich bei Ihnen um . . . — I am applying to you for . . .

zur Zeit — at the present time

ich würde mich sehr freuen — I would be very pleased

Grammar

The following are the items of grammar of which there are examples in the text and for which the Section B exercises provide practice. The references in parentheses refer to the relevant sections of the Grammar Summary.

(a) Use of Future and Conditional (12.8(b); 12.14(a)3).
(b) Reflexive verbs — *sich freuen, sich bewerben* (7.2(e)).
(c) Forms of first person — *ich, mich, mir, mein*, etc. (7.1).
(d) *als* with professions (*als Maschinenschlosser*) (3.2(a)).

(iii) **Exercises — Section B**

1. From the brief notes given, construct sentences following the example given.

   Model: Uwe — Stelle — Maschinenschlosser
   Response: Uwe bewirbt sich um eine Stelle als Maschinenschlosser.

   (a) Holger — Ausbildungsplatz — Tischler.
   (b) Beate — Stelle — Friseurin.
   (c) Petra — Ausbildungsplatz — Verkäuferin.
   (d)–(f) Now put the sentences you have written into the Future tense — for example, *Uwe wird sich um eine Stelle als Maschinenschlosser bewerben.*

2. Fill in the gaps in the passage below with the correct part of the first person pronoun (*ich, mich, mir*) or with the first person possessive adjective (*mein*) in its correct form.

(a) Ich bewerbe . . . . . . bei Ihnen um eine Stelle.

(b) . . . . . . Leistungsschwerpunkt liegt deutlich in Mathematik.

(c) Das Praktikum hat . . . . . . in . . . . . . Berufswunsch bestärkt.

(d) Hier sind Kopien . . . . . . Zeugnisse.

(e) Könnten Sie . . . . . . Gelegenheit zu einer persönlichen Vorstellung geben?

3. The last sentence of Uwe's letter gives an example of a conditional sentence: *Ich würde mich sehr freuen, wenn Sie mir bald Gelegenheit zu einer persönlichen Vorstellung geben würden.* The English rendering of this could be: 'I would be very pleased if you would give me an early opportunity for a personal introduction.' In each of the examples below begin your sentence *ich würde mich sehr freuen, wenn . . .,* and complete the clause, following the example already given.

(a) . . . wenn . . . . . . Ausbildungsplatz gewinnen.

(b) . . . wenn . . . . . . die Schule verlassen.

(c) . . . wenn . . . . . . eine Stelle finden.

(d) . . . wenn . . . . . . Geld verdienen.

4. You see the following advertisement in a German newspaper, and decide to apply for a summer-holiday job working at a hotel. Write a formal letter to the manager, telling him your age and any other information asked for in the advertisement. Give the dates when you are free and give any other information which you think he might wish to know.

Süddeutschland (Bayerische Alpen). Arbeitskräfte werden für die Sommersaison (Juli–August) gesucht. Wir stellen junge Leute als Kellner und Zimmermädchen an. Mindestalter 16 Jahre. Erfahrung im Hoteldienst erwünscht, aber nicht erforderlich. Gute Deutsch- und Englischkenntnisse. Schreiben Sie mit Zeugnissen, Lichtbild und Lebenslauf an den Direktor, Hotel zur Post, Mittenwald.

8.2 Listening Materials 📼

8.2.1 Was ich im Leben machen möchte

Listen to a number of 16-year-olds saying what their immediate plans are, as the time approaches for them to leave school. Then answer the questions below.

1. Ich bin Klaus. Ich weiß nicht so genau, was ich machen werde. Ich werde vielleicht sofort arbeiten gehen. Ich möchte sofort gut verdienen.

2. Ich heiße Martina. Ich werde einen Ausbildungsplatz suchen. Ich möchte Friseurin werden.

3. Mein Name ist Ute. Ich möchte nicht sofort arbeiten gehen. Für mich ist es, glaube ich, besser, weiterzulernen, und dann das Abitur zu machen. Vielleicht sogar später auf die Uni zu gehen.

4. Ich bin Manfred. Ich habe mich schon um einen Ausbildungsplatz beworben. Ich möchte als Mechaniker arbeiten.

5. Ich heiße Ulrike. Ich möchte wie Ute weiterzulernen, aber nicht für das Abitur. Für mich ist eine berufliche Ausbildung besser. Deshalb habe ich mich für eine berufsbildende Schule entschieden.

(i) *Falsch/Richtig*

Against the name of each of the people who have spoken are a number of statements. Decide whether you think that these statements are right or wrong.

1. Klaus: is not quite sure what he wants to do.
            does not want to work immediately.
            would like to earn money quickly.
2. Martina: is going to look for a training place.
              would like to be a sales person in a shop.
3. Ute: does not want to work straight away.
          does not like the idea of going on with her studies.
4. Manfred: has already applied for a training place.
              wants to become a mechanic.
5. Ulrike: wants to go on studying.
             would like to study for her Abitur like Ute.
             has decided to go to a vocational school.

(ii)   *Say it in German*

Assume you are asked what you would like to do, when the time comes to leave school. Make two or three statements of the kinds above, starting *ich möchte . . .; ich werde . . .*, etc. A place on a training scheme can be referred to as *ein Aus-bildungsplatz.*

8.2.2 Petra hat Erfolg

Petra hat Erfolg und bekommt eine Lehrstelle als Verkäuferin in einem Großkauf-haus. Wir stellen einige Fragen über ihre Arbeit und ihre Zukunft.

Interviewer: Wenn du an diene Zukunft denkst, hast du da schon genaue Vorstel-lungen?

Petra: Auf jeden Fall will ich früh selbständig werden, will meine eigene Wohnung haben, heiraten und Kinder haben. Später will ich nur halbtags arbeiten, denn das lange Stehen im Geschäft strengt doch sehr an. Und Haushalt und Familie machen ja auch viel Arbeit. Aber Geld verdienen will ich auf jeden Fall.

Interviewer: Du siehst deine Zukunft ja ganz positiv.

Petra: Für mich ist es wichtig, solche Träume zu haben, gute Vorstellungen von dem, was kommt. Und vielleicht wird ja auch alles gut. Das wichtigste für mich ist jetzt meine Lehre. Ich verdiene nicht viel Geld, aber mir macht mein Beruf sehr viel Spaß. Ich versuche, zu meinen Kunden immer nett und freundlich zu sein. Ich habe jetzt schon einige Stammkunden, die immer zu mir kommen. Die wollen nur von mir bedient werden. Und das macht mich stolz und selbstsicher. Mein Traum für die Zukunft wäre, mit zwei, drei Leuten später mal eine Boutique aufzumachen. Mann kann dann selbständiger arbeiten und alles nach den eigenen Vorstellungen gestalten.

Interviewer: Jetzt willst du aber erst mal deine Lehre fertig machen?

Petra: Ja, in einem Großkaufhaus erhält man wirklich eine gute Ausbildung. Man kann viele Lehrgänge besuchen und sich weiterbilden. Das ist für mich sehr wichtig. Nächstes Jahr habe ich meine erste Prüfung, danach muß ich noch weiter lernen und Erfahrung sammeln. Und dann kommt die Hauptprüfung.

Interviewer: Wie geht es dann weiter?

Petra: In einem Großkaufhaus werden die meisten Ausgebildeten nach der Lehre gleich übernommen, fest angestellt. Auch ich hätte dann wahrscheinlich keine Probleme, hier einen Arbeitsplatz zu finden.

© *Scala Jugendmagazin* 2/3, April 1982

(i) *Comprehension Questions*

1. What does Petra say she wants in the future?
2. What is the most important thing at the moment for her?
3. What does she try to do in her work?
4. What sort of plans does she have for work later on?
5. What are the advantages of doing one's training with a big department store?
6. Does she expect to get a job with her present firm?

(ii) Use of *wäre* and *hätte*

In the Grammar Summary (12.14) you will find an explanation of the way in which the Imperfect Subjunctive (for example, *wäre* and *hätte*) can be used instead of the Conditional. For example, *mein Traum für die Zukunft wäre . . .* could be translated: 'my dream for the future would be . . .'.

Die Abteilung für Damenkleider in einem großen Kaufhaus

Write down three things that you would like in the future, then make them into three sentences beginning *mein Traum für die Zukunft wäre . . . .* For example: *mein Traum für die Zukunft wäre, viel Geld zu verdienen.*

Now look at the statement *auch ich hätte dann wahrscheinlich keine Probleme*, meaning: 'I too would probably have no problems then'. Following the pattern of this sentence, make up more sentences saying the things that you would have, or would not have, in the future — for example: *auch ich hätte dann Kinder; auch ich hätte dann kein Geld.*

(iii) *Plans for the Future*

Assume that a German friend puts to you the question *wie siehst du deine Zukunft?* First of all make some notes about the sort of things you might say in answer to that question. Take Petra's answers as examples, and talk about possible further training, jobs, family, future prospects. Then, using your notes as a basis, talk about the future. Note that Petra makes a lot of use of *ich will*, and note expressions like *in Zukunft; später; das ist für mich wichtig.* Also include *wäre* and *hätte* as practised above.

(iv) *Explanations*

Select Vocabulary

die **Zukunft** — future	die **Lehre** (—n) — apprenticeship
die **Vorstellung** (—en) — idea	ker **Kunde** (—n) — customer
selbständig — independent	der **Stammkunde** — regular customer
heiraten — to marry	**selbstsicher** — self-confident
anstrengen — to strain	**gestalten** — to shape; to form
der **Beruf** (—e) — profession	der **Lehrgang** (⸚) — course of training
der **Traum** (⸚e) — dream	die **Erfahrung** (—en) — experience

Expressions and Idioms

auf jeden Fall — in any case
vielleicht wird ja auch alles gut — perhaps everything will turn out for the best after all
mir macht mein Beruf sehr viel Spaß — I get a lot of fun from my job
die wollen nur von mir bedient werden — they only want to be served by me
wie geht es dann weiter? — what happens then?
die meisten Ausgebildeten werden fest angestellt — most trainees are given a permanent job

---

9 Sport und Freizeit

9.1 Reading Materials

Leisure activities have been one of the major areas of growth in all European societies in recent years. Television means that many people are now able to watch international sporting events, such as the Decathlon described in the first passage. The pre-eminence of the GDR in many sporting events is astonishing for such a relatively small country. One such sport is bobsleighing, and the second passage describes how the GDR team won the world championships in 1985. But interest in sport is not limited to watching others perform, and the third reading passage looks at the growth in popularity of walking tours in the Federal Republic.

9.1.1 Was versteht man unter einem Zehnkampf?

Beim Zehnkampf müssen die Athleten in zwei Tagen zehn verschiedene Wett-kämpfe austragen. Am ersten Tag: 100-Meter-Lauf, Weitsprung, Kugelstoßen, Hochsprung, 400-Meter-Lauf. Am zweiten Tag: 110-Meter-Hürdenlauf, Diskus-werfen, Stabhochsprung, Speerwerfen, 1500-Meter-Lauf. Zehnkämpfer sind sehr vielseitig trainierte Sportler. Sie werden deshalb die „Könige der Athleten genannt".

(i) *Comprehension Questions*

Using the picture to help you, and information you can guess from the words used, list, in English, the events which have to be performed by decathletes.

1. On the first day.
2. On the second day.

(ii) *Compound Nouns*

The words in the right-hand column below all refer to types of general athletic events — for example, *Sprung* means 'jump' of any kind. These words can form a variety of compound nouns with words from the left-hand column, so that they then refer to particular activities — for example, *Hochsprung* means 'high jump'. Link up words from the two columns and see how many events you can make which form part of the decathlon.

Stab-	Hürdenlauf
1500-Meter-	Lauf
Weit-	Sprung
Speer-	Stoßen
100-Meter-	Hochsprung
Diskus-	Werfen
Hoch-	
Kugel-	

(iii) *Explanations*

Select Vocabulary

der Kampf (¨e) — contest; battle   der Wettkampf — competition
der Zehnkampf — decathlon   austragen (u, a) — to deal with; to engage in

Expressions and Idioms

beim Zehnkampf — in the decathlon
sehr vielseitig trainierte Sportler — sportsmen who are trained in a great variety of
   ways
sie werden „Könige der Athleten" genannt — they are called 'kings of the athletes'

9.1.2 Schnelle DDR-Bobs

Für einen überragenden Triumph sorgten die DDR-Sportler bei den Weltmeister-schaften der Zweier-Bobs auf der 1520 Meter langen Natureisbahn im italienischen Cervinia. Bei nahezu idealen Witterungs- und Bahnverhältnissen, erkämpften die

"Laß mich auch mal vorne sitzen"

© *Für Dich*, Berlin (DDR)

Titelverteidiger Wolfgang Hoppe/Dieter Schauerhammer unter 29 Bobs aus 16 Ländern in vier Wertungsläufen den WM-Titel, wobei sie insgesamt drei neue Bahnrekorde erzielten. Den zweiten Rang eroberten ihre Klubkameraden Detlef Richter und Steffen Grummt. Steffen war wie Dieter Schauerhammer früher Zehnkämpfer und stieg erst im September vergangenen Jahres als „Bremser" in den Bob.

© *Neue Berliner Illustrierte* 4/85

(i) *Comprehension Questions*

1. What competition were the GDR teams taking part in?
2. Where was the competition held?
3. What were the weather conditions like?
4. How many runs did they have to make for the title?
5. How many new track records did they set?
6. What nationality came in second place?
7. What was Steffen Grummt before becoming a member of the bobsleigh team?

(ii) *Numerals (Grammar Section 9)*

Write out in full the numerals in passages 9.1.1 and 9.1.2. For example, *1500-Meter-Lauf = Fünfzehnhundert-Meter-Lauf.*

(iii) *Explanations*

Select Vocabulary

überragend — overwhelming
sorgen (für) — to take care (of)
der WM-Titel = der Weltmeisterschaftstitel
  — the world championship title
der Titelverteidiger (—) — defender of the
  title
nahezu — very nearly
die Witterung — weather
die Witterungsverhältnisse — weather
  conditions

die Bahn (—en) — track
die Wertung — evaluation; assessment
der Wertungslauf (ⸯe) — competition
  run
erzielen — to achieve
erobern — to conquer
der Bremser (—) — brake-man (in a
  bob team)

"Nun spring endlich auf, du Blödmann!"

© *Für Dich*, Berlin (DDR)

9.1.3 Wohlauf ihr Wandersleut'

Die Schuhe geschnürt, den Rucksack geschultert — so kann man Millionen von Bundesbürgern antreffen, allein oder in Gruppen, auf stillen Wegen oder lauten Routen. Wandervereine und Jugendherbergen melden Rekordzahlen. Der neue Volkssport, den Touristikunternehmen fördern und Mediziner befürworten, scheint die Sehnsucht der Menschen nach Natur zu befriedigen — in einer Zeit, da sie ihr ferner sind denn je.

Die Deutschen wandern wieder. Was ist Wandern? Heiner Weidner, Pressesprecher der Gebirgs- und Wandervereine: „Wandern ist, wenn man sich mehr als zwei Kilometer vom Parkplatz oder Ausgangspunkt entfernt und mehr als einein-halb Stunden unterwegs ist."

Neu am Wandern ist nicht die Tatsache, daß Millionen Menschen es betreiben, sondern daß man darüber spricht, und daß der Fremdenverkehr die Sehnsucht der Menschen nach Natur kommerziell nutzt. Die Gründe für das Wandern liegen scheinbar auf der Hand. Fluchttraum, mal rauskommen aus der Stadt, den Alltag für einige Stunden oder sogar Tage hinter sich lassen, heile Welt, abschalten — deshalb wandern die Leute. Zu keiner Zeit war die Mehrzahl der Menschen von der Natur so weit entfernt wie heute.

Die klassischen Übernachtungsstätten für Wanderer sind die Jugendherbergen. Kaum ein Mensch, der nicht eine Nacht in einer der rund 570 Herbergen geschlafen hätte. Ideal für den Wanderer ist eine netzartige Verteilung der Herbergen in Abständen von 20 bis 25 Kilometern. Dieses Netz ist in beliebten Wandergebieten schon vorhanden.

Norbert Klugmann
adapted from © *Zeit Magazin* 36/1981

Wohlauf ihr Wandersleut'

(i) Exercises – Section A

The exercises in this section are concerned with comprehension and recognition, and should be attempted before you look at explanations of grammar or vocabulary.

1. In reading German, your understanding of the text can always be helped by recognising how many longer words are compounds built up from smaller words which you may know or be able to guess. Some such compounds are common – for example, *Jugendherberge*. Others may be unusual, or even made up by the writer of the text – for example, *Fluchttraum*. You may already know that *Traum* means dream, and you may connect *Flucht* with English 'flight' or with the verb *fliehen*, 'to flee' or 'to escape'.

   Without looking back at the text, link words from the two lists below to form compound nouns. When you have composed the words, have a guess at their meaning. Sometimes, when two words join to form a compound, an 's' is inserted between them, and this 's' is shown in parentheses with the words where it occurs – for example, *Volk (s) Sport = Volkssport*.

der Bund (es)	die Zahl
die Jugend	der Verkehr
der Rekord	die Stätte
das Volk (s)	der Sport

die Touristik	der Traum
die Presse	die Herberge
der Ausgang (s)	der Punkt
der Fremde (n)	der Sprecher
die Flucht	der Bürger
die Übernachtung (s)	das Unternehmen

Remember that compound nouns always take the gender of the second part of the word.

2. (a) Translate into English the definition of *Wandern* given in the text: *Wandern ist . . . unterwegs ist.*

(b) Name two things that are said to be new about the current vogue for rambling (*Neu am Wandern ist . . .*).

3. What are the reasons given for the craze for *Wandern* (*Die Gründe für das Wandern . . .*)?

(ii) **Explanations**

Select Vocabulary

geschnürt — laced up
antreffen (a, o) — to meet up with
melden — to announce
fördern — to promote
befürworten — to approve
betreiben (ie, ie) — to pursue;
 to carry on (an activity)

heil — healthy
abschalten — to switch off
die Mehrzahl — majority
netzartig — forming a network
vorhanden — available; existing

Expressions and Idioms

in einer Zeit, da sie ihr ferner sind denn je — in an age when they are further away (from nature) than ever
die Gründe liegen scheinbar auf der Hand — the reasons appear to be obvious
Kaum ein Mensch, der . . . nicht geschlafen hätte — there is hardly anyone who has not slept . . .
in Abständen von 20 bis 25 Kilometern — at distances of 20 to 25 kilometres

Grammar

The following are the items of grammar of which there are examples in the text and for which the Section B exercises provide practice. The references in parentheses refer to the relevant sections of the Grammar Summary.

(a) Varieties of subordinate clause (after *da, wenn, daß*, relatives) (13.2).
(b) *sondern* after negative (13.1(a)1).
(c) Various prepositions (14).
(d) *scheinen . . . zu* (12.12(b)).

(iii) **Exercises — Section B**

1. The following sentences have been translated from the German text. Translate them back into German, attempting to get as close as possible to the original.

(a) The new peoples' sport which tourist firms are promoting.
(b) Walking is when you get more than two kilometres away from the car-park or the starting point.

(c) There is hardly anyone who has not slept a night in a youth hostel.

(d) The new thing about walking is the fact that people talk about it.

2. Construct sentences using *nicht nur . . . sondern auch*, following the example given.

Model: Die Leute sind allein oder auch in Gruppen.
Response: Die Leute sind nicht nur allein, sondern auch in Gruppen.

(a) Sie sind auf stillen Wegen und lauten Routen.

(b) Touristikunternehmen und Mediziner fördern den Sport.

(c) Sie sind zwei Kilometer vom Parkplatz entfernt und eineinhalb Stunden unterwegs.

(d) Sie lassen den Alltag für einige Stunden hinter sich und schalten ab.

3. Fill the gaps in the following sentences with appropriate prepositions, chosen from the list given.

(a) Man kann Millionen . . . . . . Bundesbürgern antreffen, allein oder . . . . . . Gruppen, ... stillen Wegen oder lauten Routen.

(b) Die Gründe . . . . . . das Wandern liegen scheinbar . . . . . . der Hand.

(c) . . . . . . keiner Zeit war die Mehrzahl der Menschen . . . . . . der Natur so weit entfernt wie heute.

(d) Ideal . . . . . . den Wanderer ist eine netzartige Verteilung der Herbergen . . . . . . Abständen . . . . . . 20 . . . . . . 25 Kilometern.

für; auf; in; von; zu; bis.

9.1.4 Brief an eine Jugendherberge

Leipzig, den 12. Juni

Lieber Herbergsvater!

Meine Freunde und ich möchten gern vom 25. bis zum 28. Juni drei Nächte in Ihrer Herberge übernachten. Haben Sie für diese Zeit noch Betten frei? Wir sind zwei Mädchen und ein Junge und studieren in Leipzig. Können Sie uns bitte drei Betten auf die Namen Thomas Wegner, Karin Albrecht und Martina Leopold reservieren? Wir würden am Freitag, den 25. Juni gegen 18 Uhr eintreffen und bis Montagmorgen 8 Uhr bleiben.

Wie teuer ist eine Übernachtung pro Person, und ist der Preis einschließlich Frühstück und Abendessen? Besteht auch die Möglichkeit selbst zu kochen? Müssen wir eigenes Eßbesteck mitbringen, und sind eigene Schlafsäcke gestattet?

Wir waren noch nie im Harz und wären Ihnen sehr dankbar, wenn Sie uns einige Prospekte und Broschüren von der Gegend schicken könnten, so daß wir schon ein bißchen im voraus planen können. Was gibt es in Quedlingburg und Umgebung zu sehen?

Meine Adresse lautet: Martina Leopold,
(bei Winkelmann),
703 Leipzig,
Mozartstraße 9.

Vielen Dank für Ihre Bemühungen.
Mit freundlichen Grüßen,

Martina Leopold

(i) *Translation*

Translate the whole of the letter at the bottom of p. 98 into English.

(ii) *Letter-writing*

Now write a similar sort of letter to a youth hostel in one of the German-speaking countries. Use some of the turns of phrase in Martina's letter, and be sure to state some of the following information: dates; how many nights; how many boys and girls in the group; date and time of arrival; price; any other queries.

(iii) *Explanations*

Select Vocabulary

eintreffen (a, o) — to arrive   das Eßbesteck — knife, fork and spoon
einschließlich — including   gestattet — allowed

Expressions and Idioms

besteht auch die Möglichkeit . . .? — is there also a possibility . . .?
wir wären Ihnen auch dankbar, wenn Sie uns einige Prospekte schicken könnten —
    we would also be grateful if you could send us some prospectuses
so daß wir . . . im voraus planen können — so that we can do some planning in
    advance

9.2 Listening Materials 📼

9.2.1 Was machst du gern in deiner Freizeit?

Listen to the following short extracts of conversations.

Spielst du gern Fußball?
Ja, sehr, und du?
Nicht so gern. Ich spiele lieber Volleyball.

Gehst du gern wandern?
Ja, sehr gern. Ich bin jedes Wochenende unterwegs.
Ich auch. Nächstes Wochenende wandere ich im Harz. Kommst du mit?
Ja, sehr gern.

Betreibst du einen Wintersport?
Bis jetzt noch nicht, aber ich möchte gern skilaufen.
Ich bin schon skigelaufen. Das ist ein toller Sport.

 (i) Name four sports which you hear mentioned in these exchanges.
(ii) Listen again to the exchanges and then answer the following questions:

    1. How do you ask someone whether they like football?
    2. How would you say that you are going walking next week-end?
    3. How would you say 'not yet'?
    4. Tell someone that you have already been skiing, or that you have not yet
       been skiing, whichever is true in your case.
    5. How would you tell someone 'that is a great sport'?

9.2.2 Freizeitinteressen

Karin: Hallo, Tina, was machst du Freitagabend? Hast du Lust, mit zur Disco zu kommen?

Martina: Mensch, du weißt doch, daß ich freitags immer zum Training gehe. Ich spiele nun mal so gern Volleyball. Außerdem haben wir bald ein Meisterschaftsspiel und sind noch nicht in bester Form. Warum gehen wir nicht am Sonnabend zur Disco?

Karin: Da haben wir doch schon etwas anderes vor. Hast du vergessen? Wir wollen doch zusammen ins Kino gehen.

Martina: Ach ja, auf den französischen Krimi habe ich mich schon die ganze Woche gefreut.

Thomas: Was höre ich da? Wer will da mit wem ins Kino gehen? Ich sehe mir nämlich auch gern gute Filme an. Darf ich mitkommen?

Karin: Tut mir leid, Thomas, die Vorstellung ist ausverkauft. Ich hatte Glück, daß ich noch zwei Karten bekommen habe.

Martina: Geh doch lieber mit Karin morgen zur Disco. Sie geht nicht gern allein.

Thomas: Das läßt sich machen. Hauptsache, ich bin nicht so k.o. nach dem Rudern.

Martina: Du ruderst? Und ich dachte immer, du bist unsportlich.

Thomas: Nur keine Beleidigung. Ich rudere sehr gern und gut. Das kann dir mein Trainer bestätigen.

Karin: Wir glauben dir auch so. Mir macht Rudern auch Spaß, aber ich schwimme lieber. Kommst du morgen abend mit zur Disco?

Thomas: Abgemacht. Ich werde dich abholen. Übrigens, was macht ihr im Sommer? Ich suche noch jemanden zum Bergsteigen in der Tatra.

Karin: Ich kann nicht. Im Juli und August fahre ich als Rettungsschwimmer vier Wochen an die Ostsee.

Martina: Das Angebot klingt nicht schlecht, aber ich laufe lieber Ski. Frag mich im Dezember, ob du jemanden zum Skilaufen brauchst.

Thomas: Aber jetzt haben wir erstmal Sommer. Da willst du doch nicht etwa zu Hause sitzen?

Martina: Nein, ich werde arbeiten. Ich brauche das Geld, um mir ein Moped zu kaufen. Das wollte ich immer so gern haben.

Karin: Willst du nicht lieber verreisen? Das ist doch langweilig, nur zu arbeiten.

Martina: Vielleicht werde ich an den Wochenenden zelten und Paddelboot fahren. Bei uns in der Nähe gibt es viele schöne Seen. Oder ich wandere mit ein paar Freunden, und wir übernachten in Jugendherbergen.

Thomas: Können wir drei auch nicht so etwas am Wochenende machen?

(i) *Word List*

Under the names of each of the speakers, list all the free-time activities that each refers to. As an example, one item has been given in each list to start you off:

Martina	*Karin*	*Thomas*
Training	Disco	Rudern

(ii) *Comprehension Questions*

1. What does Tina do every Friday?
2. What have the two girls got planned for Saturday?
3. Why can Thomas not come with them on Saturday?
4. What is his favourite sport?

5. What plans has he got for the summer?
6. What is Karin doing in the summer?
7. How will Martina spend the summer, and why?
8. What will she do at week-ends?

(iii) *Say it in German*

You have already learned the German for quite a few sporting and free-time activities. Add to these any others which you might personally be interested in, by looking them up in a dictionary, and then make up your own reply to the question: *Was machst du gern in deiner Freizeit?* Refer to the different seasons (*im Sommer, im Herbst, im Winter, im Frühling*) and months (*im Juli, im Januar,* etc.). Refer also to the past (*letztes Jahr, letzte Sommerferien*) and to the future (*in den nächsten Ferien, nächstes Jahr*). Use as many phrases from the conversation between Tina, Karin and Thomas as you can; phrases such as: *ich spiele nun mal so gern . . .; mir macht . . . Spaß.*

(iv) *Explanations*

Select Vocabulary

freitags — every Friday
ausverkauft — sold out
bestätigen — to confirm
abgemacht — that's settled

der Rettungsschwimmer (—) — lifesaver
verreisen — to go away (on a journey)
die Beleidigung (—en) — insult

Expressions and Idioms

Hast du Lust, mit zur Disco zu kommen? — would you like to come to the disco with me?
ich spiele nun mal so gern . . . — I do so much like playing . . .
ich freue mich auf den Film — I am looking forward to the film
das läßt sich machen — that's quite possible; no problem
mir macht Rudern auch Spaß — I like rowing too
ich laufe lieber Ski — I prefer skiing
du willst doch nicht etwa zu Hause sitzen — don't say you are just going to sit at home
das wollte ich schon immer so gern haben — I've always so much wanted one
willst du nicht lieber verreisen? — wouldn't you rather go away somewhere?

10 Gesundheit und Krankheit

10.1 Reading Materials

Everybody always hopes, of course, that they will never be ill or unwell when they are abroad. The complications of different health systems, added to the language problems of explaining what is wrong with you, mean that such an experience can be a very testing one. However, just in case the worst should ever happen, if not to you personally, then to a friend or member of your family, the language of this chapter should help you with some of the problems. First of all, see whether you can recognise some of the language in instructions for taking tablets and in an advertisement for a hotel. Then there is a letter from a German girl to her English pen-friend, telling her about a recent illness.

10.1.1 Lesestücke

(i)

> (i) *SCHNUPFEN-TABLETTEN*
> Gebrauchsinformation — Sorgfältig lesen
> Falls vom Arzt nicht anders verordnet, gelten die folgenden Empfehlungen.
> Am 1. Tag werden dreimal 2 Tabletten, an den folgenden Tagen dreimal täglich eine Tablette mit etwas Wasser eingenommen.
> ARZNEIMITTEL SORGFÄLTIG AUFBEWAHREN.
> VOR KINDERN SICHERN.

(ii)

> *HOTEL KURHAUS IM SCHWARZWALD*
> Tip für Individual-Kur in einem Landschaftsparadies.
> ● Heilbad mit Wasser aus eigener Quelle
> ● chinesische Akupunktur
> ● Ozontherapie
> ● Schlankheitskuren
> NÄHERE INFORMATIONEN DURCH UNSEREN PROSPEKT.

1. The tablets are for
   (a) coughs.
   (b) stomach ache.
   (c) cold in the head.
   (d) toothache.
2. The daily dose is
   (a) 2 tablets.
   (b) 1 tablet.
   (c) 2 tablets first day, then 1.
   (d) 1 tablet first day, then 2.

1. What is the landscape like in the area of the hotel?
2. What do you think the word *Kur* means?
3. What might be the medical purpose of a *Heilbad*?
4. What sort of people might want to go for *Schlankheitskuren*?
5. What should you do if you want more information?

3. Medicines should be
   (a) given to children.
   (b) bought from children.
   (c) kept safe from children.
   (d) opened in front of children.

10.1.2 Dagmar schreibt über ihre Krankheit

Schwerin, den 15. März

Liebe Debbie!

Den Brief muß ich gleich mit einer Entschuldigung anfangen. Es tut mir leid, daß ich so lange nicht auf Deinen letzten Brief geantwortet habe, aber ich war eine Zeitlang krank. Ich konnte sogar eine Woche lang nicht zur Schule gehen, weil ich im Bett liegen mußte.

Es fing alles ganz harmlos an. In den Winterferien war ich mit meiner Klasse vierzehn Tage im Erzgebirge, wo wir in einer Jugendherberge übernachtet haben. Tagsüber sind wir viel gewandert und gerodelt, und abends war meist viel los in der Herberge, Discos, Vorträge u.s.w. Es hat alles riesig Spaß gemacht. In der zweiten Woche hatte ich mir dann eine herrliche Erkältung zugelegt, weil die Schlafsäle sehr kalt waren, aber das war nicht weiter schlimm.

Erst zu Hause merkte ich, daß etwas nicht ganz in Ordnung war. Plötzlich tat mir mein Kopf weh und ich bekam starke Ohrenschmerzen. Dazu kam noch Fieber, und ich war den ganzen Tag müde. Mir war auch ein bißchen übel, und meine Mutter war schon verzweifelt, weil ich keinen Appetit mehr hatte. So mußte ich natürlich zum Arzt gehen, der eine Mittelohrentzündung feststellte. Das Schlimmste war, daß ich auf einem Ohr so schlecht hören konnte. Ich mußte alle ständig bitten, lauter zu sprechen. Es war wirklich nicht schön, halbtaub zu sein.

Nun ist aber alles wieder in Ordnung. Ich mußte jedoch ein bißchen für die Schule nachholen. Wir schreiben nächste Woche wieder drei Klassenarbeiten. Da muß ich noch pauken, weil ich einiges versäumt habe.

„Keine Angst, er steckt nicht mehr an!"

Ich hoffe, Du hast den Winter gut überstanden. Ostern ist bald hier, dann habe ich mehr Zeit zum Schreiben. Schreib mir mal, wie Ihr Ostern feiert.

Viele herzliche Grüße,

Deine Dagmar

(i) *Exercises – Section A*

The exercises in this section are concerned with comprehension and recognition, and should be attempted before you look at explanations of grammar or vocabulary.

1. *Comprehension questions*
   (a) Why has Dagmar not been able to write to Debbie?
   (b) How long did she have to stay away from school?
   (c) Where did she catch cold?
   (d) What symptoms did she have when she got home?
   (e) What did the doctor say to her?
   (f) What was the worst thing about her infection?
2. The gaps in the following text are all missing past participles. Rewrite the passage, inserting appropriate past participles from the list given below, and without looking back at Dagmar's letter.

Es tut mir leid, daß ich so lange nicht auf Deinen Brief . . . . . . habe. In den Winterferien sind wir viel . . . . . und . . . . . . Es hat alles riesig Spaß . . . . . . Dann habe ich mir eine Erkältung . . . . . . Meine Mutter war . . . . . ., weil ich keinen Appetit mehr hatte. Leider habe ich einiges in der Schule . . . . ., aber das habe ich alles doch gut . . . . . .

zugelegt; geantwortet; überstanden; gemacht; gerodelt; verzweifelt; gewandert; versäumt.

(ii) *Explanations*

Select Vocabulary

die Entschuldigung (en) – excuse; apology
die Zeitlang – period; spell of time
rodeln – to toboggan
die Erkältung (–en) – cold; chill
der Schmerz (–en) – pain
die Ohrenschmerzen – earache

verzweifelt – in despair
die Entzündung (–en) – inflammation
ständig – constant
halbtaub – half deaf
nachholen – to catch up
pauken – to cram; to swot up (school work)

Expressions and Idioms

es tut mir leid, daß . . . – I am sorry that . . .
abends war meist viel los – usually there was a lot going on in the evenings
ich konnte nicht zur Schule gehen – I could not go to school
ich hatte mir eine Erkältung zugelegt – I had caught a chill
das war nicht weiter schlimm – then, it wasn't so bad
erst zu Hause – not until I got home
mir war auch ein bißchen übel – I also felt a bit sick
alles ist wieder in Ordnung – everything is fine again

> *Grammar*
>
> The following are the items of grammar of which there are examples in the text, and for which the Section B exercises provide practice. The figures in parentheses refer to the relevant sections of the Grammar Summary.
>
> (a) Revision of Imperfect tense (12.8(c)).
> (b) Imperfect tense of modal verbs (12.11).
> (c) Impersonal expressions (12.2).

(iii)   *Exercises – Section B*

1. Rewrite the following sentences, putting the verbs underlined into the Imperfect tense:

   (a) Ich <u>kann</u> eine Woche lang nicht zur Schule gehen, weil ich im Bett liegen <u>muß</u>.
   (b) Wir <u>sind</u> im Erzgebirge, und abends <u>ist</u> viel los in der Herberge.
   (c) Ich <u>merke</u>, daß etwas nicht in Ordnung <u>ist</u>.
   (d) Mir <u>ist</u> ein bißchen übel, und ich <u>muß</u> zum Arzt gehen. <u>Er stellt</u> eine Mittelohrentzündung fest.
   (e) Ich <u>kann</u> so schlecht hören, und ich <u>muß</u> alle ständig bitten, lauter zu sprechen.
   (f) Ich <u>will</u> jetzt für die Schule ein bißchen nachholen.

2. Make sentences by using either *es tut mir leid daß*... or *es freut mich daß*... with the following statements. For example: *es tut mir leid, daß ich nicht zur Schule gehen konnte.*

   (a) Ich habe mir eine Erkältung zugelegt.
   (b) Die Schlafsäle waren so kalt.
   (c) Ich habe die Arbeit versäumt.
   (d) Ich konnte nicht zur Schule gehen.
   (e) Du hast den Winter gut überstanden.

3. Following the general lines of Dagmar's letter, write a letter of about 150 words to a friend in Germany, explaining that you have not been able to write because you have been feeling sick and unwell. Explain that you had to stay away from school, and say what happened when you went to see the doctor.

10.2   Listening Materials 📼

10.2.1 Was ist los?

Listen to the short dialogues on tape before looking at the written text.

Was ist los, Martina?
Ich habe Kopfweh und mir ist etwas übel.

Und was ist mit dir, Klaus?
Ich habe eine Erkältung. Es ist nicht so schlimm, aber ich muß etwas aufpassen.

Heinz, du siehst nicht gut aus.
Ich habe etwas Fieber und der Hals tut mir weh.

Gabi, ist dir schlecht? Du siehst etwas blaß aus.
Ja, mir ist übel, und mein Bauch tut so weh.
Du mußt sofort zum Arzt.

(i) **Say it in German**

Can you imagine that these German speakers are staying over here in Britain, and you have to act as interpreter when they go to the doctor. Explain to the doctor what is wrong with each of them:

Martina —

Klaus —

Heinz —

Gabi —

(ii) **Role Play**

Your friend does not look too good. You find out what is the matter.

You: (Say he doesn't look well. Ask what is the matter.)

Freund: Ich habe so furchtbare Zahnschmerzen.

You: (Say he should go to the dentist.)

Freund: Ich gehe morgen früh zum Zahnarzt. Früher kann ich nicht gehen.

You: (Say he looks pale. Has he taken an aspirin?)

Freund: Ja, aber es geht mir nicht besser.

You: (Say you have something special for pain. Your friend must take two tablets, then go and lie down.)

10.2.2 Beim Arzt

Dagmar: Guten Tag, Doktor Langenfeld.

Arzt: Tag, Dagmar. Nimm bitte Platz. Na, wo fehlt es denn? Du siehst sehr blaß aus.

Dagmar: Ja, ich weiß nicht recht. Seit ich von der Klassenfahrt zurück bin, habe ich mich nicht wohl gefühlt.

Arzt: Hast du irgendwelche Schmerzen? Mir scheint, du bist auch ziemlich erkältet.

Dagmar: Das ist nicht weiter schlimm, aber mein rechtes Ohr tut mir seit ein paar Tagen so weh, und ich habe ständig Kopfschmerzen.

Arzt: Na, laß mal sehen. Ja, das sieht nicht besonders gut aus. Tut das weh, wenn ich hier drücke?

Dagmar: Oh, ja. Das war sehr unangenehm.

Arzt: Ist dir auch manchmal übel?

Dagmar: Ja, übel und schwindlig, und ich fühle mich so müde und kaputt den ganzen Tag.

Arzt: Du hast eine Mittelohrentzündung. Laß mich mal deine Temperatur messen . . . . Ja, die ist auch erhöht. Das Beste wäre, du bleibst eine Woche im Bett.

Dagmar: Oh je, die Schule fängt in zwei Tagen wieder an. Dann werde ich einiges versäumen.

Arzt: Das kannst du schon wieder nachholen. Gesundheit geht vor. Ich schreibe dir ein paar Schmerztabletten und Ohrentropfen auf. Nimm sie bitte dreimal täglich, dann wirst du dich etwas besser fühlen, aber die Entzündung wird erst in einer Woche langsam zurückgehen. Du wirst wahrscheinlich auch eine Zeitlang auf dem Ohr nur schlecht hören können.

Dagmar: Ja, das merke ich jezt schon.

Arzt: Komm in einer Woche wieder. Dann will ich mir die Sache nochmal ansehen. Mach bitte für nächsten Dienstag einen Termin aus. So, hier ist das Rezept.

Dagmar: Vielen Dank, Doktor Langenfeld. Auf Wiedersehen.
Arzt: Wiederschauen, Dagmar, und gute Besserung.

(i) *Say it in German*

Listen again to the dialogue and write down the expressions which you think mean the following:

1. What is the trouble?
2. I haven't felt well.
3. It seems to me you have got a bit of a cold.
4. I've got a constant headache.
5. Do you sometimes feel sick?
6. Health comes first.
7. Take them three times a day.
8. Make an appointment for next Tuesday.

(ii) *Comprehension*

List, in English, the various symptoms which Dagmar describes to the doctor.

(iii) *Role Play*

In the following role play you play the part of the patient.

Arzt: Guten Tag. Wo fehlt es denn?
Patient: (Say you don't know, but you do not feel well. You have headaches and feel sick.)
Arzt: Haben Sie sonst Schmerzen?
Patient: (Say your ear hurts, and you feel a little sick and dizzy.)
Arzt: So, lassen Sie mich sehen. Ja, das ist eine Entzündung, und die Temperatur ist auch erhöht. Sie müssen einige Tage im Bett bleiben.
Patient: (Say you have to go to school. You will miss some work.)
Arzt: Gesundheit geht vor. Sie können die Arbeit schon wieder nachholen. Kommen Sie in einer Woche wieder und nehmen Sie diese Tabletten. Und Sie müssen unbedingt im Bett bleiben.
Patient: (Say, of course. Thank him and say goodbye.)
Arzt: Auf Wiedersehen, und gute Besserung.

(iv) *Future Tense*

There are several examples of the Future tense used in the conversation between Dagmar and the doctor — for example, *du wirst dich etwas besser fühlen*. There is also an example of the Future tense of a modal verb: *du wirst auch eine Zeitlang auf dem Ohr nur schlecht hören können*. Read section 12.11 of the Grammar Summary, on the Future tense of modal verbs, and then put each of the following sentences into the Future, following the example of the sentence quoted above.

1. Du mußt die Tabletten dreimal täglich nehmen.
2. Ich darf nicht in die Schule gehen.
3. Ich kann auf dem Ohr nur schlecht hören.
4. Der Arzt muß die Temperatur messen und Tabletten aufschreiben.
5. Ich kann nicht eine ganze Woche im Bett bleiben.

(v) *Explanations*

Select Vocabulary

schwindlig — dizzy   das Rezept (—e) — prescription; recipe
aufschreiben (ie, ie) — to prescribe   der Termin (—e) — appointment

Expressions and Idioms

wo fehlt es denn? — what is the matter?
mir scheint . . . — it seems to me . . .
das Beste wäre, . . . — the best thing would be . . .
dann will ich mir die Sache nochmal ansehen — then I'll take another look at things
Gesundheit geht vor — health comes first
gute Besserung — get well soon

11 Typisch Deutsch?

Generalisations about national characteristics are not always very helpful. They may do nothing more than underline prejudices and cannot present a very accurate view of what individuals are really like. The first reading passage shows that some of the traditional views about characteristics of the Germans are still widely held. The second passage, however, gives the views of foreign students in the Federal Republic, who find that the reality does not always coincide with their expectations.

11.1   Reading Materials

11.1.1 Was denken Ausländer über die Deutschen?

Wenn Ausländer an die Deutschen denken, dann fallen ihnen folgende Dinge ein:
   Starke Wirtschaft;
   solide Autos;
   perfekte Organisation;
   gute Musik.
Sie denken auch an den **Fußbali** und ans deutsche **Bier.**
Franzosen, Engländer, Italiener, Niederländer und Amerikaner z.B. halten die Deutschen in der Bundesrepublik Deutschland für:

fleißig	91,4%
sauber, ordentlich ⎫	
pünktlich ⎬	89,4%
demokratisch	75,8%
höflich	74,2%
friedlich	55,4%

© adapted from *Scala Jugendmagazin*, Nov./Dez. 1984

(i)   *Comprehension Questions*

1. Which of the following items do foreigners consider typical of the Germans? Write down those items in the list which you consider to be a correct English version of things mentioned in the text. Then write the German version opposite the English. For example, if you think 'perfect organisation' is mentioned, write out:

perfect organisation — *perfekte Organisation*

good music	perfect organisation
fine painting	excellent doctors
good roads	reliable cars
strong economy	beautiful buildings

2. Now look at the list which shows the percentages of foreigners using certain adjectives to describe Germans. Below is a list of English adjectives, some of which are equivalent to the German ones. Choose the English adjectives which

you think translate those in the German list, and against each one write the German word and the percentage of people who hold that opinion. For example: 'hard-working' — *fleißig*, 91.4%.

clean	peaceful	democratic
polite	punctual	lazy
aggressive	argumentative	hard-working
good-natured	tidy	authoritarian

(ii) **Explanations**

11.1.2 Bei deutschen Schülern zu Gast

Fünf Studentinnen aus Asien und Lateinamerika waren eine Woche lang bei deutschen Schülern zu Gast. Sie berichten darüber, was ihnen auffällt, wenn sie uns besuchen.

Jugend (Lita Patua, Indonesien):   Bei uns zu Hause sagt man, die Deutschen haben besonders viel Disziplin. Als ich das erste Mal in einer deutschen Universität war, habe ich mich dann sehr gewundert. Die Studenten und Studentinnen bringen oft Wurstbrötchen, Kaffee oder Cola mit in den Unterricht. Stricken und Rauchen sind fast schon eine Gewohnheit. Wenn ein Student nicht mehr hören will, geht er aus dem Raum, ohne sich beim Lehrer zu verabschieden. So etwas wäre in meinem Heimatland unmöglich.

Familie (Sun Ying, Volksrepublik China):   Ich habe viele deutsche Freunde kennengelernt. Aber viele von ihnen sind unverheiratet oder sind schon geschieden. Das kommt mir sehr fremd vor. Gibt es in Deutschland keine richtige Familie mehr? Doch! In Brilon habe ich eine richtige deutsche Familie kennengelernt, mit fünf Personen: Vater, Mutter und drei Kinder, und natürlich ein Hund! Es gibt sehr viele Hunde hier! Besonders interessant war für mich die Stellung der Eltern in der Familie. Sie besitzen nicht dieselbe Autorität wie bei uns. Die Eltern sind fast wie gute Freunde, und die Kinder sagen frei ihre Meinung und können dabei sogar den Eltern widersprechen. Das finde ich gut. Das gibt es bei uns zu Hause nicht.

Disziplin (Zhang Xhiaohong, Volksrepublik China):   In China hört man oft, daß die Deutschen immer pünktlich sind. Aber in Deutschland erlebe ich oft das Gegenteil. Hat ein Student Verspätung, so fragt ihn der Professor nicht nach dem Grund, denn das gehört zum Privatbereich.

Erziehung (Cecilia Careamo, Peru):   Ich habe in Peru Deutsch studiert. Ich dachte immer, daß deutsche Lehrer strenger sind als bei uns. Aber jetzt glaube ich, daß das Gegenteil stimmt. Die deutschen Schüler dürfen frei ihre Meinung sagen und sie lernen früh über ihr eigenes Leben zu entscheiden.

© adapted from *Scala Jugendmagazin*, Nov./Dez. 1984

(i) *Exercises – Section A*

Attempt the exercises in this section before consulting the Explanations section.

1. *Comprehension questions*
   (Lita Patua)
   (a) What do people say about the Germans in Indonesia?
   (b) What do the German students bring into lectures?
   (c) What does a student do when he does not want to listen any more?

   (Sun Ying)
   (d) What seems strange to Sun Ying about many of his German friends?
   (e) What does he find in Brilon?
   (f) What does he find particularly interesting in the family?

2. *True or false?*   From your reading of the text, decide whether the following statements are true or false:

   (a) The Chinese think the Germans are always punctual.
   (b) When Zhang is in Germany, he sees that this is true.
   (c) A professor never asks a student why he is late.
   (d) Cecilia finds that teachers are very strict in Germany.
   (e) German students are allowed to express their opinions freely.

(ii) *Explanations*

Select Vocabulary

berichten — to give a report
sich wundern — to be astonished
stricken — to knit
sich verabschieden — to take one's leave
kennenlernen — to get to know
unverheiratet — unmarried
geschieden — divorced
die Stellung (–en) — position
besitzen — to possess

die Meinung (–en) — opinion
widersprechen — to contradict
erleben — to experience
gehören zu — to belong to
streng — strict
selbstbewußt — self-confident
Kritik üben — to engage in criticism
die Erfahrung (–en) — experience

Expressions and Idioms

. . . was ihnen auffällt — the sort of things that occur to them
so etwas wäre . . . unmöglich — that sort of thing would be impossible
das kommt mir sehr fremd vor — that seems very strange to me
ich erlebe oft das Gegenteil — I very often experience the opposite

Grammar

The following are the items of grammar of which examples occur in the text, and for which the Section B exercises give practice. The references in parentheses refer to the relevant sections of the Grammar Summary.

(a) More practice of the Perfect tense (12.6).
(b) Expression of condition by *wenn* clause or by inversion (12.14(a)).

(iii) *Exercises — Section B*

1. *Translate into English*
   (a) bei deutschen Schülern.
   (b) ohne sich beim Lehrer zu verabschieden.
   (c) Die Kinder sagen frei ihre Meinung und können dabei sogar den Eltern widersprechen.
   (d) bei uns zu Hause.
   (e) Ich dachte immer, daß deutsche Lehrer strenger sind als bei uns.

2. Answer the following questions in German, with your answer in the Perfect tense, and using information from the text.

   Model: Wie hast du dich gefühlt, als du das erste Mal an einer deutschen Universität warst?
   Response: Ich habe mich dann sehr gewundert.

   (a) Was haben die Studenten in den Unterricht mitgebracht?
   (b) Was hat der Student gemacht, als er nicht mehr hören wollte?
   (c) Hat Sun Ying deutsche Freunde kennengelernt?
   (d) Was hat Zhang Xhiaohong in China über die Deutschen gehört?
   (e) Wo hat Cecilia Deutsch studiert?

3. Fill in the gaps in the following exercises with the correct form of *viel.*

   (a) Die Deutschen haben besonders . . . . . . Disziplin.
   (b) Ich habe . . . . . . deutsche Freunde kennengelernt.
   (c) Die Studenten stricken und rauchen . . . . . .
   (d) . . . . . . deutsche Kinder sagen frei ihre Meinung.
   (e) Wie . . . . . . Deutsche hast du kennengelernt?
   (f) Es gibt sehr . . . . . . Hunde hier.

4. The text shows two ways of expressing a condition in German — either by using *wenn: Wenn ein Student nicht mehr hören will, geht er aus dem Raum* or by inverting the verb and subject: *Hat ein Student Verspätung, so fragt ihn der Professor nicht nach dem Grund.* In the three sentences below, inversion is used to express the idea of 'if . . .'. Rewrite these sentences, using *wenn.*

   (a) Hat ein Student Verspätung, so fragt ihn der Professor nicht nach dem Grund.
   (b) Will ein Kind seine Meinung sagen, so sagt es sie frei heraus.
   (c) Ist man das erste Mal an einer deutschen Universität, so wundert man sich.

5. Translate the following sentences into German, using either of the constructions for expressing 'if'.

   (a) If the students are hungry, they bring sandwiches into lectures.
   (b) If a student does not want to listen, he leaves the room.
   (c) If the children want to express their opinion, they do so freely.

6. Construct sentences using modal verbs by combining elements from the three columns below. You can make any sentence, as long as it makes sense.

Die deutschen Schüler	dürfen	frei ihre Meinung sagen.
Die Studenten	können	nicht mehr hören.
Die Kinder	wollen	den Eltern widersprechen.
Der deutsche Student	müssen	nicht mehr pünktlich sein.
Der Professor		nicht nach dem Grund fragen.

7. Now read section 12.11 in the Grammar Summary, which explains how to form the Perfect tense of modal verbs. Then write out all the sentences you have constructed in the Perfect tense. For example,

Present tense: Die Kinder dürfen frei ihre Meinung sagen.
Perfect tense: Die Kinder haben frei ihre Meinung sagen dürfen.

Die deutschsprachigen Länder

11.2 Listening Materials

Listen to these statements by foreigners staying in the Federal Republic. Then answer the questions in exercise (i) before looking at the written version of the text.

11.2.1 Wo kommen Sie her?

Ich komme aus England. Mein Name ist Andrew Jones, und ich bleibe vier Wochen hier in der Bundesrepublik. Ich halte die Deutschen für sehr freundlich.

Guten Tag. Ich bin aus Thailand. Ich bin für ein Jahr in Deutschland, und ich halte die Deutschen für höflich und sehr fleißig.

Ich komme aus Schottland. Das ist mein erster Besuch in Deutschland, aber ich finde alle sehr freundlich und höflich. Ich bin schon vier Tage hier.

Ich komme aus der Volksrepublik China. Ich halte die Deutschen für sehr nette und freundliche Leute, aber pünktlich sind sie nicht. Aber ich bin erst einige Tage hier in der Bundesrepublik.

Ich bin aus Frankreich. Ich habe viele deutsche Freunde kennengelernt. Sie sind alle freundlich und sehr höflich. Ich bin schon einen Monat hier.

(i) *Comprehension Exercise*

When you have listened to the tape, try to fill in the table below:

Where is she/he from?	How long in Germany or how long staying?	What do they think of the Germans?

11.2.2 Preuße und Bayer

We said earlier that generalisations about national character are unlikely to be very true. That becomes even more clear when you consider the differences between, say, a Bavarian and a Prussian. For most of their history Prussia and Bavaria were separate kingdoms, and the people are different in temperament and in their dialect. Some of the old differences between the two are still jokingly kept alive, as you will see from the following conversation between two Bavarians, Gabi and Stephan, and a North German, Achim.

Gabi, Stephan und Achim unterhalten sich. Gabi und Stephan kommen aus Süddeutschland. Achim kommt aus Norddeutschland, lebt aber seit 10 Jahren in Süddeutschland.

Gabi: Grüß dich, Achim, alter Preuße, wie geht's?

Achim: Jetzt lebe ich schon seit 10 Jahren in Bayern, und immer noch bezeichnet mich jeder als Preußen.

Stephan: Mach dir nichts daraus. Du bist einer der wenigen netten Preußen.

Gabi: Du hast auch Gott sei Dank deinen preußischen Dialekt abgelegt. Nur dein typisch preußisches Sprechtempo ist immer noch nicht langsamer geworden.

Stephan: Ja, ja, die Preußen sprechen schneller als sie denken können.

Achim: Wenigstens denken die Preußen. Wenn man das Denken den Bayern überlassen hätte, lebten die Deutschen heute noch im Steinzeitalter.

Stephan: Ich weiß: Preußen ist das Gehirn Deutschlands. Dafür ist Bayern schon immer das Herz Deutschlands gewesen. Die bayerische Gemütlichkeit hat ja auch genug Preußen in unser Land gezogen.

Gabi: Wer will auch schon in der flachen Landschaft des Nordens leben? Dort sieht man ja schon am Montag, wer am Donnerstag zu Besuch kommt.

Stephan: Und trotzdem haben die Preußen noch immer alles Preußische dem Bayerischen vorgezogen. Sie haben immer alles besser gewußt als die Bayern. Sie haben sogar versucht, ihre straffe, preußische Organisation in unser Bayern zu exportieren.

Gabi: Und warum haben uns die Preußen erklärt, sie tränken nur deshalb so viel von unserem bayerischen Bier, weil es viel schwächer als das norddeutsche sei?

Achim: . . . weil auch der steife Preuße Humor hat, den der gemütsvolle Bayer aber offensichtlich nicht versteht.

Stephan: Okay, okay, hört auf damit! Unsere Freundschaft ist schließlich über die rassistischen, bayerischen und preußischen Vorurteile erhaben.

(i) *Comprehension Questions*

1. How long has Achim lived in Bavaria?
2. Achim has lost his Prussian dialect, but in what way does he still speak more like a North German?
3. If Prussia is supposed to be the brain of Germany, which part is Bavaria?
4. What does Stephan think has attracted so many Prussians to the south?
5. Can you translate the joke about living in the flat lands of the North?
6. How do the Prussians excuse the fact that they drink so much Bavarian beer?

(ii) *Question Practice*

The conversation introduces several question words: *wie?* ; *warum?* ; *wer?* See whether you can form the following questions as if you were asking Achim.

1. Ask him how he is.
2. Ask him how long he has lived in South Germany.
3. Ask him why he lives in South Germany.
4. Ask him who speaks faster, the Bavarians or the Prussians.
5. Ask him why the Prussians drink a lot of Bavarian beer.
6. Ask him why Bavarians do not understand Prussian humour.

(iii) *Practice with* weil

Three of the above questions begin *warum?* and you would expect an answer beginning *weil*, meaning 'because'. *Weil* introduces a subordinate clause which sends the verb to the end of the clause, as in the example from the text: *weil auch der steife Preuße Humor hat.* Here are the answers to the three *warum?* questions above. Write them out again, but start each answer with *weil*, and place the verb in the correct position.

1. Er arbeitet in Süddeutschland.
2. Sie haben das bayerische Bier sehr gern.
3. Sie verstehen nur ihren eigenen, bayerischen Humor.

(iv) *Say it in German*

Listen again to the conversation, and pick out the German phrases for the following expressions:

1. Don't let it worry you.
2. At least the Prussians think.
3. They have always known everything better than the Bavarians.
4. That will do!

(v) *Explanations*

Select Vocabulary

sich **u**nterhalten (ie, a) — to chat
   together
be**ze**ichnen — to call; to name
ablegen — to lose; to get rid of
wenigstens — at least
das **Ste**inzeitalter — stone age
das Gehirn (—e) — brain

die Gemütlichkeit — geniality; cosiness
vorziehen (o, o) — to prefer
straff — rigid
steif — stiff
offensichtlich — obviously

Expressions and Idioms

wie geht's? — how are you?
jetzt lebe ich schon seit 10 Jahren in Bayern — I've been living for 10 years in
   Bavaria now
mach dir nichts daraus — don't let it bother you
wenn man das Denken den Bayern überlassen hätte — if thinking had been left to
   the Bavarians
unsere Freundschaft ist über die . . . Vorurteile erhaben — our friendship is above
   the prejudices

12 Umwelt

12.1 Reading Materials

Throughout Western Europe, and in many other societies all over the world, environmental questions have grown in importance over the last few years, and the public awareness of such questions is particularly strong in the Federal Republic. There *die Grünen*, the political party which has made environmental issues one of the main planks of its policy, has gained seats in parliament. Questions such as the problems of *Waldsterben* as a result of acid rain, and the pollution of the environment by the motor-car, seem much more part of public debate than is the case in the United Kingdom. In the first passage below, you are given some statistics about the problem of disposing of rubbish in modern society. Then follows a passage about the particular pollution problems presented by the motor-car.

12.1.1 Hausmüll
Nur aus unseren privaten Haushalten türmen sich allein pro Jahr

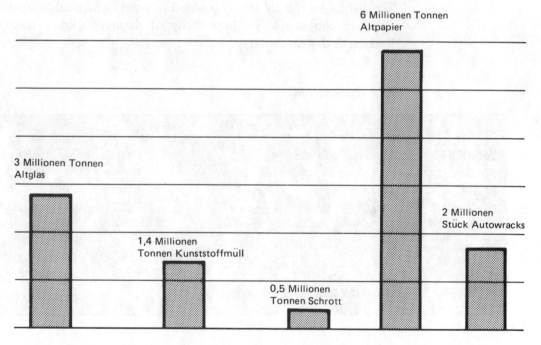

6 Millionen Tonnen
Altpapier

3 Millionen Tonnen
Altglas

1,4 Millionen
Tonnen Kunststoffmüll

0,5 Millionen
Tonnen Schrott

2 Millionen
Stück Autowracks

Rund die Hälfte unseres Hausmülls machen die schönen Verpackungen aus: die Dosen; die Becher; die Büchsen; die Pappkartons; die Tuben; die Kisten; die Folien; die Tüten; die Taschen.

(i) *Comprehension Questions*

1. What forms the bulk of the rubbish?
2. How many old cars are dumped each year?
3. What proportion of household rubbish is made up of packs and containers of different kinds?

Freizeitglück und ungetrübte Lebensfreude an Europas Sonnenstränden können durch das gelegentliche Auftauchen kleiner Zivilisationsspuren nur noch gesteigert werden

© Loriot, Diogenes Verlag, Zürich

4. What weight of old bottles is dumped?
5. The list under the table is composed of words which all mean different sorts of packs or containers. See how many of these you know or can guess, before looking at the vocabulary.

(ii)   *Explanations*

Select Vocabulary

der Müll (no plural) — rubbish; garbage
der Kunststoffmüll — rubbish from plastics, etc.
sich türmen — to pile up
der Schrott (no plural) — scrap metal
das Autowrack (—s) — wrecked car

Containers
die Dose (—n) — tin
der Becher (—) — tub (for ice cream, yoghurt)

die Büchse (—n) — tin
der Pappkarton (—s) — cardboard container
die Kiste (—n) — box
die Folie (—n) — foil wrapping
die Tube — tube
die Flasche (—n) — bottle
die Tüte (—n) — packet; plastics bag
die Tasche (—n) — bag

12.1.2 Auto und Umwelt

Das Auto ist unverzichtbar, es ist aber auch eines unserer größten Umweltprobleme. Das müssen wir wissen, und das müssen wir ändern.

Autos brauchen Straßen — Straßen fressen Natur.

Straßen und Autobahnen zerschneiden die Landschaft und beeinträchtigen das Leben in den Städten. In vielen Stadtbereichen wird die Lebensqualität immer geringer. Viele wollen oder können nicht mehr in der Stadt wohnen. Das bedeutet immer mehr Straßen und Autos. Und damit immer mehr Umweltbelastung. Damit die Räder rollen können, haben wir in der Bundesrepublik mehr als 175 000

Mindestens 98 Prozent der Männer halten sich für ausgezeichnete und begabte Autofahrer

© Loriot, Diogenes Verlag, Zürich

Kilometer Landstraßen, 7800 Kilometer Autobahnen und 335000 Kilometer Bundesstraßen.

Autos sind Luftverschmutzer.

Jährlich werden vierzig Millionen Tonnen Kraftstoff durch unsere Automotoren gepumpt und verbrannt. Die dabei freigesetzten Schadstoffe stinken und vergiften unsere Atmosphäre mit Giften wie Kohlenmonoxid, Schwefeldioxid und Blei.

Wir müssen handeln!!

Deshalb machen Sie mit bei unserem Plan für den umweltbewußten Umgang mit dem Auto.

1. Ein freiwilliger AUTOFREIER SONNTAG am letzten Sonntag im September.

2. Besonders umweltbelastend sind Kurzstreckenfahrten. Da geht der Umweltfreund lieber zu Fuß oder benutzt das Fahrrad.

3. Fahren Sie nur mit umweltschonenden Fahrzeugen.

4. Besonders umweltschonend ist die Zauberformel Tempo 100 beim Autofahren. Denn über 100 km/h steigen alle Werte stark an.

5. Bereits beim Autokauf, außer auf Sicherheit, Qualität und Kosten, muß man auch auf den Umweltschutz Rücksicht nehmen.

© *Umweltbundesamt*

(i) *Exercises – Section A*

The exercises in this section are concerned with comprehension and recognition, and should be attempted before you look at explanations of vocabulary and grammar.

1. *Word search*   There will be a few rather technical words in the passage, which you may not know but which you might be able to guess from the context. Find the German words which you think are equivalent to the following English words and phrases:

to cut up, or cut through	vehicle
to spoil, damage or harm	besides
air polluters	to take note of
harmful products/materials	protection of the environment
poisons	

2. Translate into English from the beginning as far as *Umweltbelastung.*

(ii) *Explanations*

Select Vocabulary

die **Umwelt** — environment
and note also
all the compounds formed from *Umwelt*
das **Umweltproblem** (—e) — environmental problem
die **Umweltbelastung** (and the adjective
  umweltbelastend) — burden on the
  environment
umweltbewußt — conscious of environmental problems
umweltschonend — sparing the environ-
  vironment; protecting the environment
der **Umweltschutz** — protection of the
  environment
der **Umweltfreund** (—e) — friend of the
  environment

unverzichtbar — indispensable
zerschneiden (zerschnitt; zerschnitten)
  — to cut up; to chop up
beeinträchtigen — to harm; to damage
verbrennen (verbrannte; verbrannt) —
  to burn up
der **Schadstoff** (—e) — harmful substance
vergiften — to poison
das **Kohlenmonoxid** — carbon monoxide
das **Schwefeldioxid** — sulphur dioxide
das **Blei** — lead (metal)
freiwillig — voluntary
die **Kurzstreckenfahrt** (—en) — short journey
die **Zauberformel** (—n) — magic formula
ansteigen (ie, ie) — to increase

Expressions and Idioms

die Lebensqualität wird immer geringer — the quality of life gets less and less
das bedeutet immer mehr Straßen — that means more and more roads
da geht der Umweltfreund lieber zu Fuß — in that case the person who is aware of
  environmental problems prefers to go on foot
man muß auf den Umweltschutz Rücksicht nehmen — one must take note of the
  need to protect the environment

Grammar

The following are the items of grammar of which there are examples in the text
and for which the Section B exercises provide practice. The references in parentheses give the section of the Grammar Summary where the particular points of
grammar are explained.

(a) Use of the Passive voice (12.8(e)2).
(b) *damit* followed by clause with modal verb (12.14(c)).

(iii) *Exercises — Section B*

1. Translate the following sentences into German. All the vocabulary will be
   found in the text, but all these sentences are phrased so that the Passive voice is
   required.

   (a) Harmful substances are released.
   (b) The atmosphere is poisoned.
   (c) Attention is paid to safety.
   (d) The landscape is cut up by roads.
   (e) Life is harmed by cars.

2. Answer the following questions, using a *damit* clause, as in the model.

Model: *Warum wollen viele Menschen nicht mehr in der Stadt wohnen? (Ihr Leben kann besser werden.)*
Response: *Damit ihr Leben besser werden kann.*

(a) Warum werden immer mehr Straßen gebaut? (Die Menschen vom Land können schnell in die Städte fahren.)
(b) Warum werden wir einen autofreien Sonntag haben? (Es wird weniger gefahren.)
(c) Warum geht der Umweltfreund lieber zu Fuß? (Das Auto wird weniger benutzt.)
(d) Warum nimmt man Rücksicht auf den Umweltschutz? (Die Umweltbelastung kann zurückgehen.)

3. *Retranslation*   The following passage is translated from elements in the text. Translate it back into German without looking at the original version until you have finished.

We must act! The motor-car is our biggest environmental problem. Cars harm the quality of life in towns. Every year 4 million tons of petrol are pumped through our engines. Therefore, join in our plan for a voluntary car-free Sunday. We want to travel in vehicles which spare the environment. When you are buying a car, you must take account of environmental protection.

12.2   Listening Materials 🖭

12.2.1 Spaziergang im Wald

Claudia: Ist es nicht schön, im Wald spazieren zu gehen, und Schmutz und Lärm der Großstadt hinter sich zu lassen?

Renate: Es wäre schön! Aber was, glaubst du, bedeuten die weißen Kreuze, die auf die Bäume gemalt sind?

Jens: Sie zeigen, daß die Bäume sehr krank oder sogar schon abgestorben sind. Es gibt immer mehr abgestorbene Bäume hier.

Claudia: Aber warum tut man denn nichts dagegen? Kann man die Fabriken nicht zwingen, ihre Abgase zu reduzieren?

Jens: Doch, und seitdem die Grünen in Deutschland so populär geworden sind, hat man auch schon einiges getan, um die Umweltverschmutzung zu bekämpfen.

Renate: Aber das Waldsterben ist ein internationales Problem. Es wird durch den sauren Regen ausgelöst. Fabriken verschmutzen die Luft mit Abgasen. Diese Abgase werden vom Wind teilweise Hunderte von Kilometern weit getragen und fallen dann mit dem Regen wieder zu Boden. Deutschland allein kann wenig gegen das Waldsterben tun.

Claudia: Aber warum schließen sich dann nicht alle Länder in Europa zusammen, um das Problem zu lösen?

Jens: Nicht alle Länder haben Angst um ihre Wälder. In England gibt es beispielsweise noch kein Waldsterben. Der Wind trägt den englischen Schmutz in die skandinavischen Länder und schädigt dort die Wälder. Aber den englischen Wäldern geht es noch ganz gut. Deshalb reden die Engländer nicht viel von diesem Problem.

Renate: Außerdem haben die Engländer genug wirtschaftliche Sorgen. Es scheint ihnen keine Zeit mehr zu bleiben, sich um ihre Umwelt zu kümmern.

Jens: Dabei geht es unserer Umwelt immer schlechter. Langsam aber sicher machen wir uns unseren eigenen Lebensraum völlig kaputt.

Claudia: Aber wir brauchen doch unsere Wälder!

(i) *Comprehension Questions*

1. What is painted on some of the trees?
2. What do the signs on the trees mean?
3. How would you translate *Waldsterben* into English, and how is it caused?
4. How far are factory emissions carried?
5. What effects does the waste from English factories have?

Blick auf den Schwarzwald

(ii) *Say it in German*

In the reading passages and in the dialogue you have learned a good deal of the vocabulary associated with environmental problems. Despite what Klaus said in the dialogue, there have been quite a number of initiatives made in the United Kingdom to deal with environmental problems. Write to a German friend on this subject, saying whether you think it is important to deal with the environmental problems of the modern world and suggesting some of the ways in which this can be done by individuals and local groups – such as using the car less.

(iii) *Explanations*

13 Die Deutsche Sprache Heute

13.1 Reading Materials

A living language never stands still. Words, phrases and concepts change constantly, to produce the linguistic resources for dealing with new situations. The first reading passage talks about some of the most marked changes in the vocabulary of the seventies, bringing the growing consciousness about environmental issues already discussed in the previous chapter, and also a whole range of new terms to cope with developments in politics, computers and the changes in the use of leisure time. Another major element of change for the German language has been the development of new social structures in the GDR, and the development also, therefore, of new terms to describe the changes. German has always been a language of regional diversity, particularly with regard to the Swiss and Austrian varieties of the language. The second passage below describes how the difference has now increased with the changes brought about in the GDR.

13.1.1 Neu in den siebziger Jahren

Jede Epoche in der Geschichte hat ihre eigene Sprache. Auch in den siebziger Jahren sind neue Begriffe in die Schlagzeilen der Zeitungen gekommen.

Protestbewegungen gehören zum Alltag der 70er. Nie gab es so viele *Bürgerinitiativen*. Man wartet nicht auf die nächste Wahl, man sagt den Politikern sofort und direkt die Meinung. Bürger — vor allem junge Leute — demonstrieren gegen neue Straßen und Flugplätze, gegen Arbeitslosigkeit, gegen politische Entscheidungen jeder Art.

Atomkraft? — Nein, Danke ist eine Parole der *Kernkraftgegner*. Die *Friedensbewegung* protestiert gegen die Raketenrüstung.

Computer werden kleiner, besser — und gefährlicher. Ihre Datenlisten geben Informationen über jeden einzelnen Bürger. *Datenschutz*, der Schutz des Individuums vor dem Super-Wissen der Computer, wird notwendig.

Die *Alternativen* sind Leute, die neue Wege gehen wollen: weniger Technik, weniger Streß und natürliche Ernährung sollen den Menschen gesund machen. Im *Bio-Laden* kann man Lebensmittel von *Öko-Bauern* kaufen — Gemüse und Brot ohne Chemie.

Umweltverschmutzung ist der Preis für die schnelle industrielle Entwicklung in den 50er und 60er Jahren. Der *Umweltschutz* ist eine der wichtigsten politischen Forderungen der 70er. Die politische Partei der *Grünen* entsteht. Mehr *Lebens-*

qualität wollen die Bürger in den Städten. In den 70er Jahren entstehen überall *Fußgängerzonen*.

Die Arbeitszeit wird kürzer, die Freizeit länger. Die *Freizeit-Gesellschaft* erfindet neue Spiele. Man erlebt Abenteuer in der Natur beim *Drachenfliegen* und *Windsurfen*. Die Menschen in den Städten wollen sich bewegen. Den größten Erfolg hat die Mode-Sportart *Jogging*, der Dauerlauf durch die Parks der Stadt.

adapted from © *Scala Jugendmagazin*, Mai–Aug. 1984

(i)   *Exercises – Section A*

The exercises in this section are concerned with comprehension and recognition, and should be attempted before you look at explanations of vocabulary or grammar.

1. The sort of social developments which have given rise to the German vocabulary described in the passage have also occurred to a greater or lesser extent in the United Kingdom. Give English equivalents for the words in italics in the text.
2. *Comprehension questions*
   (a) Against what sort of things do young people demonstrate?
   (b) What are the dangers of computers?
   (c) What are the advantages offered by alternative ways of living?
   (d) What earlier developments have brought about our present environmental problems?
   (e) Why is there at present a boom in various sports?

Den größten Erfolg hat die Mode-Sportart „Jogging"

(ii) *Explanations*

Select Vocabulary

der Begriff (–e) – concept
die Schlagzeile (–n) – headline
die Wahl (–en) – election; choice
die Parole (–n) – slogan

der Schutz (no plural) – protection
die Ernährung – nourishment; feeding
das Drachenfliegen – hang-gliding
der Dauerlauf – jogging

Grammar

The following are the items of grammar of which there are examples in the text, and which form the basis for the Section B exercises. The references in parentheses give the section of the Grammar Summary where the particular points of grammar are explained.

(a) Comparative and superlative of adjectives (6(a), (b)).
(b) Revision of prepositions and cases (14).
(c) Use of *jeder* (8.5(k)).

(iii) *Exercises – Section B*

1. Answer the following questions in German, following the indications given by the English in parentheses.

Model: Hat Jogging einen großen Erfolg gehabt? (Yes, jogging has had the greatest success.)
Response: Ja, Jogging hat den größten Erfolg gehabt.

(a) Man demonstriert, aber sollte man nicht auf eine Wahl warten? (Perhaps one should wait for the next election.)
(b) Computer sind jetzt klein und gut, nicht? (Yes, but they are also more dangerous.)
(c) Gibt es im heutigen Leben viel Streß? (Yes, there is more and more stress in modern life.)
(d) Ist der Umweltschutz eine wichtige Forderung? (Yes, the protection of the environment is one of the most important demands of the modern world.)
(e) Ist die Arbeitszeit immer noch lang? (No, working time is getting shorter.)
(f) Hat man jetzt mehr Freizeit? (Yes, leisure time is longer.)
(g) Warum entstehen Fußgängerzonen? (Because people want more quality of life.)

2. Fill in the gaps with a suitable preposition chosen from the list below, and add the correct ending to the word following the preposition.

(a) Jede Epoche . . . . . . d– Geschichte hat ihre eigene Sprache.
(b) Auch . . . . . . d– siebiziger Jahren sind neue Begriffe . . . . . . d– Schlagzeilen der Zeitungen gekommen.
(c) Protestbewegungen gehören . . . . . . Alltag der 70er.
(d) Man wartet nicht . . . . . . d– nächste Wahl.
(e) Der Schutz des Individuums . . . . . . d– Super-Wissen der Computer wird notwendig.
(f) Die Datenlisten geben Informationen . . . . . . jed– einzeln– Bürger.
(g) Die Friedensbewegung protestiert . . . . . . d– Raketenrüstung.
(h) Umweltverschmutzung ist der Preis . . . . d– industrielle Entwicklung in den 50er Jahren.

(i) Man erlebt Abenteuer . . . . . . d— Natur.

(j) Jogging ist der Dauerlauf . . . . . . d— Parks der Stadt.

gegen; durch; zum; vor; in; auf; gegen; über; für.

3. *Translate into German*

(a) Decisions of every kind.

(b) Information about each individual citizen.

(c) Every age has its own language.

(d) Every newspaper has new concepts in its headlines.

(e) Every town has pedestrian precincts.

(f) Every person wants less stress.

13.1.2 Die deutsche Sprache im „anderen" Deutschland

Die unterschiedliche Entwicklung der beiden Teile Deutschlands nach dem 2. Weltkrieg hat Auswirkungen im Bereich der deutschen Sprache. Neue Wörter und Wortbildungen und fremdsprachliche Einflüße sind oft kommentiert worden. Die sprachlichen Entwicklungen in Ost und West führten bereits in den fünfziger Jahren zu der Frage, ob die Teilung des Landes nicht auch zu einer Teilung der Sprache führe, so daß sich der Deutsche in Ost und der Deutsche in West sich eines Tages kaum mehr verstehen würden. Es gab Diskussionen darüber, ob das Deutsche Ost und das Deutsche West nicht eigentlich nur Varianten der einen deutschen Sprache seien, so wie das Schweizerdeutsch und das Österreicherdeutsch auch. Die deutsche Sprache als grammatisches System bleibt weitgehend unberührt. Es ist vor allem der Wortschatz, der hüben und drüben von Wandlungen betrofffen ist. Die Zahl neu gebildeter Wörter ist auf beiden Seiten groß. Sie wird mit Sicherheit in der DDR größer sein, als in der Bundesrepublik. Erfahrungen der letzten Jahre zeigen, daß die Leute in der DDR, vermutlich durch intensive Nutzung westdeutscher Fernsehsendungen, im Hinblick auf neue Wörter in der Bundesrepublik kaum Schwierigkeiten haben. Es ist anders in der BRD. Die große Menge des neuen DDR-Wortschatzes ist in der BRD weithin unbekannt geblieben.

adapted from introduction to *Kleines Wörterbuch des DDR-Wortschatzes*, by M. Kinne and B. Strube-Edelmann, © Verlag Schwann, Düsseldorf

Here are a few terms from the vocabulary of the GDR, and some of the abbreviations which are also widely used and which have no equivalent in the Federal Republic:

polytechnische Oberschule (POS) — the all-through comprehensive school (ages 6–16)

Bestarbeiter — a worker who has achieved outstanding results

Blauhemd — member of the FDJ (see below)

FDJ — Freie Deutsche Jugend — the state youth organisation

FDGB — Freier Deutscher Gewerkschaftsbund — the main trade union organisation

HO — Handelsorganisation — state organisation for hotels and restaurants

LPG — Landwirtschaftliche Produktionsgenossenschaft — collective farm

VEB — Volkseigener Betrieb — state-run company or industry

(i) *Exercises — Section A*

The exercises in this section are concerned with comprehension and recognition, and should be attempted before you look at explanations of vocabulary or grammar.

1. *Comprehension questions*
   (a) What political change has brought changes in the German language?
   (b) What question was raised in the fifties?
   (c) What might be the result of two separate German languages growing up?
   (d) What part of the language has been most affected by change?
   (e) How do citizens of the GDR keep up with linguistic changes in the Federal Republic?
   (f) Are language developments in the GDR well known in the West?

2. *Sentence structure* This passage contains a number of complex sentences. To help you sort out the structure of these sentences, it is important to be able to distinguish between main clauses and subordinate clauses. In the following exercise, insert into the gaps the most appropriate subordinating conjunction, choosing from the list given below the exercise. Do this without looking back at the original text.

   (a) Die Entwicklungen führten zu der Frage, ... die Teilung des Landes nicht auch zu einer Teilung der Sprache führe, ... sich der Deutsche in Ost und der Deutsche in West eines Tages sich kaum mehr verstehen würden.
   (b) Es gab Diskussionen darüber, ... das Deutsche Ost und das Deutsche West nicht eigentlich nur Varianten seien.
   (c) Es ist vor allem der Wortschatz, ... hüben und drüben von Wandlungen betroffen ist.
   (d) Erfahrungen in den letzten Jahren zeigen, ... die Leute in der DDR kaum Schwierigkeiten haben.

   so daß; der; ob; daß.

(ii) **Explanations**

Select Vocabulary

unterschiedlich — varied
die Auswirkung (—en) — effect
der Einfluß (⸚e) — influence
unberührt — untouched
hüben und drüben — on both sides
   (often used with the particular sense
   of the two German states)
die Wandlung (—en) — change
vermutlich — presumably

im Hinblick auf — with regard to
Note: der Deutsche — the German (man)
   die Deutsche — the German (woman)
   das Deutsche — the German language
   (= die deutsche Sprache)
See further explanations in Grammar
Summary section 4(e)2.

Grammar

The following are the items of grammar of which there are examples in the text, and for which the Section B exercises provide practice. The references in parentheses give the section of the Grammar Summary where the particular points of grammar are explained.

(a) Uses of the Subjunctive and Conditional (12.14).
(b) Use of the Perfect tense of the Passive voice (12.8(e)(iii)).
(c) Complex sentence structure (15 (f)).

(iii) **Exercises – Section B**

1. Use the statements given below to make sentences which begin: *wir müssen uns fragen, ob . . .* or *es gibt Diskussionen darüber, ob . . . .*

Model: Die Teilung des Landes führt zu einer Teilung der Sprache.
Response: Wir müssen uns fragen, ob die Teilung des Landes zu einer Teilung der Sprache führe.

(a) Die beiden Sprachen sind nur Varianten der einen Sprache.
(b) Der Wortschatz ist von Wandlungen betroffen.
(c) Die Zahl der Wörter ist groß.
(d) Es ist anders in der BRD.
(e) Die deutsche Sprache als grammatisches System bleibt unberührt.

2. *Conditional sentences* In the following exercise you are given pairs of short sentences in the Present tense. Following the example of the model, rewrite each pair as a single sentence, expressing a condition, and with the correct sequence of tenses.

Model: Es geht so weiter. Wir verstehen uns nicht mehr.
Response: Wenn es so weiter ginge, würden wir uns nicht mehr verstehen.
Or: Wenn es so weiter gehen würde, würden wir uns nicht mehr verstehen.

(a) Die Sprache entwickelt sich rasch. Es führt zu einer Teilung.
(b) Das System bleibt unberührt. Die beiden Sprachen sind nur Varianten.
(c) Die Leute in der DDR sehen westdeutsche Fernsehsendungen. Sie kennen den neuen westdeutschen Wortschatz.

3. The text contains an example of the Perfect tense of the Passive voice: *Neue Wörter . . . sind oft kommentiert worden*, which could be rendered into English as: 'new words have often been commented upon'. Following this pattern, translate the following sentences into German:

(a) Linguistic developments have been seen in both parts.
(b) The language as a system has not been touched.
(c) West German TV has been watched by citizens of the GDR.

4. As an aid to the analysis of complex sentences, look again at the three sentences listed below, and, in each case, write out the main clause and the subordinate clauses of the sentences. Then try translating the sentences into English. Do not be afraid to break up the German into a number of smaller sentences in English, if this seems to make better sense in English.

(a) Die sprachlichen Entwicklungen . . . . . . verstehen würden.
(b) Es gab Diskussionen . . . . . . das Österreicherdeutsch auch.
(c) Erfahrungen . . . . . . kaum Schwierigkeiten haben.

13.2 Listening Materials 🖭

13.2.1 **Wiedersehen nach vielen Jahren** (old friends now living on different sides of the German frontier show some of the problems of comprehension)

Sabine: Nun erzähl mir doch bloß mal, was sich bei euch in den letzten Jahren alles getan hat.

Herbert: Tja, wo soll ich da anfangen? Ich bin schon seit einigen Jahren mittlerer Leistungskader in unserem Kombinat und plage mich zur Zeit mit der Qualifizierung. Unsere Brigade unterstützt mich aber dabei, und die Parteileitung hilft auch.

Sabine: Verstehe ich das richtig? Du willst dich beruflich weiterbilden, aber warum in der Armee?

Herbert: Nicht in der Armee, in unserem Betrieb, wo ich Brigadeleiter bin.

Sabine: Meinst du vielleicht Vorarbeiter?

Herbert:	Ja, natürlich. Bei uns heißt das Brigadier. Gisela hat mit der Schule viel zu tun und ist auch nach Feierabend viel unterwegs. Heute abend muß sie zum Elternaktiv. Der Dieter fährt diesen Sommer wieder ins Pionierlager. Da hilft Gisela auch bei der Organisation mit.
Sabine:	Was ist denn ein Elternaktiv?
Herbert:	Das sind auserwählte Eltern, die mit der Schule zusammenarbeiten.
Sabine:	Und euer Sohn macht auch schon beim Militär mit?
Herbert:	Nein, der ist ein Thälmannpionier. So heißt bei uns eine Jugendorganisation. Mit vierzehn bekommt er dann ein Blauhemd und gehört zur FDJ.
Sabine:	Das klingt mir alles sehr spanisch. Was macht denn eure Elke? Die muß doch schon sechzehn sein.
Herbert:	Ja, wir sind sehr stolz auf sie. Sie hat nämlich den Sprung zur EOS geschafft. Das ist hier gar nicht leicht.
Sabine:	Und was ist die EOS?
Herbert:	Na, die Erweiterte Oberschule, wo sie ihr Abitur machen kann.
Sabine:	Ach so. Wie steht es denn mit eurem Wochenendhaus? Ist das nicht bald fertig?
Herbert:	Unsere Datscha? Ja, die ist fast einzugsreif. Es fehlen nur noch Kleinigkeiten. Letzten Sonnabend konnten wir leider nicht dort bauen. Wir hatten im Betrieb einen Sobotnik.
Sabine:	Einen was?
Herbert:	Oh, einen freiwilligen und unbezahlten Arbeitseinsatz. Das machen wir ein- oder zweimal im Jahr.
Sabine:	Ich glaube, ich muß bei euch erstmal richtig DDR-Deutsch lernen, bevor ich mitreden kann.

(i) *Comprehension Questions*

1. List the words used by Herbert, and which Sabine does not understand because they are 'DDR-Deutsch'. From the explanations given by Herbert, explain in English what these terms mean.

2. What do you learn about the other members of Herbert's family? Write down the names and as much information as you can after listening to the tape.

Gisela —
Dieter —
Elke —

(ii) *Explanations*

Select Vocabulary

der Vorarbeiter (—) — foreman
der Feierabend (—e) — end of the working day
auserwählt — selected
einzugsreif — ready to move into
freiwillig — voluntary
unbezahlt — unpaid
der Arbeitseinsatz (¨e) — work session

Expressions and Idioms

erzähl mir doch bloß mal . . . — now just you tell me . . .
ich plage mich mit der Qualifizierung — I'm struggling to get my qualifications
das klingt mir alles sehr spanisch — that all sounds double dutch to me
wir sind sehr stolz auf sie — we are very proud of her

„Wenn die dem Jungen weiterhin Vieren und Fünfen geben, machst du einfach nicht mehr mit im Elternaktiv!"

© *Für Dich*, Berlin (DDR)

sie hat nämlich den Sprung zur EOS geschafft — you see, she has managed to make the jump to the Sixth Form College

es fehlen nur noch Kleinigkeiten — there are just a few little things left to do

Further Items of „DDR-Deutsch"

The point was made earlier that most changes in the German of the GDR affect vocabulary — in particular, the vocabulary which refers to different patterns of social and political organisation, such as schools, factories, etc. For anyone visiting the country, there are no more problems in speaking and understanding German than in any other area where German is spoken. One of the features worth noting also is that, whereas the language of the Federal Republic has absorbed a very large number of English (and American) words, this influence is not present in the GDR. There is an influence from Russian (for example, words in the dialogue such as *Datscha* and *Sobotnik*), but this influence is much less than that of English in the West. Among the specialised vocabulary mentioned in the dialogue were the following:

der mittlere Leistungskader — middle-ranking manager/foreman

das Kombinat — group of factories

die Brigade — group of workers

der Brigadier — foreman

das Aktiv — group of people working for a particular cause

das Pionierlager — pioneer camp

der Thälmannpionier — the Pioneers are a youth organisation named after Ernst Thälmann, a German communist who died in concentration camp. The great majority of young people between 6 and 14 years old belong to the Pioneers, after which they join the FDJ

die EOS = Erweiterte Oberschule — equivalent to a Sixth Form College, this is the school following the POS, the basic 6–16 comprehensive school

die Datscha — country cottage; week-end house

der Sobotnik — a working Saturday when workers offer their labour free

14 Lesestücke aus Anderen Deutschsprachigen Ländern

The form of this chapter varies from that of the others in this book. The aim is to offer more extensive reading passages with possibilities for developing and extending reading skills. There are no exercises concerned specifically with points of grammar, although the passages, of course, contain a wide range of examples of structures in context, which will allow students to extend their knowledge of grammatical forms and structures encountered already in the book.

The point has been made a number of times that German is a language spoken in four European countries, and although the Federal Republic contains the largest number of German speakers, the differences between the four cultures should not be forgotten. Indeed, these differences contribute to the value of learning German. The three passages chosen here seek to represent some of this variety by offering insights into Switzerland, Austria and the GDR. (The Federal Republic is amply represented elsewhere in the book.)

14.1 Warum ich gern Österreicherin bin

Wenn ich an meine Heimat Österreich denke, dann entsteht vor mir zuallererst das Bild meiner nächsten Umgebung, meiner Wohngemeinde, vertrauter Plätze, an denen ich gern meine Freizeit verbringe. Österreich ist ein äußerst reizvolles Land, und bietet für den Großteil seiner Menschen, was man heute Umwelt- und Lebensqualität nennt. Diesem landschaftlichen Reiz ist wahrscheinlich der rege Fremdenverkehr zu verdanken, der seit jeher eine starke Säule der Wirtschaft bildet.

Österreich ist ein freies Land mit einer demokratischen Gesellschaftsordnung. Diese Tatsache ist keine Selbstverständlichkeit. Schließlich folgten nach dem Krieg zehn Jahre Besatzung, und der Staatsvertrag, in dem sich Österreich zu einer neutralen Position in Europa verpflichtet, kam auch mit dem Einverständnis der Sowjetunion zustande.

Österreich kann stolz sein auf seine wissenschaftlichen und kulturellen Leistungen und seine Tradition in der Geschichte. Schließlich haben bis zum ersten Weltkrieg zahlreiche slawische Völker zusammen mit Ungarn, Italienern und deutschprachigen Österreichern in einem großen Reich relativ friedlich gelebt. Heute spricht man von der alten Monarchie als einem frühen Modell eines vereinten Europa, und die Gesinnung der Völkerverständigung ist beim Österreicher der Gegenwart sehr lebendig.

Ich lebe auch gern in diesem Land, weil die Menschen in der Lage sind, Differenzen vernünftig, ohne Gewaltanwendung, auszutragen. Die Suche nach Kompromissen in ideologischen, sozialen oder wirtschaftlichen Fragen ist gewissermaßen ein politisches Prinzip geworden. Herausragendes Beispiel ist die sogenannte Sozialpartnerschaft, die das Verhältnis zwischen den Arbeitgebern und dem Gewerkschaftsbund kennzeichnet. In Österreich hat es seit Jahren, wenn nicht Jahrzehnten, keinen großen Streik gegeben, weil die Sozialpartner sich über die wichtigen politischen Fragen verständigen konnten. Das Netz der sozialen Sicherheit ist gut, die sozialen Unterschiede scheinen mir viel geringer als anderswo und auch das Hauptproblem der letzten Jahre, die steigende Arbeitslosigkeit, ist nur in abgeschwächter Form spürbar.

(i) *Comprehension Questions*

1. The writer of this piece is a young Austrian teacher spending a year in England. What is the first thing she thinks of when asked about her native Austria?

Österreich ist ein äußerst reizvolles Land — besonders in den Bergen

2. What does she describe as 'a strong pillar of the economy'?
3. What do you learn about Austria in the post-war period?
4. The old Austrian monarchy was swept away by World War 1, but what do people now say about the monarchy?
5. What countries and peoples combined to form the old Austrian monarchy?
6. What does the author feel is special about her fellow-countrymen?
7. What is the 'social partnership' referred to by the author?

(ii)   *Words in Context*

The passage contains a number of difficult words, which you might be able to guess in context. Below are some of these words, with a German definition. With the help of the definitions and the context try to find English equivalents for these words:

Besatzung — das Besetzthalten eines Gebietes durch Soldaten
Einverständnis — Zustimmung
die Leistung — gut ausgeführte Tat oder Arbeit
Gesinnung — Grundhaltung; Einstellung; Denkart
die Gewaltanwendung — Gewalt = Macht
                    Anwendung = Gebrauch

(iii)   *Jumbled Sentences*

The following sentences from the passage have been jumbled. Rewrite the sentences with correct word order.

1. für Menschen nennt Österreich Großteil Land und Umwelt- und Lebensqualität ein bietet seiner den ist reizvolles was heute äußerst man.
2. Land Gesellschaftsordnung Österreich ist freies mit einer ein demokratischen.
3. Gewaltanwendung Differenzen ich Land weil Menschen Lage vernünftig auszutragen lebe in diesem die sind ohne der auch gern in.

(iv)   *Translation*

Translate the following section of the passage into English: In Österreich hat es seit Jahren . . . spürbar.

(v)   *Select Vocabulary*

zuallererst — first of all
vertraut — familiar
der Großteil — the greater part; majority
die Säule (—n) — pillar
die Wirtschaft (—en) — economy
die Selbstverständlichkeit (—en) — self-evident truth; foregone conclusion
die Besatzung (—en) — occupation
der Staatsvertrag (—e) — state treaty
sich zu etwas verpflichten — to undertake to do something
das Einverständnis (—se) — agreement
die Leistung (—en) — achievement
friedlich — peaceful
das Reich (—e) — empire

die Gegenwart — present day
die Gewaltanwendung — use of force
austragen (u, a) — to deal with
gewissermaßen — to a certain extent
herausragend — outstanding; prominent
das Verhältnis (—se) — relationship
der Arbeitgeber (—) — employer
der Gewerkschaftsbund — trade union organisation
kennzeichnen — to characterise
das Jahrzehnt (—e) — decade
sich verständigen — to come to an agreement
die soziale Sicherheit — social security
anderswo — elsewhere

vereint — united; unified
die Gesinnung — way of thinking;
  basic attitude
die Völkerverständigung — mutual
  understanding between peoples

die Arbeitslosigkeit — unemployment
in abgeschwächter Form — on a
  reduced scale
spürbar — noticeable; perceptible

14.2 Ein Mädchen aus Schwerin in der DDR schreibt ihrer englischen Brieffreundin und beschreibt ihre Heimatstadt

Schwerin, den 5. Mai

Liebe Debbie!

Wir haben zur Zeit Ferien, und nun will ich endlich, wie schon lange versprochen, Dir mehr von meiner Heimatstadt erzählen. Schwerin ist eine wunderschön gelegene Stadt. Man nennt sie auch die Stadt der sieben Seen, weil sie von so viel Wasser umgeben ist. Es wird behauptet, daß sie früher Zuarin geheißen hatte, was soviel wie „Tierpark" bedeutet. Auch heute ist die Stadt noch von vielen Wäldern und schönen Parks umgeben.

1160 erhielt Schwerin das Stadtrecht. Vorher war es eine Siedlung der Obotriten gewesen, mit einer Burg des Slawenfürsten Niklot. Später wurde aus dieser Burg das Schloß, in dem die Herzöge von Mecklenburg regierten. In der Stadt selbst befinden sich noch viele andere schöne Bauwerke, wie zum Beispiel der Dom, das Theater und das Museum. Aber früher war die Stadt eine ziemlich ruhige Provinzstadt gewesen.

Heute hat sich das geändert. Schwerin ist mittlerweile eine interessante Großstadt geworden, und es gibt jetzt auch Industriezweige hier. Früher hatte nur die Landwirtschaft eine große Rolle gespielt. Unser Theater beispielsweise hat in der ganzen Republik einen guten Ruf, und es finden hier oft sehr interessante Aufführungen statt.

Inzwischen hat Schwerin 120 000 Einwohner, und die Altstadt mit dem Einkaufszentrum ist eigentlich viel zu klein für so viele Menschen. Das macht das Einkaufen oft problematisch, und im Sommer kannst du vor den Frischobstständen lange Schlangen sehen. In den letzten zwanzig Jahren ist in Schwerin viel gebaut worden. Die Neubauviertel befinden sich alle am Stadtrand und sind mit der Straßenbahn schnell vom Zentrum zu erreichen. Diese Wohnhäuser sehen allerdings ein bißchen eintönig aus, und so versuchen die Leute, die dort wohnen, ihre Balkons individuell zu gestalten. Es gibt hier viele ausgezeichnete Möglichkeiten, Sport zu treiben, z.B. Segeln, Rudern, Kanufahren, Tennis und andere. Wir haben auch eine große Sport- und Kongreßhalle, wo oft interessante Veranstaltungen stattfinden. Ich will auch nicht unseren schönen Tierpark vergessen, der ein beliebtes Ausflugsziel für die ganze Familie ist.

Schreib mir doch mal, wie es in Deiner Heimatstadt aussieht.

Herzliche Grüße,

Deine Dagmar

(i) *Comprehension Questions*

1. Why is Schwerin called the town of seven lakes?
2. What happened in 1160?
3. What do you learn about the theatre?
4. Has the shopping centre kept pace with the growth of the town?
5. What can you say about the new estates?
6. What sort of sporting activities are mentioned?
7. What is said about the *Tierpark*?

(ii) *Pluperfect Tense*

Read Grammar Summary section (12.8(f)) about the Pluperfect, and then find three sentences in the letter which contain a Pluperfect tense.

(iii) *Translation*

Translate into English the section from *Schwerin ist eine wunderschön gelegene Stadt* as far as *eine ruhige Provinzstadt gewesen.*

(iv) *Letter-writing*

At the end of her letter, Dagmar asks Debbie to write and tell her about the town where she lives in the United Kingdom. Write a letter of about 200 words describing your town or village, perhaps saying a little about its history and describing how it looks today. What sort of sporting and leisure-time activities does it offer?

(v) *Explanations*

wie schon lange versprochen — as was promised ages ago	die Frischobststände — fresh fruit stalls
weil sie von so viel Wasser umgeben ist — because it is surrounded by so much water	die Schlange (—n) — queue (also snake)
das Stadtrecht — town charter	ist viel gebaut worden — there has been a lot of building
die Siedlung (—en) — settlement	das Neubauviertel (—) — new building development; housing estate
der Slawenfürst — slavonic prince	sind schnell zu erreichen — can be quickly reached
das Bauwerk (—e) — construction; building	allerdings — however; though; mind you
mittlerweile — in the meantime	eintönig — monotonous
der Industriezweig (—e) — branch of industry	individuell zu gestalten — to arrange in an individual way
die Landwirtschaft — agriculture	ausgezeichnet — excellent
hat einen guten Ruf — has a good reputation	die Veranstaltung (—en) — event
die Aufführung (—en) — theatre production	das Ausflugsziel (—e) — destination for an excursion
	wie es in Deiner Heimatstadt aussieht — what it looks like in your home town

14.3 Luzern — Meine Heimatstadt

A teenage Swiss boy writes an essay about his home town.

Luzern, die Leuchtenstadt im Herzen der Schweiz, ist weltweit sehr bekannt. Viele Ausländer kennen diese Stadt besser und lieben sie mehr als Bern oder Zürich. Nur Genf erfreut sich einer größeren Popularität. Aber warum ist Luzern eine solche Touristenstadt geworden?

Die Lage, sagen die einen; die vielen Attraktionen und Sehenswürdigkeiten, behaupten die anderen. Tatsache ist, in Luzern findet der Tourist alles, was er sich kulturell und geographisch unter der Schweiz vorstellt; hohe, felsige Berge, grüne Alpen, einen sauber scheinenden, bläulich schimmernden See, und eine Stadt, vollgepackt mit historischen Bauten. Zudem hat Luzern das „Glück", direkt an der Nord-Süd Verbindung zu liegen. Die Stadt mit ihren 65 000 Einwohnern hat deshalb überaus viele einmalige Übernachtungen. Doch nur der Reisende, der ein paar Tage in Luzern verweilen kann, kommt voll auf seine Rechnung. Tagsüber stehen zahlreiche Museen, wie zum Beispiel das Naturhistorische Museum oder das Verkehrshaus zur Besichtigung bereit. Für das leibliche Wohl sorgen die zahlreichen Restaurants, die vom günstigen Schnellimbiß über die gutbürgerlichen Restaurants bis zu den edelsten Lokalen hin reichen. Hier können sich die „ausländischen Gäste'' auch mit unserer Küche vertraut machen. Da diese aber oft nicht mit unseren Eßgewohnheiten vertraut sind, sieht man nicht selten, daß manche Japaner oder auch Amerikaner bei 30 Grad Hitze genüßlich an einem Käsefondue sitzen und mit einem Löffel bewaffnet, die gelbe Masse vertilgen. Wer kann da einem Schweizer verübeln, wenn er mitleidig leicht zu lächeln beginnt?

Nach dem kräftigen Essen trotten sie dann, mit den Foto-, Film- und Video-kameras bewaffnet, durch die Altstadt. Schnell ist ein Objekt gefunden, das sich zum Fotografieren lohnt. Die Einheimischen sehen diesem Treiben gelassen zu und nehmen davon kaum noch Notiz, denn sie wissen, daß die Touristen einen ordentlichen Happen Geld in unserem Städtchen zurücklassen. Dadurch können viele Arbeitsplätze gesichert werden. Natürlich stehen nicht nur die vielen Bauten und die Gaumenfreuden im Mittelpunkt. Eine Schiffsreise auf dem Vierwald-stättersee oder auch ein Sonnenaufgang auf der Rigi gehören schon fast zum Obligatorium der Reisegesellschaften.

Doch in der Nacht gehört Luzern wieder den Luzernern. Dazu gehören ein Kinobesuch in einem unserer 11 Lichtspieltheater, ein gemütlicher Abend in der „Stammbeiz'' oder eine aufregende Nacht in einer der unzähligen Bars oder in einem Nightclub. Rundum, Luzern ist eine gemütliche Stadt, in der es sich gut leben läßt.

(i) *Comprehension Questions*

1. What are the attractions of Lucerne's geographical setting?
2. Besides the landscape, there are other reasons why Lucerne has grown up at that particular place. What are these reasons?
3. What examples are given of the places you can visit in Lucerne?
4. How does the author describe the range of restaurants available to the tourist?
5. What is the attitude of local people to the many tourists?
6. After eating, what else is practically a necessity if one is a tourist in Lucerne?
7. What sort of night life is there in the town?

(ii) *Translation*

Translate into English the following passage: From *Aber warum ist Luzern eine solche Touristenstadt geworden?* as far as *kommt voll auf seine Rechnung.*

(iii) *Gapped Text*

In the following extract from the passage the adjectives have been omitted. Re-write the passage below, filling in the gaps with adjectives chosen from the list below. Be sure to add the correct adjectival endings.

Für das . . . . . . Wohl sorgen die . . . . . . Restaurants, die vom . . . . . . Schnellimbiß über die . . . . . . Restaurants, bis zu den . . . . . . Lokalen hin reichen. Hier können sich die . . . . . . Gäste auch mit unserer Küche vertraut machen. Nach dem . . . . . . Essen trotten sie dann durch die Altstadt. Zum Nachtprogramm gehören ein . . . . . . Abend in der „Stammbeiz'' oder eine . . . . . . Nacht in einer der . . . . . . Bars.

ausländisch; kräftig; leiblich; unzählig; zahlreich; edelst; gemütlich; günstig; aufregend; gutbürgerlich.

(iv) *Explanations*

die Leuchtenstadt — town of lights
sich erfreuen (+ Genitive) — to enjoy
die Lage (—n) — position
sich vorstellen — to imagine
zudem — in addition
überaus viele — very many
verweilen — to stay; to linger
kommt voll auf seine Rechnung — has
   his money's worth
das Verkehrshaus — transport museum
   in Lucerne
das leibliche Wohl — physical well-being
gutbürgerliche Küche — good, plain
   cooking
edel — fine; noble

die Eßgewohnheiten — eating habits
das Käsefondue — cheese fondue
   (Swiss dish)
vertilgen — to demolish
jemandem etwas verübeln — to blame
   someone for something
mitleidig — sympathetically
bewaffnet — armed
gelassen — in a relaxed way
der Happen — a good catch
die Gaumenfreude (—n) — pleasures
   of the palate
der Vierwaldstättersee — Lake Lucerne
das Lichtspieltheater (—) — cinema
rundum — all in all

Part II

REFERENCE SECTION

Key to Exercises

Chapter 1 Familie und Zuhause

1.1.1 *(i)*

1. (a) Niece. (b) Grandson. (c) Aunt. (d) Sister-in-law. (e) Grandmother.
2. *geborene* refers to the woman's maiden name. English usually makes use of the French term *née*.
3. (a) Karl's brother Rolf is aged 20. He is married and his wife is also 20 and is called Renate. (b) The grandparents on Karl's father's side of the family are called Wilhelm and Luise. Wilhelm is aged 72 and Luise is 70. Luise's maiden name was Müller. On Karl's mother's side of the family the grandparents are called Karl and Ottilie Schröder. They are aged 68 and 69, and Ottilie's maiden name was Stett.

1.1.1 *(ii)*

1. (a) Meine Schwester heißt Gabi; sie ist 12 Jahre alt. (b) Meine Mutter heißt Sophie; sie ist 42 Jahre alt. (c) Meine Schwägerin heißt Renate; sie ist 20 Jahre alt.
2. (a) and (b) will depend upon your age and the names and ages of your family. Follow the pattern of the statements made above.

1.1.2 *(i)*

1. The family offers opportunities for playing.
2. They are mostly babies and small children, but also, sometimes, schoolchildren.
3. Usually the maximum number of children looked after is four or five.
4. Yes, the families are paid, and this is arranged privately with the parents.
5. (a) tagsüber. (b) regelmäßig. (c) zumeist. (d) in der Regel. (e) bezahlt.

1.1.2 *(ii)*

(a) wie viele Kinder? (b) was ist das? (c) wie? (d) welche Kinder?

1.1.2 *(iii)*

(a) What is a day-family? (b) How many mothers and fathers go to work? (c) How many children are in a day-family? (d) Which parents look after the children? (e) How do the parents pay? (f) What do the children play? (g) What sort of children stay in a day-family?

1.1.3 *Exercises – Section A*

1. (a) In Germany only the richer families can afford a house. (b) They live in a flat, either owned by them, or rented. (c) They saved up for 12 years. (d) She is

surprised to learn how often Helen has moved house. (e) She lived on the outskirts of the town. (f) Although Munich is a big city it keeps the atmosphere of a small town. (g) She feels quite sad that she has moved away from home.

2. (a) Ich kann mir gar nicht vorstellen. (b) Die meisten Familien. (c) Ich war verblüfft. (d) Stadtviertel. (e) Heimatstadt. (f) Sportverein.

1.1.3 Exercises – Section B

1. (a) Gabi hat von ihrer Familie und ihrem Haus geschrieben. (b) Gabis Eltern haben Geld für ein Haus gespart. (c) Helen ist sehr oft umgezogen. (d) Gabi ist endlich von zuhause fortgezogen. (e) Sie ist immer schnell sowohl im Grünen als auch in der Stadtmitte gewesen. (f) Ich habe es in München schön gefunden. (g) Man hat München die Großstadt mit Kleinstadtatmosphäre genannt. (h) Die Jugendlichen der Gegend haben sich kennengelernt.

2. (a) Als ich von unserer Wohnung fortgezogen bin, haben wir ein neues Haus gekauft. (b) Als ich bei meiner Familie wohnte, habe ich am Stadtrand gewohnt. (c) Wenn ich in München bin, wohne ich bei meinen Eltern. (d) Als ich in München gewohnt habe, war unser Haus am Stadtrand. (e) Wenn man in einem freundlichen Stadtviertel wohnt, spürt man nichts von der Anonymität der Großstadt. (f) Wenn ich Dir von meiner Kindheit schreibe, finde ich est fast schade, daß ich von diesem Zuhause fortgezogen bin.

3. (a) Ich schreibe von meinem Haus und meiner Familie. (b) Wir haben schon immer in unserem Haus gewohnt. (c) Wohnst du noch bei deinen Eltern? (d) Ich bin mit meiner Familie umgezogen. (e) In unserem Viertel hat man nie etwas von der Anonymität der Großstadt gespürt. (f) Ich bin von meinem Zuhause fortgezogen. (g) Ihr habt mir von Eurem Haus geschrieben.

4. The content of the letter will depend on the place where you live, and your own family circumstances.

1.2.1

Name	Age	Brothers	Sisters	Father	Mother
Rolf Schmidt	18	1	1	Heinrich	Sophie
Johann Weiß	17	0	0	–	Karin
Hans Schwarz	16	2	3	Hermann	Brigitte
Jürgen	16	0	1	Simon	Greta

1.2.2 (i)

The correct answers are as follows: 1. (c) 2. (a). 3. (b). 4. (a). 5. (c).

1.2.2 (ii)

1. Ich auch nicht. 2. Aus Rostock. 3. Nach Leipzig. 4. Was studierst denn du? 5. Lehrer, das will ich auf keinen Fall werden. 6. Das glaube ich. 7. Oh, wie schön!

1.2.2 (iii)

1. Where do you come from, then? 2. By the way, my name is Karen. 3. Where are you going to, then? 4. That really is funny. 5. Is your father a journalist, I wonder? 6. Well, I have often been there. 7. You see, I have three brothers and sisters. 8. That really is fun. 9. Well, at least you have your peace and quiet.

1.2.2 *(iv)*

Ich auch nicht. Wo kommen Sie denn her? ...

... Ich heiße — , und ich fahre nach München ...

... Ich bin auch Student. Ich bin Engländer(in), und ich studiere Deutsch ...

... Ich bin aus — . Ich bin schon drei Stunden mit diesem Zug gefahren ...

... Es ist eine schöne, kleine Stadt. Ich wohne in der Stadtmitte ... Wo wohnen Sie in Hamburg? ...

... Ich habe drei Geschwister ...

... Ich bleibe drei Wochen bei einem Brieffreund in München.

(Change the details about town and family to fit in with your own life.)

Chapter 2 Transport und Reisen

2.1.1 *(i)*

1. Is the car in order? 2. Passports. 3. The documents for the children. 4. Führerschein; Versicherungskarte. 5. Street maps and guides. 6. Are any jabs necessary?

2.1.1 *(ii)*

1. Ist der Wagen nicht in Ordnung? 2. Sind Päße erforderlich? 3. Sind die Reiseausweise für Kinder noch gültig? 4. Brauchen Sie eine grüne Versicherungskarte? 5. Sind Straßenkarten nötig? 6. Haben Sie schon einen internationalen Führerschein? 7. Sind Reiseausweise und Impfungen erforderlich?

2.1.2 *(i)*

1. The visitor has chosen Great Britain for a holiday; or he/she has an appointment for a meeting; or he/she just wants to go to London shopping. 2. By train and ship. 3. No; from many German cities trains travel direct to the channel. 4. By travelling with London Transport. 5. It is practical, safe, cheap and fast.

2.1.2 *(ii)*

The answers to the questions should be as follows:
1. Wählen Sie Großbritannien. 2. Fahren Sie über Oostende nach Dover. 3. Nein, fahren Sie mit der Bahn. 4. Lernen Sie nur London kennen. 5. Fahren Sie mit London Transport.

2.1.3 *Exercises — Section A*

1. (a) They wanted to travel on the longest tram line in the world. (b) They went up to where the number 79 tram was waiting. (c) It was noisy and swaying and reminded one of the first trams in the town, 80 years before. (d) The lines were carried overhead on pillars and bridges. (e) Diagonally opposite. (f) It had travelled past Europe's biggest inland harbour. (g) 10 years ago it was very dirty; now, water lilies are growing there. (h) Essen used to be a noisy, smoky industrial city. Now it is becoming a garden city. (i) They see the monotonous outskirts of an industrial city. (j) The outskirts of Dortmund. (k) The express tram brought them back in about an hour.

2. (a) Kreuz und quer durch das Ruhrgebiet. (b) Schräg gegenüber. (c) Europas größter Binnenhafen. (d) Sehr verschmutzt. (e) Und so ging es weiter. (f) In etwa einer Stunde.

1. Hinter Lohausen wurde es leiser. Der Zug fuhr neben der Straße mitten durch Äcker und Wiesen . . . . Die Bahn fuhr über die Ruhr. Wir stiegen wieder um in die Bahn nach Essen. Sie fuhr in der Mitte der breiten Bundesstraße 1. Wieder wurde es grau. Draußen regnete es. Von Gelsenkirchen nach Bochum waren die Wagen überfüllt. Und so ging es weiter, bis die Linie 409 uns zum Endpunkt unserer Reise brachte.

2. (a) The correct prepositions in sequence are: nach . . . mit . . . nach . . . über . . . mit . . . in . . . in . . . mit.
   (b) Unsere Reporter wollten mit der längsten Straßenbahnlinie der Welt fahren. Sie fuhren kreuz und quer durch das Ruhrgebiet von Düsseldorf bis nach Dortmund. Die Fahrt über die alten Gleise erinnerte an die ersten Trambahnen in den Städten vor 80 Jahren. Zwischen Düsseldorf und Duisburg wurde es leiser. Der Zug fuhr neben der Straße mitten durch Äcker und Wiesen. Von hier aus ist es nicht mehr weit zum Hauptbahnhof. Schräg gegenüber hielt die Linie 901. Sie war vorher an Europas größten Binnenhafen vorbeigefahren. Die Bahn fuhr über die Ruhr.

3. (a) Die billigste Fahrt ist die einfache Fahrt zweiter Klasse von Bonn nach London. (b) Die einfache Fahrt von Düsseldorf nach London ist billiger als die einfache Fahrt von Frankfurt nach London. (c) Die Hin- und Rückfahrt von Hannover nach London ist teurer als die Hin- und Rückfahrt von Bonn nach London. (d) Die Hin- und Rückfahrt erster Klasse von Berlin nach London ist die teuerste Fahrt.

4. The following are possible sentences: Die längste Fahrt ist die Fahrt von Berlin nach London. Die kürzeste Fahrt ist die Fahrt von Bonn nach London. Von Frankfurt nach London ist eine längere Fahrt als von Düsseldorf nach London. Von Hannover nach London ist eine kürzere Fahrt als von Hamburg nach London. Von Berlin nach London ist länger als von Frankfurt nach London. u.s.w.

5. am besten; eindruckvollst–; faszinierendst–; praktischst–; billigst–; sicherst–; schnellst–; größt–; längst–.
   Der schnellste Weg nach Großbritannien. London ist die faszinierendste Stadt Europas. Duisburg hat den größten Binnenhafen Europas. Von Düsseldorf bis nach Dortmund ist die längste Straßenbahnlinie der Welt. London ist eine der eindrucksvollsten Hauptstädte der Welt. Essen war einmal die größte Bergbaustadt Europas.

6. Am schnellsten fährt man mit dem Flugzeug. Am bequemsten fährt man mit dem Taxi. Am preiswertesten fährt man mit dem Fahrrad. Am praktischsten fährt man mit dem Autobus. Am sichersten fährt man mit dem Zug. Am teuersten fährt man mit dem Flugzeug. Am langsamsten fährt man mit dem Fahrrad.

2.2.1 *(i)*

1. The Orient Express is arriving. 2. The train is leaving. 3. *Achtung* means 'take care!' 4. The train from Munich to Milan. 5. It is posted on ticket office window number 1. 6. Because there is building work on the line.

2.2.2 *(i)*

The correct answers are: 1. (a). 2. (c). 3. (a).

2.2.2 *(ii)*

1. The 17.20 means that she would have to change in Bonn, but the 17.44 is direct. 2. She asks him whether he could write the information down. 3. A day-return ticket costs 5 marks less. 4. He says that she must go to the ticket window.

2.2.2 *(iii)*

Wann fährt der nächste Zug nach Braunschweig? . . .
. . . Muß ich umsteigen oder fährt er direkt? . . .
. . . Fährt ein Zug so um fünf Uhr zurück? . . .
. . . Wann kommt er an? . . .
. . . Könnten Sie vielleicht das alles aufschreiben? . . .
. . . Vielen Dank, auf Wiedersehen.

Chapter 3 Ferien

3.1.1 *(i)*

1. In Innsbruck. 2. They are leaving the next day. 3. Yes, they have had fine weather. 4. They are going for a stroll round the town, then some shopping. 5. In the evening, they are going to the theatre.

3.1.1 *(ii)*

1. gestern; gestern abend; heute; morgen; schönes Wetter. 2. Make up your own post-card, like the one in the chapter.

3.1.2 *(i)*

1. On the Danube. 2. It has the highest church tower in the world. 3. Splendid buildings and pretty fountains. 4. Every Saturday on the Minster square. 5. Delicacies of Swabian cooking. 6. Dancing or theatres.

3.1.2 *(ii)*

1. (a) nach. (b) in. (c) am. (d) auf. (e) durch. (f) ins.
2. mit . . . mit . . . im.
3. (a) auf. (b) am.
4. (a) Wir machen einen Einkaufsbummel, und danach machen wir eine Pause. (b) Am Münsterplatz ist ein Schild aufgestellt, und darauf steht „jeden Samstag Wochenmarkt". (c) Ich habe ein Päckchen bekommen, und darin war ein Reiseführer von Ulm.

3.1.3 *Exercises – Section A*

1. The following statements are correct: (a); (b); (d); (f); (g).
2. (a) erobern. (b) bremsen. (c) wohltuend. (d) erfreulich. (e) beherbergen. (f) sich erholen. (g) Annehmlichkeit.

3.1.3 *Exercises – Section B*

1. (a) Als wir an das Erholungsheim kamen, eroberten wir als erstes die Schwimmhalle. (b) Als man das Heim familienfreundlich plante, baute man Zimmer

für die Kinder. (c) Als das Haus 1980 eröffnet wurde, kamen sofort viele Gäste.
2. (a) Erfreulich, daß man familienfreundlich plant und denkt. (b) Wir erhielten die Nachricht, daß Badesachen mitzubringen sind. (c) Wir wissen, daß 120 000 Werktätige sich hier erholt haben. (d) Wir freuen uns, daß Schwimmen groß-geschrieben wird.
3. (a) beim Bau moderner Wohnblocks; beim Bau neuer Heime; beim Bau schöner, neuer Wohnungen. (b) Die Annehmlichkeiten des neuen Heimes; die Annehm-lichkeiten des schönen Ortes; die Annehmlichkeiten des modernen Hotels; die Annehmlichkeiten der malerischen Stadt.
4. (a) Sie fühlen sich wohl. (b) Sie erholen sich. (c) Sie können sich schönere Ferien nicht vorstellen.

3.1.4 *Exercises – Section A*

1. (a) She found it in a list of hotels. (b) A double room for two weeks. (c) It is important that the room should have a peaceful position. (d) She wants to know the price for bed and breakfast per person per night. (e) She wants a prospectus so that she can find out the exact position and size of the hotel, the sort of furnishings and a description of the way to get there. (f) She will come by car. (g) She wants to know what there is to see, and whether there are possibilities for walking, sport, sailing and evening entertainment.
2. (a) Ich hätte gern ein Zimmer mit Blick auf den See. (b) Könnten Sie mir bitte den Preis für eine Übernachtung mit Frühstück pro Person und pro Nacht mitteilen? (c) Ich möchte Sie bitten, mir einen Prospekt zu schicken, dem ich die genaue Lage und Größe des Hotels, die Art der Ausstattung von Zimmern entnehmen kann. (d) Es wäre für mich auch wichtig zu wissen, ob Sie einen bewachten Hotelparkplatz oder andere Parkmöglichkeiten in der Nähe haben. (e) Gibt es Sehenswürdigkeiten im Gebiet? Besteht die Möglichkeit, am See Segelboote auszuleihen? Bieten die Orte Unterhaltung am Abend?

3.1.4 *Exercises – Section B*

1. (a) Ich möchte gern ein Zimmer mit ruhiger Lage. (b) Ich hätte gern ein Zimmer mit Blick auf den See. (c) Könnten Sie mir bitte den Preis für eine Übernachtung mit Frühstück mitteilen? (d) Ich würde gern ein Zimmer mit Vollpension buchen. (e) Könnten Sie mir bitte einen Prospekt schicken? (f) Es wäre für mich wichtig, Informationen über das Gebiet zu haben. (g) Ich möchte gern, zwei Wochen in der Schweiz verbringen.
2. (a) Ich möchte wissen, ob Sie einen bewachten Parkplatz haben. (b) Ich möchte Sie fragen, ob es zumindest Parkmöglichkeiten in der Nähe gibt. (c) Ich möchte Sie fragen, ob Sie ein Doppelzimmer mit Bad und WC haben. (d) Ich möchte wissen, ob man ein Zimmer mit Vollpension buchen kann. (e) Ich möchte fragen, ob Sie mir Informationen über das Gebiet schicken können. (f) Ich möchte wissen, ob die Orte Unterhaltung am Abend bieten.
3. The correct sequence of prepositions and articles is as follows:
in der; im; auf den; mit dem; über das; am; am.
4. (a) Es ist mir wichtig, ein Zimmer mit einer ruhigen Lage zu haben. (b) Könn-ten Sie mir bitte den Preis für ein Zimmer mit Frühstück mitteilen? (c) Ich möchte Sie bitten, mir einen Prospekt von Ihrem Hotel zu schicken. (d) Es ist mir wichtig, zu wissen, ob Sie einen bewachten Parkplatz haben. (e) Könnten Sie mir bitte Informationen über das Gebiet schicken?
5. You might make up a list like the following:
Hotelverzeichnis
Informationen über das Gebiet

Sport- und Wandermöglichkeiten
Segelboote
Pferdereiten
Unterhaltung am Abend
Theater, Kino, Tanzlokale
Restaurants

Your own list might have other things that you want to ask. The following letter is a possible way of asking for some of the information.

Städtisches Verkehrsamt,
Goslar.

Sehr geehrte Damen und Herren!
Ich würde gern im Sommer nächsten Jahres drei Wochen im Harz verbringen, und ich möchte Sie deshalb bitten, mir Informationen über die Stadt Goslar und ihre Umgebung zu schicken. Es wäre mir wichtig, ein Hotelverzeichnis zu haben, und ich möchte auch wissen, was für Sport- und Wandermöglichkeiten in der Umgebung sind. Ich interessiere mich auch für Segeln und Pferdereiten, und ich möchte wissen, ob die Möglichkeit besteht, Segelboote und Pferde auszuleihen. Ferner möchte ich Sie bitten, mir Informationen über die Unterhaltung am Abend zu schicken. Hat die Stadt ein Theater und Kinos? Oder gibt es vielleicht Tanzlokale? Hätten Sie auch ein Verzeichnis der Restaurants in der Stadt?

Vielen Dank für Ihre Mühe
Mit freundlichen Grüßen

3.2.1 *(i)*

1. A handful of dollars. 2. By air. 3. The beach. 4. Ancient traditions are combined with modern efficiency. 5. In Mexico.

3.2.2

1. (a) Ja, Gasthaus „zum Goldenen Adler". (b) Ja, wir haben noch Zimmer frei. (c) Wir haben ein Doppelzimmer mit Dusche zu DM 46 . . . Ich kann Ihnen nur ein kleines Zimmer ohne Dusche für DM 26 anbieten. (d) Ja, Frühstück und Bedienung sind inbegriffen.

2. (a) Wir sind vier Personen, meine Eltern, meine Schwester und ich. (b) Ein Doppelzimmer für meine Eltern und zwei Einzelzimmer. [oder: ein Zweibettzimmer]. (c) Meine Eltern möchten ein Doppelzimmer mit Bad oder mit Dusche. Für die Einzelzimmer geht es auch ohne Dusche. (d) Was kosten die Zimmer? Hätten Sie vielleicht etwas Billigeres? Gut, also das geht. (e) Sind Frühstück und Bedienung im Preis inbegriffen? (f) Wir werden wahrscheinlich erst um 21 Uhr ankommen. Wäre es noch möglich, so spät ein Abendessen zu bekommen? (g) Vielen Dank. Auf Wiederhören.

3.2.3

1. (a) He is the leader of the group. (b) There are seven pupils in the group and they have three tents plus Mr Brown's own one-man tent. (c) The minibus costs 6 DM per day extra. (d) 5 days. (e) The numbers are to hang on their tents. (f) They must get coins or tokens at the reception desk.

2. (a) Wir sind vier Personen. (b) Ja, wir haben unser eigenes Zelt. (c) Wir haben ein Auto. (d) Wir wollen drei Tage bleiben. (e) Haben Sie noch Platz? (f) Was kostet die Übernachtung? (g) Wo sind die Toiletten und die Waschräume?

Chapter 4 Städte der Bundesrepublik

4.1.1 *(i)*

1. Sunny and very warm. 2. In the west. 3. Starting cloudy, but otherwise clear and without rain. 4. From east to south. 5. Both cloudless. 6. Because it is the highest mountain in Germany.

4.1.2 *(i)*

The correct statements are as follows: 2.; 3.; 5.; 6.

4.1.2 *(ii)*

1. An die Fußgänger denkt kaum einer. 2. Die Autofahrer haben es gut. 3. Die Frankfurter haben mich auch positiv überrascht. 4. In anderen Ländern hält man die Großstädter für arrogant. 5. Es fiel uns also leicht, vierzehn Tage hier zu verbringen. 6. Sie möchten nicht mit der neuesten Mode imponieren. 7. Sie lieben mehr die gemütlichen Innenhöfe. 8. Fremden gegenüber sind sie trotzdem offen.

4.1.3 *Exercises — Section A*

1. (a) No; it lies on the Elbe about 100 km from the North Sea. (b) It is the biggest port in Germany. (c) Containers, gas, oil, cars, coffee, timber, etc. (d) At five o'clock in the morning. (e) It is a suburb of the city, and lies on the Elbe and on a small hill. (f) A mixture of people — for example, sailors and fishermen, but also politicians and film stars.
2. (a) Hamburg hat den größten und wichtigsten Hafen Deutschlands. (b) Am Sonntagmorgen um fünf Uhr kann man hier schon einkaufen. (c) Von oben hat man eine schöne Aussicht auf die Elbe und in das flache Land hinter den Elbdeichen. (d) Wenn man genug Geld hat, oder wenn man schon lange hier wohnt.

4.1.3 *Exercises — Section B*

1. The letter you write will depend on the place where you live.
2. The correct endings for the adjectives are as follows:
   frischen; größten; wichtigsten; regelmäßige; flüssige; feste; zollfreie; anderes; frische; alte; lebende; heiße; interessante; hohen; schöne; flache; alte; berühmten.

4.2.1 *(i)*

1. Domplatz. 2. Friedrich-Wilhelm-Straße. 3. Rathaus. 4. die Burg.

4.2.2 *(i)*

1. She has been doing school-work all day and needs a change. 2. She suggests that they might have an ice and then go to the cinema. 3. She says that she could buy a cinema programme on the way to the café. 4. They decide to meet in the café. 5. No; they are right next to the cinema. 6. At six o'clock. 7. She will come on her bicycle.

4.2.2 *(ii)*

1. Hast du heute abend schon etwas vor? 2. Ich brauche unbedingt eine Abwechslung. 3. Treffen wir uns im Café? 4. Gleich beim Kino. 5. Das ist mir gleich. 6. Muß ich rechts oder links abbiegen? 7. Bis dann!

4.2.2 *(iii)*

Nein, heute abend bin ich frei . . .
Ja, gerne. Hast du etwas Bestimmtes vor? . . .
Ja, gut; das würde ich gerne tun. Weißt du, was für gute Filme momentan laufen? . . .
Das Café kenne ich nicht, aber den Dom kenne ich schon . . .
Ja, um fünf Uhr, das geht. Bis dann!

Chapter 5 Essen und Trinken

5.1.1 *(i)*

1. Kalte Vorspeisen — cold starters. Warme Vorspeisen — hot starters. Hauptgerichte — main courses. Dessert — desserts. Getränke — drinks. 2. Oxtail soup and French onion soup. 3. Veal and pork. 4. Various ice-creams. 5. ¼ litre.

5.1.1 *(ii)*

You choose your own meal, but you might say something like this:
Ich nehme zuerst Ochsenschwanzsuppe, und dann als Hauptgericht Kalbsrahmbraten. Als Dessert möchte ich einen Eisbecher. Und ich trinke dazu ein Viertel Moselwein bitte.

5.1.2 *(i)*

1. Honey; sugar; butter; salt; coffee. 2. Until the honey and the butter melt. 3. Do not put the mixture in the fridge. 4. Pour into the dish and stir. 5. It must cook for 20 minutes in a hot oven. 6. The icing must not get too thin.

5.1.2 *(ii)*

Pour water into a frying-pan. Place a saucepan in the water. Boil the water and then turn down to low heat. Melt the fat in the saucepan. Add the icing sugar. Add hot water carefully and stir. The icing must not get too thin.

5.1.3 *Exercises — Section A*

1. (a) Black bread or rolls, butter, jam and honey. (b) Because one has more time at week-ends. (c) An egg, cheese or sausage. (d) Because school finishes at midday. (e) Potatoes, rice or noodles and vegetables or salad. (f) Because the regions all have their own specialities. (g) Coffee and cakes. (h) Black bread; wholemeal bread; butter; different cheeses; cold meats; tea; lemonade or beer.
2. The missing words are as follows: Frühstück; Deutschen; Marmelade; Kaffee; Ei; Wurstsorten; Mittagessen; Beilagen; Reis; Kuchen; Abendessen; Käsesorten; Tee.

1. (a) Es hat mich sehr gefreut, den Tag mit Semmeln zu beginnen. (b) Es hat mich sehr gefreut, am Sonntag Kuchen und Schlagrahm zu frühstücken. (c) Es hat mich sehr gefreut, eine bayerische Spezialität zu probieren. (d) Es hat mich sehr gefreut, nachmittags Kaffee und Kuchen zu essen. (e) Es hat mich sehr gefreut, Bier zum Abendessen zu trinken.

2. (a) Da du einen Aufsatz schreiben mußt, gebe ich Dir einige Tips. (b) Da man sich mehr Zeit lassen kann, ißt man Käse und Wurst. (c) Da jede Gegend in Deutschland ihre eigenen Spezialitäten hat, gibt es kein typisch deutsches Gericht. (d) Da es die Schwarzwälderkirschtorte nur an Festtagen gibt, ißt man unter der Woche einfachere Kuchen. (e) Da die Hauptmahlzeit normalerweise das Mittagessen ist, essen wir abends kalt.

3. (a) Ich will gleich mit dem Frühstück anfangen. (b) Die meisten Deutschen wollen den Tag mit Semmeln beginnen. (c) Die Kinder müssen zum Mittagessen nach Hause kommen. (d) Nachmittags will ich Kuchen essen und Kaffee trinken. (e) Am Sonntag wollen viele Familien Kaffee, Kuchen und Schlagrahm frühstücken.

4. The correct forms of the adjectives are as follows:
   (a) Deutsche; deutsche; (b) weiches; (c) deutsches; eigenen; (d) einfachere; (e) meisten; (f) verschiedene; (g) englischen; leichtes; deutsches.

5.2.1 *(ii)*

Herr Lange: Breakfast — a lot of coffee, and perhaps a bread roll with butter and jam.
Peter: Lunch — a chop with potatoes or chips and a side salad. He might drink a beer with his meal.
Frau Stett: Afternoon tea — cakes and tea or coffee. She prefers tea.
Bruno: Supper — cold meats, cheese. He drinks lemonade.

5.2.1 *(iii)*

Follow the patterns given by the other speakers, but talk about your own meals.

5.2.2 *(i)*

1. She suggests having a party. 2. They have not had a party for ages. 3. Ten. 4. They might make a giant pizza. 5. Everybody is doing pizzas at the moment. 6. An oriental meal such as a curry. 7. It is too complicated, and you can't get the right spices. 8. They are fed up with eating potato soup and bockwurst. 9. She had a Chinese meal with her parents. 10. She thinks that they may need special vegetables and sauces. 11. They decide to try a Chinese meal. 12. The guests will bring their own drink.

5.2.2 *(ii)*

1. Hallo. Wollen wir vielleicht eine Party geben?
   . . . Wollen wir diesmal vielleicht etwas kochen zur Abwechslung? . . . Sagen wir zehn . . .
   Wie wäre es mit einer Pizza? Und wir könnten Bier oder Wein trinken . . .
   Ja, du hast recht. Es ist besser, etwas Einfaches vorzuschlagen. Wollen wir das probieren? Treffen wir uns morgen, um Pläne zu machen.
2. Guten Tag, Bruno. Komm herein! . . .

Das ist eine tolle Idee. Es ist schon lange her, seitdem wir zusammen im Restaurant gegessen haben. Was schlägst du vor? . . .

Curry esse ich nicht so gern. Hast du schon mal chinesisch gegessen? . . .

Es gibt ein neues chinesisches Restaurant in der Marktstraße. Das könnten wir beide probieren . . .

Bis dann!

Chapter 6 Einkaufen und Post

6.1.1 *(i)*

1. No, you can telephone to make your purchase. 2. It is especially quiet. 3. The pictures are always sharply focused. 4. On holiday. 5. Prices start at 199 DM. 6. They claim that it makes work easy in the house and garden. 7. A fully automatic washing machine.

6.1.1 *(ii)*

1. Ist das das Kaufhaus Hertie? 2. Ich möchte eine Quarzuhr kaufen. 3. Ist der Preis immer noch 45 DM? 4. Muß ich zum Kaufhaus kommen, oder können Sie die Uhr mit der Post schicken? 5. Kann ich mit einem Scheck bezahlen, oder soll ich lieber bar bezahlen?

6.1.2

1. Geflügel; Obst und Gemüse; Kindermöbel; Geschenkartikel; Handschuhe; Damenhüte; Fundbüro; Bettwäsche; Süßwaren.
2. 2nd floor (alles für das Kind); 1st floor (Schürzen); 1st floor (Sportartikel); Ground floor (Schirme); Ground floor (Schmuck); 5th floor (Gardinen); 4th floor (Küchenmöbel).
3. Entschuldigen Sie bitte. Können Sie mir sagen, wo die Cafeteria ist?
   Entschuldigen Sie bitte. Wie komme ich zum Teeraum?
   Entschuldigen Sie bitte. Wo finde ich die Herrenbekleidung?
   Entschuldigen Sie bitte. Wissen Sie, wo die Taschentücher sind?

6.1.3 *Exercises – Section A*

1. (a) The booklet of postal charges (*Postgebührenheft*) has the complete list of charges. (b) The letter should have the complete address. (c) The name of the person sending the letter; the stamp; any special instructions (e.g. registered mail); the name of the recipient, together with the street, house number and the postal code and name of the town. (d) It can be sent by airmail or by express mail.
2. (a) Mitteilung; (b) Gebühren; (c) Empfänger; (d) befördern; (e) Eilbote.

6.1.3 *Exercises – Section B*

1. (a) Wer ein längeres Schreiben im Umschlag versenden will, muß einen Brief schicken. (b) Wer einen gedruckten Glückwunsch mit Unterschrift versenden will, kann ihn als Drucksache schicken. (c) Wer eine gedruckte Einladung mit handschriftlichen Zusätzen versenden will, kann sie als Briefdrucksache schicken.
2. (a) Damit die Sendung schnell zum richtigen Empfänger kommt, muß man die Briefmarke rechts oben aufkleben. (b) Damit die Sendung schnell zum richtigen Empfänger kommt, muß man unter der Briefmarke rechts oben besondere

Angaben machen. (c) Damit die Sendung schnell zum richtigen Empfänger kommt, muß der Name des Empfängers in der Mitte des Umschlags stehen. (d) Damit die Sendung schnell zum richtigen Empfänger kommt, muß die Postleitzahl vor dem Namen der Stadt stehen. (e) Damit die Sendung schnell zum richtigen Empfänger kommt, muß die Nummer des Postamts nach dem Namen des Ortes kommen.

3.   16. September 1986

Sehr geehrte Damen und Herren!

Ich bin Schüler in einer englischen Schule, und ich interessiere mich sehr für Briefmarken. Ich sammle gern alle Briefmarken, und ich habe eine große Briefmarkensammlung. Ich lerne Deutsch in der Schule, und deshalb interessiere ich mich besonders für die Briefmarken der Bundesrepublik. Ich möchte sehr gern eine vollständige Reihe der bundesdeutschen Briefmarken haben. Wäre es vielleicht möglich, mir eine solche Reihe zu schicken? Ich wäre Ihnen sehr dankbar.

Mit freundlichen Grüßen

Abs: J. Smith
    4 School Rd,
    Chelmsford,
    England.
            An den
            Bundesminister für das Post- und
                            Fernmeldewesen,
            Dienstgebäude,
            Adenauerallee 81,
            5300 BONN 1,
            Federal Republic of Germany

6.2.1 *(i)*

1. 1st floor. 2. Special offers. 3. Articles in the leather department. 4. French perfumes at greatly reduced prices. 5. There are smart skirts in summery colours. 6. They are being sold at half price.

6.2.1 *(ii)*

1. Solange der Vorrat reicht. 2. Vergessen Sie nicht. 3. Lassen Sie sich diese Chance nicht entgehen! 4. Zu stark reduzierten Preisen. 5. In sommerlichen Farben.

6.2.2 *(i)*

1. She has not much time. She must do her shopping. 2. Only a few minutes. 3. Once a week, on Fridays. 4. They go to the Aldi supermarket. 5. Bread, meat, sausage, fruit and vegetables. 6. A little corner-shop. 7. Supermarkets are very impersonal and nerve-racking, but things are cheaper there, and you can get special offers. 8. There is a wide choice, everything is fresh and good value. 9. She would like to be able to order by telephone, and she wishes that the supermarket had a delivery service. 10. A delivery service would be especially valuable for people who were ill or physically handicapped.

6.2.2 *(ii)*

1. Umfrage; Einkäufe. 2. Lebensmittel; Hausartikel; Bauernmarkt. 3. unpersönlich; nervenaufreibend. 4. Auswahl; preisgünstig. 5. Bestellung; die Lieferung.

6.2.2 *(iii)*

1. Ich möchte vier Brötchen und ein Vollkornbrot, bitte . . .
Ich möchte auch etwas Besonderes für den Geburtstag einer Freundin. Hätten Sie vielleicht eine Schwarzwälderkirschtorte? . . .
Was für Kuchen haben Sie? . . .
Eine Nußtorte wäre schön. . . Nein, danke, das wär's. Was macht das zusammen? . . .
Hier ist 17.50 DM. Danke schön. Auf Wiedersehen.

2. Here is an example of a possible conversation, but, of course, your suggested conversation may be different.

Verkäuferin:	Guten Tag. Was darf es sein?
You:	Ich möchte gern einige Geschenke kaufen. Was für Parfüm haben Sie?
Verkäuferin:	Zur Zeit haben wir französische Parfüms zu stark reduzierten Preisen. Möchten Sie einige probieren?
You:	Ja, das wäre eine gute Idee. Ich möchte auch gern eine Vase kaufen, oder vielleicht einen Ziergegenstand aus Porzellan.
Verkäuferin:	Hier haben wir schöne Vasen, und auch Porzellanziergegenstände. Gefallen Ihnen diese kleinen Vögel und Tiere aus Porzellan?
You:	Ja, die habe ich sehr gern. Ein Holzschnitt wäre auch eine Möglichkeit. Könnten Sie mir so etwas zeigen?
Verkäuferin:	So etwas aus Holz wäre schön als Geschenk, nicht?
You:	Ja, das ist schön, aber ich hätte doch lieber die Sachen aus Porzellan. Was kosten sie?
Verkäuferin:	Jedes Stück 28 DM.
You:	Gut, also ich nehme diese zwei. Und ich möchte auch, wie gesagt, die Parfüms probieren.
Verkäuferin:	Gerne.

Chapter 7 Schule und Erziehung

7.1.1 *(i)*

1. He studies four languages: French, English, German and Latin. 2. The answer to this question will depend on your school, but might include Social Studies (*Sozialkunde*). 3. This will depend on your own timetable. 4. One period, on Tuesdays at 11.45. 5. The answer is given above: Social Studies.

7.1.1 *(ii)*

This will depend on your own timetable.

7.1.2 *(i)*

1. Primary School (*Grundschule*). 2. Yes. 3. Yes; he often contributes ideas of his own. 4. He has fulfilled the basic requirements, and can already read short texts

from the class library on his own. 5. If he gives himself enough time, he can produce tidy and conscientious written work. 6. He is enthusiastic about painting and singing.

7.1.2 *(ii)*

1. Wenn gemalt oder gesungen wird, ist Reinhard mit Begeisterung dabei. 2. Reinhard arbeitete gern mit den anderen Kindern am Gruppentisch zusammen. 3. Oft brachte er den Unterricht durch eigene Ideen weiter.

7.1.2 *(iii)*

He likes working in groups with other children. He can maintain concentration on his work for long periods. He is reliable in completing his work. He can often make use of his own ideas for taking the lesson further. He has fulfilled basic requirements in reading, writing and mathematics. He can already read short texts on his own. When he takes his time, he can produce tidy and conscientious written work. He is an enthusiastic participant whenever there is painting or singing.

7.1.3 *Exercises – Section A*

1. The following statements are correct: (c); (e); (f); (g); (h); (i).
2. Um sechs Uhr klingelt der Wecker, und Leif steht um 6.10 auf. Um sieben Uhr frühstückt er, und er verläßt das Haus um halb acht. Er muß zuerst zehn Minuten zu Fuß gehen, und dann auf den Bus warten. Der Bus kommt um dreiviertel acht, und fährt etwa 20 Minuten zur Schule. Um 8.10 ist die erste Stunde, Mathematik, und um dreiviertel zehn ist die große Pause.
   Am Morgen hat er sechs Stunden, und um 1.10 ist das Schlußklingeln, und die Schule ist aus. Um dreiviertel zwei kommt er nach Hause, ißt sein Mittagessen und legt sich ein bißchen hin. Um halb drei fängt er mit den Hausaufgaben an.

7.1.3 *Exercises – Section A*

1. The correct forms of the relative pronouns are as follows:
   (a) der. (b) die. (c) die. (d) die. (e) die. (f) das.
2. (a) Ich gehe um halb acht aus dem Haus, weil der Bus um dreiviertel acht fährt. (b) Viele Leute stehen da, weil der Bus etwas Verspätung hat. (c) Wir langweilen uns, weil der Unterricht nicht sehr interessant ist. (d) Alle stürzen ins Freie, weil die Schule aus ist. (e) Ich lege mich hin, weil ich mittags immer total erschöpft bin. (f) Ich fange mit den Hausaufgaben an, weil ich viel zu tun habe.
3. (a) Ich gehe um halb acht aus dem Haus, denn der Bus fährt um dreiviertel acht. (b) Viele Leute stehen da, denn der Bus hat etwas Verspätung. (c) Wir langweilen uns, denn der Unterricht ist nicht sehr interessant. (d) Alle stürzen ins Freie, denn die Schule ist aus. (e) Ich lege mich hin, denn ich bin mittags immer total erschöpft. (f) Ich fange mit den Hausaufgaben an, denn ich habe viel zu tun.
4. This letter will depend on your own school day and timetable. Use Leif's account of his day to help you, and also the key to exercise 2 in Section A above.

7.1.4 *Exercises – Section A*

1. (a) About one hour. (b) Because she has come with her mother. (c) She shows her what she has found. (d) No, he is frightened by the new surroundings and

unknown people. (e) He starts to leave his mother when someone brings him a big lorry to play with. (f) The assistant must look after each child as if it were her own. (g) She must first of all get to know the child. (h) The first visit lasts an hour, which can be a long time for the child. (i) After the first visit, there is a discussion to see whether it is felt that the mother should come again.

2. The words to fill the gaps are as follows, in the order in which they should appear: fremd; gekommen; aufgeregt; gelaufen; was; unterwegs; zunächst; über; fremden; fest; versiegen; beobachten; los; bringt; Zimmer.

7.1.4 *Exercises – Section B*

1. (a) Silka sagt ihr, was sie gerade getan hat. (b) Die Erzieherin zeigt Markus, was sie gebracht hat. (c) Die Leiterin der Krippe erklärt, was dort gemacht wird. (d) Die Erzieherin muß wissen, was für das Kind besonders wichtig ist.

2. (a) Heute ist Silkas erster Tag in der Krippe, in der sie schöne Tage erleben wird. (b) Er ist erschrocken über die fremden Menschen, mit denen er sich zum ersten Mal zusammenfindet. (c) Die Kinder lieben die Erzieherinnen, mit denen sie den ganzen Tag verbringen. (d) Das Lebensalter von einem Jahr, in dem die meisten Kinder zur Krippe kommen, ist wichtig.

3. (a) Jedes Kind soll sich bei uns vom ersten Tag an wohlfühlen. (b) Jede Erzieherin muß es so betreuen, als wäre es ihr eigenes. (c) Zunächst einmal soll die Erzieherin das Kind kennenlernen. (d) Da muß die Mama einfach da sein.

4. (a) Silka ist so glücklich, als wäre sie schon öfter hier in der Krippe gewesen. (b) Markus ist so schüchtern, als wären ihm alle Leute hier fremd. (c) Markus hält sich an der Mutter so fest, als wäre er erschrocken. (d) Jedes Kind fühlt sich hier so wohl, als wäre es hier zu Hause.

5. The correct forms of the possessive adjectives and pronouns is as follows: (a) ihrer; ihr. (b) ihr; ihr. (c) seine; ihm. (d) ihr.

7.2.1 *(i)*

Name	School	Class	Favourite Subjects	Subjects Disliked	Future Plans
Paul	Gymnasium	6	Maths/Physics	Languages	University
Petra	Realschule	8	Eng/French	Phys/Chem	Language teacher
Julia	Gesamtschule	12	Art	Maths	Art college
Manfred	Realschule	9	Maths/Eng	–	work in bank

7.2.2 *(i)*

1. Like a working day for adults. 2. He was at school in Switzerland. 3. He has a French pen-friend. 4. Because you lose concentration if you have to study for too long. 5. He has other interests besides school. 6. Because you have more time for sport, music, etc. 7. One can learn how to work without supervision. 8. One must think of the teachers as well. They need their free-time.

7.2.2 *(ii)*

The particles used are as follows: 1. ja. 2. nämlich; doch. 3. ja; ja. 4. ja; mal; mal; mal.

7.2.2 *(iii)*

1. That really is like a working day for adults. 2. You see, you don't learn anything like as much, because after four or five hours, your concentration really does start to get less. 3. Besides, you just can't do anything else in the day. I mean to say, I've certainly got other interests besides school. 4. That is something you have just got to learn as well. And then you have just got to think about the teachers. They really need some free time.

7.2.2 *(iv)*

Here are a few suggestions for what you might wish to say:
Ich finde das besser, wenn man den ganzen Tag in der Schule ist. Man braucht doch Zeit zum Lernen, und man kann ja nicht so gut zu Hause arbeiten.
Freizeit hat man schon am Abend, und auch am Wochenende. In England hat man doch zwei freie Tage am Wochende. Ich finde das schon besser, als samstags in die Schule zu gehen.
Ich meine, in England hat man mehr Sport in der Schule. Man hat ja mehr Möglichkeiten, sich ein bißchen zu bewegen. Man bleibt nicht den ganzen Tag im Klassenzimmer. Außerdem, man hat viele Klubs in der Schule und Arbeitsgruppen. Das kann ja auch interessanter sein, als nach Hause zu gehen.
Da bin ich anderer Meinung. Die Lehrer werden bezahlt, Unterricht zu geben. Sie haben schon genug Ferien und Freizeit.

Chapter 8 Von der Schule in die Arbeitswelt

8.1.1 *(ii)*

There are a variety of things you could write here. Two examples have been given already in the chapter. Here are a few more examples of statements that could be made.
The most popular job for girls is salesgirl. Only a small number of girls get jobs in a bank. Girls do not apply for jobs which have traditionally been men's jobs, such as mechanics and builders. The craft trades, such as carpenter and bricklayer, are still popular in Germany.

8.1.2 *Exercises – Section A*

1. (a) The first possibility is to find a job as soon as possible after leaving school. (b) Secondly, they could try to find training on the job, in a recognised job-training scheme. (c) Thirdly, they could take up a vocational training course in a technical school. (d) Fourthly, they could go to a technical school and attempt to improve the level of their school-leaving certificate.
2. (a) They have known each other for a few years. (b) They have to decide what to do when they leave school. (c) He or she starts off by earning quite a good wage. (d) Unqualified workers either do not get a job at times when the economy is in poor shape, or else they are the first to be given the sack.

8.1.2 *Exercises – Section B*

1. (a) Die Ausbildung dauert schon seit drei Jahren. (b) Ich besuche diese Schule seit vier Jahren. (c) Ich arbeite seit einem Jahr als Ungelernter. (d) Ich bin schon seit zwei Jahren bei dieser Firma eingestellt.

2. (a) Beate wird später eine Arbeitsstelle annehmen. (b) Petra wird nächstes Jahr eine betriebliche Ausbildung beginnen. (c) Holger wird zunächst eine berufsbildende Schule besuchen. (d) Uwe wird sich nächste Woche um einen Ausbildungsplatz bewerben.

3. (a) Beate kann später eine Arbeitsstelle annehmen. (b) Petra kann nächstes Jahr eine betriebliche Ausbildung beginnen. (c) Holger kann zunächst eine berufsbildende Schule besuchen. (d) Uwe kann sich nächste Woche um einen Ausbildungsplatz bewerben.

4. (a) Um in einem anerkannten Ausbildungsberuf zu beginnen. (b) Um einen weiterführenden Abschluß zu erreichen. (c) Um zunächst besser zu verdienen. (d) Um sich dann entscheiden zu können.

8.1.3 *Exercises – Section A*

1. (a) Ich bewerbe mich bei Ihnen um eine Ausbildungsstelle. (b) zur Zeit. (c) Ich werde im Juni 1986 die Schule verlassen. (d) Betriebspraktikum. (e) Ich übersende Ihnen. (f) Ich würde mich sehr freuen.

2. (a) He is applying for a job as an engine-fitter. (b) In June 1986. (c) Maths and Physics. (d) His work experience as a fitter. (e) It would give him particular pleasure to have a personal introduction to Herr Meyer.

8.1.3 *Exercises – Section B*

1. (a) Holger bewirbt sich um einen Ausbildungsplatz als Tischler. (b) Beate bewirbt sich um eine Stelle als Friseurin. (c) Petra bewirbt sich um einen Ausbildungsplatz als Verkäuferin. (d) Holger wird sich um einen Ausbildungsplatz als Tischler bewerben. (e) Beate wird sich um eine Stelle als Friseurin bewerben. (f) Petra wird sich um einen Ausbildungsplatz als Verkäuferin bewerben.

2. (a) mich. (b) mein. (c) mich . . . meinem. (d) meiner. (e) mir.

3. (a) Ich würde mich sehr freuen, wenn ich einen Ausbildungsplatz gewinnen würde. (b) Ich würde mich sehr freuen, wenn ich die Schule verlassen würde. (c) Ich würde mich sehr freuen, wenn ich eine Stelle finden würde. (d) Ich würde mich sehr freuen, wenn ich Geld verdienen würde.

4.   Bedford, den 17.10 1986
Direktor,
Hotel zur Post,
Mittenwald.

Betr: Bewerbung
Sehr geehrter Herr Direktor!
Ich habe neulich Ihre Anzeige in der „Zeit" gesehen, und ich möchte mich bei Ihnen als Kellner bewerben. Ich bin 17 Jahre alt, und ich besuche zur Zeit eine englische Gesamtschule. Ich studiere Deutsch seit vier Jahren, und ich suche eine Gelegenheit, meine Deutschkenntnisse zu verbessern. Für meine weiteren Studien wäre es höchst günstig, die Sommersaison bei Ihnen arbeiten zu können. Ich habe schon einige Erfahrung im Hoteldienst, denn ich habe während der Schulferien in einem englischen Hotel gearbeitet. Ich übersende Ihnen Kopien von zwei Zeugnissen, ein Lichtbild und einen Lebenslauf. Ich würde mich sehr freuen, wenn es mir gelingen würde, als Kellner in Ihrem Hotel eingestellt zu werden. Meine Sommerferien beginnen am 20 sten Juli.
                        Mit freundlichen Grüßen,
                        Peter Jones

8.2.1 *(i)*

1. Klaus is not quite sure what he wants to do but would like to earn some money quickly. 2. Martina is going to look for a training place. 3. Ute does not want to work straight away. 4. Manfred has already applied for a training place and wants to work as a mechanic. 5. Ulrike wants to go on studying and has decided to go to a vocational school.

8.2.1 *(ii)*

The answer to this exercise depends on your own plans for the future.

8.2.2 *(i)*

1. She wants to be independent, have her own flat, marry and have children. 2. The most important thing for her at the moment is her training. 3. She tries to be always pleasant and friendly to her customers. 4. She would like to open her own boutique with two or three others. 5. You get a good training because there are a lot of courses which allow you to further your education. 6. Yes, because, with a big firm, most trainees are taken on straight after their apprenticeship.

8.2.2 *(ii, iii)*

Here, again, the answers will vary according to individual plans. Use the statements in Petra's conversation to give you the phrases you need.

Chapter 9 Sport und Freizeit

9.1.1 *(i)*

1. 100 metre sprint; long jump; shot put; high jump; 400 metres. 2. 110 metres hurdles; discus; pole vault; javelin; 1500 metres.

9.1.1 *(ii)*

Stabhochsprung; 1500-Meter-Lauf; Weitsprung; Speerwerfen; 100-Meter-Lauf; Diskuswerfen; Hochsprung; Kugelstoßen.

9.1.2 *(i)*

1. World championships for two-man bobs. 2. At Cervinia, in Italy. 3. Almost ideal weather conditions. 4. Four. 5. Three. 6. Another team from the GDR. 7. He was previously a decathlete.

9.1.2 *(ii)*

Hundert-Meter-Lauf; Vierhundert-Meter-Lauf; Hundertzehn-Meter-Hürdenlauf; Fünfzehnhundert-Meter-Lauf; tausendfünfhundertzwanzig Meter; neunundzwanzig Bobs aus sechzehn Ländern.

9.1.3 *Exercises − Section A*

1. der Bundesbürger − citizen of the Federal Republic; die Jugendherberge − youth hostel; die Rekordzahl − record number; der Volkssport − people's

sport; das Touristikunternehmen — tourism enterprise; der Pressesprecher — press spokesman; der Ausgangspunkt — starting-point; der Fremdenverkehr — tourism; der Fluchttraum — dream of escape; die Übernachtungsstätte — place to spend the night.

2. (a) Walking (rambling) is when one walks more than two kilometres from the car-park or starting point, and when one is walking for more than one and a half hours. (b) The fact that people are talking about it, and that the tourist industry is making a commercial profit out of people's longing to get back to nature.

3. The reasons are apparently obvious. There is the dream of escape, of getting away from the town for a while, of leaving daily routine behind one for a few hours, or even days.

9.1.3 *Exercises — Section B*

1. (a) Der neue Volkssport, den Touristikunternehmen fördern. (b) Wandern ist, wenn man sich mehr als zwei Kilometer vom Parkplatz oder Ausgangspunkt entfernt. (c) Kaum ein Mensch, der nicht eine Nacht in einer Jugendherberge geschlafen hätte. (d) Neu am Wandern ist die Tatsache, daß man darüber spricht.

2. (a) Sie sind nicht nur auf stillen Wegen, sondern auch auf lauten Routen. (b) Nicht nur Touristikunternehmen sondern auch Mediziner fördern den Sport. (c) Sie sind nicht nur zwei Kilometer vom Parkplatz entfernt, sondern auch eineinhalb Stunden unterwegs. (d) Sie lassen nicht nur den Alltag für einige Stunden hinter sich, sondern auch sie schalten ab.

3. (a) von; in; auf. (b) für; auf. (c) zu; von. (d) für; in; von; bis.

9.1.4 *(i)*

Dear Hostel Warden,

My friends and I would like to spend three nights in your hostel from June 25th to 28th. Have you still got beds free at that time? There are three of us, two girls and a boy, and we are students in Leipzig. Could you please reserve three beds for us in the names of Thomas Wagner, Karin Albrecht and Martina Leopold? We would arrive on Friday, June 25th, at about 6.0 p.m. and stay until Monday morning at 8 o'clock.

How expensive is the overnight stay per person, and does the price include breakfast and evening meal? Is there also a possibility of doing one's own cooking? Do we have to bring our own eating utensils, and are personal sleeping-bags allowed?

We have never been to the Harz before and we should be very grateful if you could send us a few prospectuses and brochures of the area, so that we can plan a little bit in advance. What is there to see in Quedlingburg and district? My address is as follows:

9.1.4 *(ii)*

Write a similar sort of letter, putting in your own dates, numbers of people, nights of stay, etc.

9.2.1 *(i)*

Football; volleyball; walking; skiing.

9.2.1 *(ii)*

1. Spielst du gern Fußball? 2. Nächstes Wochenende wandere ich. 3. Noch nicht. 4. Ich bin schon skigelaufen. Oder: ich bin noch nicht skigelaufen. 5. Das ist ein toller Sport.

9.2.2 *(i)*

Martina	*Karin*	*Thomas*
Training	Disco	Rudern
Volleyball	Kino	Bergsteigen
Skilaufen	Schwimmen	
Zelten		
Paddelboot fahren		
Wandern		

9.2.2 *(ii)*

1. She plays volleyball. 2. They are going to the cinema. 3. All the seats are sold. 4. Rowing. 5. He is going mountain climbing in the Tatra mountains. 6. She is spending July and August as a life-saver on the Baltic. 7. She is going to work because she needs the money. 8. She may go camping and canoeing.

9.2.2 *(iii)*

Make up your own lists of activities and statements about what you like doing in your free time.

Chapter 10 Gesundheit und Krankheit

10.1.1 *(i)*

The answers to the multiple choice exercise are: 1. (c). 2. (c). 3. (c).

10.1.1 *(ii)*

1. The landscape is described as a 'paradise'. 2. The word *Kur* means 'cure', and is usually used in German when one goes to a health resort or sanatorium. 3. A *Heilbad* is a bath or pool with medicinal waters, such as one finds at a spa. 4. Overweight people would want a *Schlankheitskur*, which aims to get you to lose weight. (*schlank* = 'slim'.) 5. Write for a prospectus.

10.1.2 *Exercises – Section A*

1. (a) She has been ill. (b) One week. (c) On a school trip to the Erzgebirge, staying in a youth hostel. (d) She had headaches and earache. Also a high temperature and she felt tired all day, and rather sick. (e) The doctor diagnosed inflammation of the middle ear. (f) The worst thing was that she had such poor hearing in one ear.
2. The missing past participles are as follows: geantwortet; gewandert; gerodelt; gemacht; zugelegt; verzweifelt; versäumt; überstanden.

10.1.2 *Exercises – Section B*

1. (a) konnte . . . mußte. (b) waren . . . war. (c) merkte . . . war. (d) war . . . mußte . . . stellte. (e) konnte . . . mußte. (f) wollte.

2. (a) Es tut mir leid, daß ich mir eine Erkältung zugelegt habe. (b) Es tut mir leid, daß die Schlafsäle so kalt waren. (c) Es tut mir leid, daß ich die Arbeit versäumt habe. (d) Es tut mir leid, daß ich nicht zur Schule gehen konnte. (e) Es freut mich, daß du den Winter gut überstanden hast.

3. Make up your own letter, using material from Dagmar's letter, and also taking note of other expressions for feeling unwell, which occur in the listening passages.

10.2.1 *(i)*

Martina – headache and feels sick.

Klaus – has a cold. It's not too bad, but he must take care.

Heinz – has a temperature and his neck aches.

Gabi – feels sick, and has stomach ache.

10.2.1 *(ii)*

Du siehst etwas krank aus. Was ist los? . . .

Du sollst zum Zahnarzt gehen . . .

Du siehst blaß aus. Hast du schon Aspirin genommen . . .

Ich habe etwas Besonderes gegen Schmerzen. Du mußt zwei Tabletten nehmen und dann dich ein bißchen hinlegen.

10.2.2 *(i)*

1. Wo fehlt es denn? 2. Ich habe mich nicht wohl gefühlt. 3. Mir scheint, du bist ziemlich erkältet. 4. Ich habe ständig Kopfschmerzen. 5. Ist dir manchmal übel? 6. Gesundheit geht vor. 7. Nimm sie bitte dreimal täglich. 8. Mach für nächsten Dienstag einen Termin aus.

10.2.2 *(ii)*

I have not felt well (ich habe mich nicht wohl gefühlt) . . . My right ear has been hurting for a few days (mein rechtes Ohr tut mir seit ein paar Tagen so weh) . . . I have constant headaches (ich habe ständig Kopfschmerzen) . . . I am also sick and dizzy (mir ist auch übel und schwindlig) . . . I feel so tired and washed out all day (ich fühle mich so müde und kaputt den ganzen Tag).

10.2.2 *(iii)*

Ich weiß micht recht, aber ich fühle mich nicht wohl. Ich habe Kopfschmerzen, und es ist mir auch übel . . .

Mein Ohr tut mir weh, und mir ist auch ein bißchen übel und schwindlig . . .

Ich muß zur Schule gehen. Ich werde etwas Arbeit versäumen . . .

Ja, natürlich. Vielen Dank und auf Wiedersehen.

10.2.2 *(iv)*

1. Du wirst die Tabletten dreimal täglich nehmen müssen. 2. Ich werde nicht in die Schule gehen dürfen. 3. Ich werde auf dem Ohr nur schlecht hören können.

161

4. Der Arzt wird die Temperatur messen und Tabletten aufschreiben müssen. 5. Ich werde nicht eine ganze Woche im Bett bleiben können.

Chapter 11 Typisch Deutsch?

11.1.1 *(i)*

1. good music – gute Musik; strong economy – starke Wirtschaft; perfect organisation – perfekte Organisation; reliable cars – solide Autos.
2. clean – sauber, 89.4%, polite – höflich, 74.2%; peaceful – friedlich, 55.4%; punctual – pünktlich, 89.4%; tidy – ordentlich, 89.4%; democratic – demokratisch, 75.8%; hard-working – fleißig, 91.4%.

11.1.2 *Exercises – Section A*

1. (a) The Germans are particularly well-disciplined. (b) Sausage sandwiches, coffee or Cola. (c) He leaves the room. (d) They are unmarried or divorced. (e) A real German family. (f) The role of the parents. They do not have the same authority as in China.
2. The correct statements are as follows: (a); (c); (e).

11.1.2 *Exercises – Section B*

1. (a) Among German students. (b) Without taking leave of the teacher. (c) The children express their opinions freely and, when they do so, they can even contradict their parents. (d) Where I live. (e) I always thought that German teachers are stricter than where I live.
2. (a) Sie haben Wurstbrötchen, Kaffee oder Cola mitgebracht. (b) Er ist aus dem Raum gegangen. (c) Ja, er hat viele deutsche Freunde kennengelernt. (d) Er hat gehört, daß die Deutschen immer pünktlich sind. (e) Sie hat in Peru Deutsch studiert.
3. (a) viel; (b) viele; (c) viel; (d) viele; (e) viele; (f) viele.
4. (a) Wenn ein Student Verspätung hat, fragt ihn der Professor nicht nach dem Grund. (b) Wenn ein Kind seine Meinung sagen will, sagt es sie frei heraus. (c) Wenn man das erste Mal an einer deutschen Universität ist, wundert man sich.
5. (a) Wenn die Studenten hungrig sind, bringen sie Brötchen in den Unterricht mit. Oder: Sind die Studenten hungrig, so bringen sie Brötchen in den Unterricht mit. (b) Wenn ein Student nicht mehr hören will, geht er aus dem Raum. Oder: Will ein Student nicht mehr hören, so geht er aus dem Raum. (c) Wenn die Kinder ihre Meinung sagen wollen, sagen sie sie frei heraus. Oder: Wollen die Kinder ihre Meinung sagen, so sagen sie sie frei heraus.
6. Here are a few examples of sentences you could make: (a) Die deutschen Schüler dürfen den Eltern widersprechen. (b) Die Studenten wollen nicht mehr hören. (c) Die Kinder dürfen frei ihre Meinung sagen. (d) Der deutsche Student will nicht mehr pünktlich sein. (e) Der Professor muß nicht nach dem Grund fragen.
7. (a) Die deutschen Schüler haben den Eltern widersprechen dürfen. (b) Die Studenten haben nicht mehr hören wollen. (c) Die Kinder haben frei ihre Meinung sagen dürfen. (d) Der deutsche Student hat nicht mehr pünktlich sein wollen. (e) Der Professor hat nicht nach dem Grund fragen müssen.

11.2.1 *(i)*

Where from?	How long staying?	What opinion of Germans?
England	4 weeks in Germany	friendly
Thailand	staying for a year	polite and hard-working
Scotland	4 days in Germany	friendly and polite
China	a few days in Germany	pleasant and friendly but not punctual
France	a month in Germany	friendly and polite

11.2.2 *(i)*

1. 10 years. 2. He still speaks at a faster pace than the southerners. 3. The heart. 4. Bavarian friendliness. (Note that *Gemütlichkeit* is a difficult word to translate, and can mean friendliness, informality, cosiness, etc.) 5. The land is so flat that you can already see on Monday who is coming to pay you a visit on Thursday. 6. Because they say it is so much weaker than North German beer.

11.2.2 *(ii)*

1. Wie geht es dir? 2. Wie lange wohnst du schon in Süddeutschland? 3. Warum wohnst du in Süddeutschland? 4. Wer spricht schneller, die Bayern oder die Preußen? 5. Warum trinken die Preußen so viel bayerisches Bier? 6. Warum verstehen die Bayern den preußischen Humor nicht?

11.2.2 *(iii)*

1. Weil er in Süddeutschland arbeitet. 2. Weil sie das bayerische Bier sehr gern haben. 3. Weil sie nur ihren eigenen, bayerischen Humor verstehen.

11.2.2 *(iv)*

1. Mach dir nichts daraus. 2. Wenigstens denken die Preußen. 3. Sie haben alles immer besser gewußt als die Bayern. 4. Hört auf damit!

Chapter 12 Umwelt

12.1.1 *(i)*

1. Waste-paper. 2. 2 million. 3. About half. 4. 3 million tons. 5. Check with vocabulary.

12.1.2 *Exercises – Section A*

1. to cut up – zerschneiden; to spoil – beeinträchtigen; air polluters – Luftverschmutzer; harmful products – Schadstoffe; poisons – Gifte; vehicle – Fahrzeug; besides – außer; to take note of – Rücksicht nehmen (auf); protection of the environment – Umweltschutz.
2. The Motor-car and the Environment

We cannot do without the motor-car, but it is one of our biggest environmental problems. That is something we must know and must change.

Cars need roads and roads consume the natural environment.

Roads and motorways cut up the landscape and are harmful to life in the cities. In many urban areas the quality of life is getting less and less. Many people do not want or are not able to live in the town any longer. That means even more roads and cars. And at the same time a greater burden on the environment.

12.1.2 *Exercises — Section B*

1. (a) Schadstoffe werden freigesetzt. (b) Die Atmosphäre wird vergiftet. (c) Rücksicht wird auf Sicherheit genommen. (d) Die Landschaft wird von Straßen zerschnitten. (e) Das Leben wird von Autos beeinträchtigt.
2. (a) Damit die Menschen vom Land schnell in die Städte fahren können. (b) Damit es weniger gefahren wird. (c) Damit das Auto weniger benutzt wird. (d) Damit die Umweltbelastung zurückgehen kann.
3. Wir müssen handeln! Das Auto ist unser größtes Umweltproblem. Autos beeinträchtigen die Lebensqualität in den Städten. Jedes Jahr werden vier Millionen Tonnen Kraftstoff durch unsere Motoren gepumpt. Deshalb machen Sie mit bei unserem Plan für einen freiwilligen autofreien Sonntag. Wir wollen in Fahrzeugen reisen, die die Umwelt schonen. Wenn Sie ein Auto kaufen, müssen Sie auf Umweltschutz Rücksicht nehmen.

12.2.1 *(i)*

1. White crosses. 2. That the trees are very sick or already dead. 3. Death of forests, caused by acid rain. Factories emit fumes into the atmosphere which are then carried long distances and fall with rain. 4. Often hundreds of kilometres. 5. English waste is carried over to the Scandinavian countries and harms the forests there.

12.2.1 *(ii)*

Here are some ideas for the letter you might write.
Liebe Petra!
Du hast mich in Deinem letzten Brief gefragt, ob wir in England auch so umweltbewußt sind wie Ihr in Deutschland. Ich glaube nicht, daß wir hier so weit sind wie bei Euch. Eine politische Partei wie die Grünen ist hier noch nicht so bedeutend wie in der Bundesrepublik. Und man hat hier auch vielleicht nicht so viel Angst wegen des Waldsterbens und wegen des sauren Regens wie bei Euch. Aber ich glaube schon, daß man sich der Umweltprobleme doch bewußter ist, als vor einigen Jahren. Zum Beispiel sind die großen Städte in den letzten Jahren viel sauberer geworden, auf Grund von Gesetzen, die verbieten, Kohle zu verbrennen. Es gibt noch andere Beispiele, die ich Dir erzählen könnte, wenn Du Dich dafür interessierst.
> Viele Grüße,
> Deine Mary

Chapter 13 Die Deutsche Sprache Heute

13.1.1 *Exercises — Section A*

1. Not all the German terms have exact English equivalents, so some of the following translations are approximations:
   protest movements; citizens' initiatives; atomic power — no, thank you!; opponents of nuclear power; peace movement; data protection; those with an alternative life-style; health-food shop; organic farmers; environmental pollu-

tion; environmental protection; the Greens; quality of life; pedestrian precincts; leisure society; hang-gliding; wind-surfing; jogging.

2. (a) New roads and airports; unemployment and political decisions of every kind. (b) They can store all sorts of data referring to individuals. (c) There is less technology, less stress and more natural food. (d) The fast industrial development in the fifties and sixties. (e) Because people have more and more leisure-time.

13.1.1 *Exercises — Section B*

1. (a) Ja, vielleicht sollte man doch auf die nächste Wahl warten. (b) Ja, aber sie sind auch gefährlicher. (c) Ja, es gibt immer mehr Streß im modernen Leben. (d) Ja, der Umweltschutz ist eine der wichtigsten Forderungen der modernen Welt. (e) Nein, die Arbeitszeit wird immer kürzer. (f) Ja, die Freizeit wird länger. (g) Weil die Leute mehr Lebensqualität wollen.

2. (a) in der Geschichte. (b) in den siebziger Jahren . . . in die Schlagzeilen. (c) zum Alltag. (d) auf die nächste Wahl. (e) vor dem Super-Wissen. (f) über jeden einzelnen Bürger. (g) gegen die Raketenrüstung. (h) für die industrielle Entwicklung. (i) in der Natur. (j) durch die Parks.

3. (a) Entscheidungen jeder Art. (b) Informationen über jeden einzelnen Bürger. (c) Jede Epoche hat ihre eigene Sprache. (d) Jede Zeitung hat neue Begriffe in den Schlagzeilen. (e) Jede Stadt hat Fußgär.gerzonen. (f) Jede Person will weniger Streß haben.

13.1.2 *Exercises — Section A*

1. (a) The division of Germany after World War 2. (b) Whether the political division would lead to a separation of the two languages. (c) Germans in the East and those in the West might hardly be able to understand each other. (d) The vocabulary. (e) By watching TV programmes. (f) No. Most of the new developments in the GDR are unknown in the West.

2. (a) ob . . . so daß. (b) ob . . . . (c) der. (d) daß.

13.1.2 *Exercises — Section B*

1. (a) Wir müssen uns fragen, ob die beiden Sprachen nur Varianten der einen Sprache seien. (b) Es gibt Diskussionen darüber, ob der Wortschatz von Wandlungen betroffen sei. (c) Wir müssen uns fragen, ob die Zahl der Wörter groß sei. (d) Es gibt Diskussionen darüber, ob es anders in der BRD sei. (e) Es gibt Diskussionen darüber, ob die deutsche Sprache als grammatisches System weitgehend unberührt bleibe.

2. (a) Wenn die Sprache sich rasch entwickeln würde, würde es zu einer Teilung führen. (b) Wenn das System unberührt bliebe, wären die beiden Sprachen nur Variationen. (c) Wenn die Leute in der DDR westdeutsche Fernsehsendungen sehen würden, würden sie den neuen deutschen Wortschatz kennen.

3. (a) Sprachliche Entwicklungen sind in beiden Teilen gesehen worden. (b) Die Sprache als System ist nicht berührt worden. (c) Das westdeutsche Fernsehen ist von DDR Staatsbürgern gesehen worden.

4. (a) Main clause: Die sprachlichen Entwicklungen führten bereits in den fünfziger Jahren zu der Frage . . .

   Subordinate clause 1: ob die Teilung des Landes nicht auch zu einer Teilung der Sprache führe . . .

   Subordinate clause 2: so daß sich der Deutsche in Ost und der Deutsche in West eines Tages kaum mehr verstehen würden.

Translation: Even as early as the fifties, the linguistic developments led to the question as to whether the division of the country might not also lead to a division of the language. Such a split would mean that Germans in the East and Germans in the West would hardly understand each other any more.

(b) Main clause: Es gab Diskussionen darüber, ...

Subordinate clause 2. ob das Deutsche Ost und das Deutsche West eigentlich nur Varianten der einen deutschen Sprache seien ...

Subordinate clause 2: so wie das Schweizerdeutsch und das Österreicherdeutsch auch. (In this last clause the verb *sind* is omitted, and understood, as often happens in such comparisons.)

Translation: There were discussions as to whether the German of the East and of the West were perhaps only variants of a single German language, just as with Swiss and Austrian German.

(c) Main clause: Erfahrungen der letzten Jahren zeigen ...

Subordinate clause: daß die Leute in der DDR kaum Schwierigkeiten haben. The subordinate clause here is further complicated by the inclusion of two phrases:

vermutlich durch intensive Nutzung westdeutscher Fernsehsendungen ...
im Hinblick auf neue Wörter in der Bundesrepublik.

Translation: Experience in the last few years has shown that people in the GDR have hardly any difficulty with regard to new words in the Federal Republic. This is presumably because of intensive watching of West German TV programmes.

13.2.1 *(i)*

1. mittlerer Leistungskader — middle-ranking manager/foreman; Kombinat — factory/works; Brigade — unit of workers; Parteileitung — party leadership; Brigadeleiter — foreman of a work unit; Elternaktiv — parents' committee; Pionierlager — summer camp for members of the Pioneers organisation; Blauhemd — blue shirt (uniform of the Pioneers); FJD = Freie Deutsche Jugend; EDS = Erweiterte Oberschule; Datscha — week-end cottage; Sobotnik — a voluntary, unpaid work shift.
2. Gisela has a lot to do at school, and is often busy even after work. This evening she has to go to a parents' meeting. Dieter is a member of the Pioneers, and this summer is going to the Pioneer camp, where he will help Gisela with the organisation. Elke has managed to get into the Sixth Form College and will do her A levels.

Chapter 14 Lesestücke aus anderen deutschsprachigen Ländern

14.1 *(i)*

1. The picture of her immediate surroundings at home. 2. The busy tourist industry. 3. There were ten years of occupation after the war. 4. People see the old monarchy as an early model for a united Europe. 5. Hungary, various Slav peoples, Italians and German-speaking Austrians. 6. People are able to settle their differences sensibly without resorting to the use of force. 7. This is a partnership between employers and trades unions.

14.1 *(ii)*

Besatzung — occupying force; Einverständnis — agreement; Leistung — achievement; Gesinnung — way of thinking; Gewaltanwendung — use of power.

14.1 *(iii)*

1. Österreich ist ein äußerst reizvolles Land, und bietet für den Großteil seiner Menschen, was man heute Umwelt- und Lebensqualität nennt. 2. Österreich ist ein freies Land mit einer demokratischen Gesellschaftsordnung. 3. Ich lebe auch gern in diesem Land, weil die Menschen in der Lage sind, Differenzen vernünftig, ohne Gewaltanwendung, auszutragen.

14.1 *(iv)*

In Austria there has been no big strike for years, or even for decades, because the social partners can reach agreement about the important political questions. The social security network is good, the social distinctions seem to me to be much less than elsewhere and even the main problem of recent years, rising unemployment, is only evident on a reduced scale.

14.2 *(i)*

1. Because it is surrounded by so much water. 2. In 1160 Schwerin received its charter as a city. 3. The theatre has a good reputation throughout the Republic. 4. No, the shopping centre is too small for so many people. 5. The apartment blocks on the new estates all look rather the same, so the people living there try to brighten them up by decorating their balconies. 6. Sailing, rowing, canoeing and tennis. 7. The zoo is a popular place for families to visit.

14.2 *(ii)*

1. Es wird behauptet, daß sie früher Zuarin geheißen hatte. 2. Vorher war es eine Siedlung der Obotriten gewesen. 3. Früher war die Stadt eine ruhige Provinzstadt gewesen.

14.2 *(iii)*

The town of Schwerin is beautifully situated. It is also called the town of the seven lakes, because it is surrounded by so much water. It is claimed that the town had previously been called Zuarin, which means very much the same as 'zoo'. Even today the town is still surrounded by many forests and lovely parks. In 1160 Schwerin received its charter. Previously, it had been a settlement of the Obotrites, with a fortress of the Slav prince Niklot. Later this fortress became the castle in which the dukes of Mecklenburg ruled. In the town itself there are still many other lovely buildings, such as, for example, the cathedral, the theatre and the museum. But in earlier days it had been quite a peaceful provincial town.

14.2 *(iv)*

This letter will depend on where you live, and what you can say about it. Use Dagmar's letter as an example of what to mention.

14.3 *(i)*

1. It has everything which suggests Switzerland to the tourist — high, rocky mountains, green alpine meadows, a shimmering blue lake, and a town packed with historic buildings. 2. It lies on the main north–south route. 3. There are many museums, such as the Natural History Museum and the Transport Museum.

4. Everything from snack-bars to solid, middle-class restaurants and the most aristocratic eating-places. 5. The locals view the tourists with a certain amount of amusement, particularly the way they tackle the local delicacies. But they know that the tourists bring a lot of money to the city. 6. A boat journey on the lake or watching the sun rise over the Rigi. 7. Lucerne has 11 cinemas and many bars and nightclubs.

14.3 *(ii)*

But why has Lucerne become such a tourist city? Some say it is the situation; others say that it is because of the many attractions and things to see. The fact is that in Lucerne the tourist finds everything which he imagines to be culturally and geographically a part of Switzerland. High, rocky mountains; green, alpine meadows; an apparently clean, shimmering blue lake; and a town packed full of historic buildings. In addition, Lucerne has the 'good fortune' to lie right on the main lines of communication from north to south. Therefore the town, with its 65 000 inhabitants has, in particular, many visitors who spend only one night in the town. But only the traveller who can spend a few days in Lucerne really has his money's worth.

14.3 *(iii)*

The adjectives, in the correct order, are as follows: leibliche; zahlreichen; günstigen; gutbürgerlichen; edelsten; ausländischen; kräftigen; gemütlicher; aufregende; unzähligen.

Grammar Summary

Table of Contents

1 Nouns

1.1 Gender

There are three genders for nouns in German – masculine, feminine and neuter. It is generally true to say that nouns denoting males are masculine in gender, and those denoting females are feminine. However, nouns which are not obviously male or female may be of any gender, and the only guaranteed rule for getting the gender right is to make sure that when you learn a new word, you also learn the gender. So, do not just learn *Tisch*, but also *der Tisch*. Since a knowledge of the gender affects articles, adjectival endings, plurals and so many elements in using the language correctly, this is learning-time well spent. There are a certain number of useful gender rules, according to the form of words as well as their sense, and these rules are given below.

(a) *Masculine by Meaning*

1. Names of male persons and animals: *der Onkel; der Hund; der Arzt.*
2. Most instruments and inanimate agents ending in *er: der Computer; der Wecker.*
3. Makes of cars (because of *der Wagen*): *der Ford; der Mercedes.*
4. Seasons, months, days of the week, points of the compass: *der Frühling; der Mai; der Freitag; der Norden.*

(b) *Masculine by Form*

1. Nouns ending in *ich; ig; ing; ling: der Teppich; der Honig.*
2. Foreign borrowings ending in *ant; ast; ismus: der Elephant; der Marxismus.*
3. Most nouns formed from strong verb stems, and which have no endings added: *der Biß* (from *beißen*); *der Wurf* (from *werfen*).

(c) *Feminine by Meaning*

1. Names of female persons and animals: *die Mutter; die Stute* (mare).
2. Most makes of aeroplanes: *die Boeing.*
3. Many German rivers: *die Donau; die Mosel; die Ruhr.* But note: *der Rhein; der Main.*
4. Cardinal numbers: *die Fünf; eine Eins.*

(d) *Feminine by Form*

1. Most nouns ending in *e: die Blume; die Schule.* But not when such nouns refer to male persons or animals: *der Junge; der Löwe.* Note also the group of weak masculine nouns such as *der Name* (see section 1.3). A special case is *der Käse*, which is not weak (the genitive is *des Käses*), and of which the most common plural is *die Käsesorten* (text 5.1.3). There are a few neuter nouns ending in *e: das Auge; das Ende; das Gebäude.*
2. Nouns ending in *ei; heit; keit; schaft; ung: die Möglichkeit; die Freundschaft; die Bildung.*
3. Foreign borrowings ending in *a; anz; enz; ie; ik; ion; tät; ur: die Kamera; die Biologie; die Musik; die Kapazität.*

(e) *Neuter by Meaning*

1. Most terms for the young: *das Baby; das Kind; das Lamm.*
2. Continents, and most towns and countries: *das Asien; das schöne Italien.* But note: *die Schweiz; die Tschechoslowakei; die Sowjetunion.*
3. Metals: *das Eisen; das Kupfer.* But note: *der Stahl.*
4. Infinitives of verbs used as nouns: *Stricken und Rauchen* (text 11.1.2).
5. Letters of the alphabet.
6. Fractions: *das Viertel.* But note: *die Hälfte.*

(f) *Neuter by Form*

1. Most nouns beginning *Ge: das Gebäude; das Gesicht.* But note: *der Gedanke; die Gefahr.*
2. Diminutive nouns ending in *chen; lein: das Mädchen; das Fräulein.*
3. Nouns ending in *nis: das Einverständnis; das Gefängnis.*
4. Nouns ending in *tum: das Eigentum* (property). But note: *der Irrtum.*
5. Foreign borrowings ending in *at; ett; fon; ment: das Telefon.*

(g) *Compound Nouns*

Compound nouns, which are formed from a combination of one or more simple nouns, always take the gender of the last item: *der Apfelbaum; die Haustür; das Freibad.*

1.2 Plurals

The formation of plurals is a complicated section of German grammar. As with genders, the best advice is to learn the plural when the word is learned. So, following the analogy given in 1.1 above, do not learn just *der Tisch*, but also *der Tisch, die Tische*. There are regular ways in which the plurals are formed, and the information below will help you with unfamiliar words. Note that these lists are not as complete as you will find them in a full-length grammar.

(a) *Masculine Plurals*

1. Most masculines form the plural ⁻e: *der Stuhl, die Stühle; der Paß, die Päße.* In cases where the vowel can not take an Umlaut, *e* is added: *der Tisch, die Tische.*
2. Most masculines ending in *el; en; er* do not change in the plural: *der Onkel, die Onkel; der Schatten, die Schatten; der Lehrer, die Lehrer.* Some masculines of this type add an Umlaut: *der Apfel, die Äpfel; der Bruder, die Brüder; der Garten, die Gärten; der Laden, die Läden; der Mantel, die Mäntel; der Vater, die Väter; der Vogel, die Vögel.*
3. A small number of masculines add *e* in the plural, even when there is a vowel which could take an Umlaut: *der Abend, die Abende; der Dom, die Dome; der Hund, die Hunde; der Mond, die Monde; der Ort, die Orte; der Pfad, die Pfade; der Schuh, die Schuhe.*
4. A few masculines have plurals ⁻er: *der Mann, die Männer; der Mund, die Münder; der Wald, die Wälder.*
5. A group of masculine nouns is weak — that is, they take *n* or *en* in all cases except the nominative singular: *der Bauer, die Bauern; der Herr, die Herren* (*Herrn* in other cases of the singular); *der Mensch, die Menschen.*
6. Masculines ending in *e* add *n* in the plural: *der Name, die Namen.*

(b) *Feminine Plurals*

1. The great majority of feminine nouns add *n* or *en* in the plural: *die Schule (−n); die Schwester (−n); die Tafel (−n).*
2. Two feminine nouns add an Umlaut in the plural: *die Mutter, die Mütter; die Tochter, die Töchter.*
3. A small group of feminines form the plural ⁻e: *die Bank, die Bänke* (= bench. Note *die Bank, die Banken* = bank); *die Hand, die Hände; die Nacht, die Nächte; die Stadt, die Städte; die Wand, die Wände; die Wurst, die Würste.*

(c) *Neuter Plurals*

1. Most neuter plurals are formed by ⸚*er: das Buch, die Bücher; das Glas, die Gläser.*
2. Neuters ending in *el; er; chen; lein* do not change in the plural: *das Mädchen, die Mädchen; das Ufer, die Ufer.*
3. Some monosyllabic neuter nouns add *e* in the plural: *das Bein, die Beine; das Boot, die Boote; das Ding, die Dinge; das Haar, die Haare; das Heft, die Hefte; das Jahr, die Jahre; das Meer, die Meere; das Pferd, die Pferde; das Schiff, die Schiffe; das Tier, die Tiere; das Zelt, die Zelte.*

(d) *Plural of Foreign Nouns*

1. Masculine foreign nouns:
(i) in *er* do not change: *der Revolver, die Revolver.*
(ii) Most others add *e: der Boß, die Bosse.*
(iii) Many other masculine nouns of foreign origin, and ending on a stressed syllable, are weak in declension − that is, they add *en* in all cases, singular and plural: *der Komponist, die Komponisten; der Präsident, die Präsidenten.*
(iv) Most nouns ending in *us* have plural *usse: der Autobus, die Autobusse.*
2. Feminine foreign nouns all add *n* or *en: die Armee, die Armeen.*
3. Neuter foreign nouns:
(i) do not change if they end in *en* or *er: das Examen, die Examen; das Theater, die Theater.*
(ii) Others usually add *e: das Konzert, die Konzerte; das Telegramm, die Telegramme.*
4. A large number of foreign nouns form their plural by adding *s: das Auto, die Autos; das Hotel, die Hotels; der Park, die Parks; der Klub, die Klubs.*

(e) *Further Points to Note*

1. Some nouns are used only in the plural: *die Eltern; die Ferien.* Note also *die Möbel* (furniture) is nearly always used in the plural.
2. *Weihnachten, Ostern, Pfingsten* are usually treated as plural: *fröhliche Weihnachten!* − 'Merry Christmas'.
3. Some nouns are singular in German, though plural in English: *die Brille* − 'spectacles'; *die Hose* − 'trousers'; *die Treppe* − 'stairs'. These nouns can be used in the plural when they mean, for example, several pairs of trousers.

1.3 Declension of Nouns

(a) *Forms for all Nouns except Weak Masculines:*

Singular	Masculine	Feminine	Neuter
Nominative	der Mann	die Frau	das Buch
Accusative	den Mann	die Frau	das Buch
Genitive	des Mannes	der Frau	des Buches
Dative	dem Mann	der Frau	dem Buch(e)

Plural			
Nom.	die Männer	die Frauen	die Bücher
Acc.	die Männer	die Frauen	die Bücher
Gen.	der Männer	der Frauen	der Bücher
Dat.	den Männern	den Frauen	den Büchern

173

(b) *Points to Note*

1. Masculine and neuter nouns in the Genitive usually add *s* to a word of more than one syllable (*des Wagens*) and *es* to a monosyllable (*des Buches*). Most foreign nouns add *s* only (*des Klubs*).
2. The *e* shown in parentheses after the singular of the dative neuter singular is nowadays only found in fixed expressions such as *nach Hause*, and even here it is often dropped in conversation.
3. All nouns, of whatever gender, add *n* or *en* in the Dative plural: (*man sagt den Politikern . . .* − 13.1.1).
4. Proper nouns add *s* to show possession, rather like the English 's: *Leifs Stundenplan* (7.1.1); *Silkas erster Tag* (7.1.4).
5. Family names add *s* in the plural: *die Müllers; die Schmidts.*
6. Names of countries do not change in the plural (*die zwei Deutschland*) or, in some cases, add *s*: (*die vielen Chinas*). When using the name of a country in the Genitive, either use *von* or, in the case of neuter countries, a Genitive *s: . . . der beiden Teile Deutschlands* (13.1.2).

(c) *Forms for Weak Masculines (e.g. der Junge; der Mensch)*

	Singular	Plural
N	der Junge	die Jungen
A	den Jungen	die Jungen
G	des Jungen	der Jungen
D	dem Jungen	den Jungen

(for example: *. . . sollen den Menschen gesund machen* − 13.1.1). Note also the small group of masculine nouns which follow the same pattern as *Name* below:

	Singular	Plural
N	der Name	die Namen
A	den Namen	die Namen
G	des Namens	der Namen
D	dem Namen	den Namen

(Also: *der Friede* − 'peace'; *der Gedanke* − 'thought'; *der Glaube* − 'belief'; *der Wille* − 'will').

(d) A special case is offered by *das Herz*, which has Genitive and Dative *des Herzens, dem Herzen;* (*im Herzen der Schweiz* − 14.3).

1.4 Declension of Nouns of Weight, Measure, Value

(a) Nouns which denote weight, measure or value remain in the singular when they are preceded by a cardinal number or by an adjective indicating number: *zwei Glas Bier; zehn Pfund Kartoffeln; vier Dutzend Eier.* Note that the noun following the measure stands in apposition, and is therefore in the same case as the measure, and not in the Genitive, as in English. Compare: *zwei Glas Bier* − 'two glasses of beer'.

(b) The word *Stück* is used a great deal in shopping to indicate almost any article. For example: *was kosten die Orangen? Geben Sie mir bitte drei Stück.*

(c) *Mark* and *Pfennig* are similarly used in their singular form when talking about cost: *von 98 Mark auf 49 Mark reduziert* − 6.2.1.

(d) Apart from *die Mark*, just mentioned, feminine nouns of measure are used in the plural form: *drei Flaschen Wein.*

(e) Note that many nouns denoting quantity, whether used in the singular or plural, are followed by a noun in apposition, as described in paragraph (a) above: *eine Gruppe Touristen; zwei Schachteln Zigaretten; eine Menge Geld.*

1.5 Uses of Cases

Throughout this summary there are numerous references to the four cases. Here is a brief reminder of the uses of the cases.

(a) Nominative case is used for the subject of the sentence and as the complement of the verbs *sein, werden, bleiben, heißen, scheinen.*

(b) Accusative case is used for the direct object, after certain prepositions (see Grammar Summary section 14.2) and in certain phrases of time (Grammar Summary section 11.3).

(c) Genitive case is used to express possession, and can translate English 'of': *eine der wichtigsten Forderungen* — 'one of the most important demands' (13.1.1); *welcher Art ist diese Unterhaltung?* — 'of what kind is this entertainment' (3.1.4).

There is a tendency to avoid the Genitive in conversation, where it may sound rather stilted. In conversational use the construction *von* + Dative is preferred, e.g. *das Haus von meinem Bruder*, rather than *das Haus meines Bruders.*

There are some uses of the Genitive in adverbial constructions, notably: *guter Laune* — 'in good spirits'; *schlechter Laune* — 'in bad spirits'. Note also *meines Erachtens* — 'in my opinion'; *er fährt erster Klasse* — 'he travels first class'.

There are also some expressions of uncertain time which use the Genitive: *eines Tages* — 'one day'.

(d) Dative case is used for the indirect object and after many prepositions (see Grammar Summary section 14.1). The Dative is also used in many expressions referring to health, and the way one feels: *plötzlich tat mir mein Kopf weh . . . mir war auch ein bißchen übel* (10.1.2).

2 The Definite Article

2.1 Forms

The forms of the definite article are given in the table of nouns in paragraph 1.3 (a) of this Summary. The definite article combines with certain prepositions to make contracted forms, notably: *an + das = ans; an + dem = am; auf + das = aufs; in + das = ins; in + dem = im; zu + der = zur; zu + dem = zum; von + dem = vom; bei + dem = beim.*

2.2 Uses

Many of the uses of the definite article are comparable with the use of English 'the'. The following points refer to usage which is different from English.

(a) Use of the article with abstract nouns is usual in German, although there are some variations: *man muß auf den Umweltschutz Rücksicht nehmen* — 12.1.2; *das Waldsterben ist ein internationales Problem* — 12.2.1.

(b) The article is used with nouns denoting arts, sciences, sports: *nach dem Rudern* — 9.2.2; *ich suche noch jemanden zum Bergsteigen* — 9.2.2; *nicht mal Lust zum Lesen* — 1.2.2; *. . . daß ich immer zum Training gehe* — 9.2.2.

(c) The article is used with nouns denoting species and substances. For example, *der Mensch* can mean 'mankind', as in *weniger Technik, weniger Streß sollen den Menschen gesund machen* — 13.1.1.

(d) The use of the article with parts of the body and articles of clothing is common, but not obligatory. Compare: *du wirst auch schlecht auf dem Ohr hören können* − 10.2.2 and *mein rechtes Ohr tut mir so weh* − 10.2.2. When the definite article is used, the Dative pronoun of the person is often used also: *mir hängt das zum Halse 'raus* − 5.2.2. This is a slang phrase meaning 'I've had as much of that as I can take'.

(e) The article is used in a number of cases with proper nouns. For example: (i) with the names of masculine and feminine countries: *im Herzen der Schweiz* − 14.3; *in der Bundesrepublik* − 12.1.2; (ii) with certain other geographical names, e.g. names of lakes and mountains: *in der Nähe des Vierwaldstättersees* − 3.1.4; *ich suche noch jemanden zum Bergsteigen in der Tatra* − 9.2.2; (iii) in colloquial usage, before the names of persons: *der Dieter fährt . . .* − 13.2.1.

(f) The article is used with seasons, months and meals: *frag mich im Dezember* − 9.2.2; *Was macht ihr im Sommer?* − 9.2.2; *im Winter mild* − 4.1.3; *ich werde gleich mit dem Frühstück anfangen* − 5.1.3.

(g) The article is used with *meist: die meisten Familien* − 1.1.3 = 'most families'.

(h) The article is omitted in pairs of words and enumerations: *ein Prospekt . . . aus dem ich die genaue Lage und Größe des Hotels, Art der Ausstattung von Zimmern . . . entnehmen kann* − 3.1.4.

3 The Indefinite Article

3.1 Forms

	Masculine	Feminine	Neuter
N	ein	eine	ein
A	einen	eine	ein
G	eines	einer	eines
D	einem	einer	einem

3.2 Uses

Uses of the indefinite article are comparable with English, but note the following:
(a) The indefinite article is omitted after *als* meaning 'as' and followed by an occupation: *als Hilfsarbeiter* − 8.1.2; *als Rettungsschwimmer* − 9.2.2.

4 The Adjective

(a) *Uninflected Use of the Adjective*

Adjectives are used in their simple form, without endings, when they are not immediately followed by a noun which they describe. For example: *sie halten die Deutschen für fleißig, sauber, höflich* − 11.1.1; *sie sind sehr selbstbewußt* − 11.1.2.

(b) *Inflected Use of Adjectives*

When an adjective is followed by a noun, it is inflected − that is to say, it takes adjectival endings. There are three types of declension of adjectives: weak, mixed and strong. These are described below.
1. Weak declension has only two possible endings, *e* or *en*, as shown in the following tables:

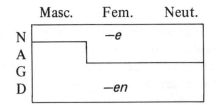

The weak endings are used following the definite article and after *dies-; jen-; jed-; welch-; manch-; solch-;* also after *alle* in the plural.

Examples:

Masc.	Fem.	Neut.	Plural
N dieser gute Wein	jene gute Suppe	welches gute Brot	alle guten Dinge
A diesen guten Wein	jene gute Suppe	welches gute Brot	alle guten Dinge
G dieses guten Weines	jener guten Suppe	welches guten Brotes	aller guten Dinge
D diesem guten Wein	jener guten Suppe	welchem guten Brot	allen guten Dingen

2. Mixed declension takes *en* in all the places where the weak declension takes *en*. The only difference, therefore, is in the masculine and neuter nominative and in the neuter accusative:

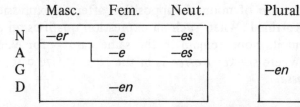

These endings are used after the indefinite article and after *kein*, and the possessive adjectives *mein, dein, sein, ihr, unser, Ihr, euer.*

Examples

Masc.	Fem.	Neut.	Plural
N ein guter Wein	eine gute Suppe	ein gutes Brot	keine guten Weine
A einen guten Wein	eine gute Suppe	eine gutes Brot	keine guten Weine
G eines guten Weines	einer guten Suppe	eines guten Brotes	keiner guten Weine
D einem guten Wein	einer guten Suppe	einem guten Brot	keinen guten Weinen

(The indefinite article has no plural form.)

It should be pointed out that adjectival endings are often made to seem very complicated, but in the great majority of cases represented by the weak and mixed declensions given above, only *e* and *en* endings are involved.

3. Strong declension is used where the adjective stands alone in front of the noun. Since there is no other word to show the case and gender of the noun, the adjective must show these features, and is therefore 'strong'.

Examples:

	Masc.	Fem.	Neut.	Plural
N	guter Wein	gute Suppe	gutes Brot	gute Weine
A	guten Wein	gute Suppe	gutes Brot	gute Weine
G	guten Weines	guter Suppe	guten Brotes	guter Weine
D	gutem Wein	guter Suppe	gutem Brot	guten Weinen

As stated above, strong endings are usual when the adjective stands alone: *auf stillen Wegen* — 9.1.3; *starke Wirtschaft, solide Autos, perfekte Organisation, gute Musik* — 11.1.1; *bei starker Hitze* — 5.1.2; *im Sommer nächsten Jahres* — 3.1.4. In addition, these endings are found after *viel, viele, ein bißchen, ein wenig, etwas*, and in the plural after *einige, manche, mehrere*, and after cardinal numbers: *viele deutsche Freunde* — 11.1.2; *drei gehäufte Teelöffel* — 5.1.2.

In all three declensions, a string of adjectives before the noun all have the same endings: *die Kopien meiner beiden letzten Zeugnisse* — 8.1.3.

(c) *Adjectival Use of Participles*

Present and past participles are often used as adjectives, and follow the rules of inflection described above. They may be uninflected when they do not precede the noun: *viele sind unverheiratet* — 11.1.2. Preceding the noun, they take the usual adjectival endings: *das weltbekannte Münster* — 3.1.2; *die freigesetzten Schadstoffe* — 12.1.2; *mit umweltschonenden Fahrzeugen* — 12.1.2. Note how German builds up adjectives in this way, creating new words to meet new concepts. Thus, *Umwelt* ('environment') is linked with the present participle *schonend* ('looking after'), or with the past participle *bewußt* ('conscious'), to make the adjectives *umweltschonend* and *umweltbewußt*.

(d) *Adjectives Preceded by a Noun of Measurement*

In 1.4 above, the use of nouns in apposition after an expression of measure or quantity was explained. When such an expression qualifies an adjective + noun, the adjective and its noun remain in the same case — for example, *eine Tasse starker Kaffee*, where *starker Kaffee* is in the Nominative case, standing in apposition to *eine Tasse*.

(e) *Adjectival Nouns*

1. Any adjective can be used as a noun. In such a case, the word is written with a capital letter and has endings as though it were followed by the word *Mann* or *Frau*. Compare *der Erwachsene* = 'grown up (person)' and the dative *bei den Erwachsenen* — 7.2.2. Note also the plural forms *die Jugendlichen* — 1.1.2; *die Deutschen* — 11.1.3, where the word *Leute* may be understood, and the adjectival noun therefore carries the weak plural ending. Note also the name of the political party *die Grünen* — 13.1.1.

Note the inflection of the adjectival noun after *etwas, nichts, alles: etwas Bestimmtes* — 4.2.2; *nichts Besonderes* — 5.2.2; *alles Gute; wir haben schon etwas Anderes vor* — 9.2.2 (see also Grammar Summary section 8.6).

2. A special case is provided by *deutsch*, the adjective for 'German', which has two forms of adjectival noun. A person is referred to by *der Deutsche/ein Deutscher* (male) and *die Deutsche/eine Deutsche* (female). *das Deutsche* is a neuter adjectival noun meaning the German language, for which one can also say *die deutsche Sprache*. See text 13.1.2, where *der Deutsche Ost und der Deutsche West* refers to the people in East and West Germany, and *das Deutsche Ost und das Deutsche West* refers to the language in East and West Germany.

(f) *Indefinite Adjectives*

The following are known as indefinite adjectives: *ander; bestimmt; einige; folgend; gewiß; mehrere; übrig; verschiedene; viele; wenige* (see also Grammar Summary section 8.6). When used with a following noun, they take endings like any other adjectives: *für einige Stunden* — 9.1.3; . . . *hat folgende Möglichkeiten* — 6.1.3; *bringt nicht so viele Vorteile* — 7.2.2; *die wenigen Menschen* — 4.1.2. Most of these indefinite adjectives are used with plural nouns. When another adjective is used between the indefinite and the noun, this adjective usually takes the strong endings: *viele interessante Leute* — 4.1.3.

(g) *Adjectives Followed by Dative*

A number of adjectives are followed by the dative case and may therefore be compared with English adjectives followed by 'to': *das kommt mir sehr fremd vor* — 11.1.2 = 'that seems very strange to me'. Other adjectives used in the same way are *ähnlich* ('similar to'); *bekannt* ('known to'); *gleich* ('all the same to'). Note that *wichtig* may be used either with the dative or with *für*. Compare *es ist mir sehr wichtig, daß . . .* — 3.1.4 and *für mich ist es wichtig, . . .* — 8.2.2.

(h) Note the use of *voller*, which is not declined, as in *voller Spannung* — 7.1.4.

(i) *Possessive adjectives* (*mein, dein, sein, ihr, unser, Ihr, euer*)
They are declined like *ein* in the singular and like *kein* in the plural: *. . . von Deiner Familie und Eurem Haus . . . mit meiner Familie* — 1.1.2; *meine Eltern* — 1.1.2.

(j) Adjectives are formed from the names of towns by adding the ending *er*, and they are then indeclinable: *erleben Sie den Ulmer Wochenmarkt* — 3.1.2; *im Cottbuser Neubauviertel* — 7.1.4.

(k) When referring to decades, i.e. 'the seventies', German forms an indeclinable adjective by adding *er* to the numeral: *neu in den siebziger Jahren* — 13.1.1.

5 The Adverb

5.1 All adjectives and participles may be used as adverbs and are then not inflected: *schnell versiegen die Tränen* — 7.1.4, where *schnell* is an adverb qualifying the verb, and would be rendered in English by 'quickly'. An adverb may also qualify an adjective: *der Unterricht ist richtig interessant* — 7.2.2 = 'the lessons are really interesting'. In English, adverbs may often differ from adjectives, particularly by adding the ending 'ly', as in the two examples given, but German has no such changes to the adverb. Note particularly that an adverb remains unchanged when a following adjective is inflected: *die Zahl neu gebildeter Wörter* — 13.1.2 = 'the number of newly created words'.
5.2 There are also a large number of words which are used only as adverbs, some of which are given below.

(a) *Adverbs of Degree*

1. *sehr* may be used with an adjective: *sehr geehrter Herr Meyer* — 8.1.3; *sehr wichtig* — 8.2.2. When used with a verb, *sehr* means 'very much', 'greatly': *ich würde mich sehr freuen* — 8.1.3; *das lange Stehen strengt doch sehr an* — 8.2.2.
2. Colloquial German makes a good deal of use of *richtig* and *total* as adverbs of degree: *ich bin mittags immer total erschöpft* — 7.1.3.

3. *zu* is equivalent to English 'too': *zu klein* — 5.2.2.
4. *weitgehend* and *weithin* are used as intensifying adverbs: *weitgehend unberührt ... weithin unbekannt* — 13.1.2.

(b) *Adverbs of Place*

1. In the questions *wo?* and *wohin?* German distinguishes between position and motion towards: *wo wohnst du denn? wohin fährst du denn?* — 1.2.2.
2. *woher?* means 'where from?' and may either be used as a single word or split, as in the following examples: *wo kommst du denn her?* — 1.2.2; *wo willst du die denn herbekommen?* — 5.2.2 = 'where will you get those from?'
3. It will be clear from the examples of *wohin?* and *woher?* that *hin* has the force of motion away from the speaker, and *her* implies motion towards the speaker. This is an important distinction because of the many verbs of motion which use *hin* and *her* to indicate direction of movement.
4. *da* and *dort* both mean 'there', but *dort* is more definite and specific: *Duisburg begann für uns dort, wo . . .* — 2.1.3; *ich war in der Schweiz. Da hatte man nicht so viel Freiheit* — 7.2.2. *da* can also have a rather indeterminate meaning similar to English colloquial 'then': *da muß ich noch pauken* — 10.1.2 = 'I'll have to get down to some school work then.'
5. *oben* and *unten* translate 'at the top of', and 'at the bottom of': *links oben . . . rechts oben* — 6.1.3; *oben wartete die Linie 79* — 2.1.3; *von oben hat man eine schöne Aussicht* — 4.1.3.
6. *hüben und drüben*, meaning 'here and over there' is often used nowadays to refer to the two Germanies, as in 13.1.2: *es ist vor allem der Wortschatz, der hüben und drüben betroffen ist.*
7. *mitten* is an adverb meaning 'in the middle' and is usually followed by a preposition: *mitten durch Äcker und Wiesen* — 2.1.3. Note also similar usage of *kreuz und quer* = 'in all directions': *kreuz und quer durch das Ruhrgebiet* — 2.1.3.
(c) *gern* (or, *gerne*) means 'gladly', 'willingly' and is most frequently used to express liking: *in München sitzt man gerne im Straßencafé* — 4.1.2 = 'people like sitting at street cafés'; *ob Sie gerne tanzen . . .* — 3.1.2 = 'whether you like dancing . . .'. The negative is also possible: *ich fahre nicht gern mit dem Zug* — 1.2.2. Other possibilities include the use of *gern* with *möchte*: *meine Freunde und ich möchten gern drei Nächte übernachten* — 9.1.4. An alternative is to use *gern* with the Imperfect subjunctive of *haben*: *wenn möglich hätte ich auch gern ein Zimmer . . .* — 3.1.4 (see also Grammar Summary section 12.11(b)3). The comparative and superlative of *gern* are *lieber* and *am liebsten*: *ob Sie gerne tanzen oder lieber ins Theater gehen* — 3.1.2 = 'whether you like dancing or prefer to go to the theatre'; *da geht der Umweltfreund lieber zu Fuß* — 12.1.2 = '. . . prefers going on foot'. Other examples are: *ich schwimme lieber . . . ich laufe lieber Ski* — 9.2.2. Note the idiomatic use: *geh doch lieber mit Karin zur Disco* — 9.2.2 = 'why don't you go with Karin to the disco instead?'

Note other ways of expressing likes and dislikes: *hast du Lust, mit zur Disco zu kommen?* — 9.2.2; *Rudern macht auch Spaß* — 9.2.2; *ich habe nicht mal Lust zum Lesen* — 1.2.2.

(d) *Interrogative Adverbs*

1. *warum?*: *warum gehen wir nicht zur Disco?* — 9.2.2 = 'why don't we go to the disco?'
2. *Wieso?* is used to query an answer, and might be translated 'how is that?', or 'how does that come about?': *Wieso, ist dein Vater etwa ein Journalist?* — 1.2.2.
3. *wie?* is an interrogative adjective of manner meaning 'how?' It may either stand

alone: *wie sind die Einkaufsmöglichkeiten?* Or it may qualify a following adjective: *wie groß sind die umliegenden Orte?*; *wie teuer ist eine Übernachtung?* —
9.1.4; *wie oft gehen Sie einkaufen?* — 6.2.2.

4. *weshalb?* can be used in the same way as *warum?* to mean 'why?' It has an additional use, however, which translates 'why' when it introduces a subordinate clause and not a question: . . . *andere Gründe, weshalb sich Jugendliche mit einem Arbeitsplatz besser stehen* — 8.1.2.

6 Comparison of Adjectives and Adverbs

(a) The usual way for adjectives and adverbs to form the comparative is similar to the English way of adding *er* to the simple form: *streng, strenger* — 11.1.2; *gering, geringer* — 13.1.2. Whereas English does not use this form for longer adjectives (e.g. 'beautiful', 'more beautiful'), German adds *er* to even the longest adjectives: *selbstverständlich, selbstverständlicher.* Adjectives and adverbs ending in *el, en, er* drop the *e* of the stem when forming the comparative: *dunkel, dunkler.*

Some of the most common monosyllabic adjectives add an Umlaut in the comparative: *kürzer . . . länger* — 13.1.1. Other adjectives following this pattern are: *alt/älter; jung/jünger; stark/stärker; schwach/schwächer; klug/klüger; warm/ wärmer; kalt/kälter; groß/größer; arm/ärmer; hart/härter; krank/kränker; oft/öfter; scharf/schärfer; schwarz/schwärzer.*

(b) The superlative is formed by adding *st* to the adjective or adverb (*est* after the final consonants *s, ß, x, z*): *streng, strengst; gering, geringst.* The superlative of adjectives normally appears preceded by the definite article, and the usual adjectival endings are added: *mit der neuesten Mode* — 4.1.2; *Hamburg hat den größten und wichtigsten Hafen Deutschlands* — 4.1.3. Sometimes the superlative may be used omitting the noun 'thing', which is understood — for example: *das wichtigste für mich* — 8.2.2 = 'the most important thing for me'. The superlative of adverbs has the same form as that just described for adjectives, but it is preceded by *am* and not by the definite article: *wir treffen uns am besten* — 4.2.2; *London lernt man am besten mit London Transport kennen* — 2.1.2; *am stärksten* — 8.1.1. The adjective used as a noun may also appear in the superlative: *bist du die Älteste?* — 1.2.2; *das Schlimmste war . . .* — 10.1.2; *das Beste wäre . . .* — 10.2.2.

(c) The following adjectives and adverbs form irregular comparatives and superlatives:

bald	eher	am ehesten = 'soon', 'sooner', 'soonest'
gern	lieber	am liebsten = 'gladly', 'rather', 'best of all'
groß	größer	der größte = 'big', 'bigger', 'biggest'
gut	besser	der beste = 'good', 'better', 'best'
hoch	höher	der höchste = 'high', 'higher', 'highest'
nah	näher	der nächste = 'near', 'nearer', 'nearest/next'
viel	mehr	der meiste = 'much', 'more', 'most'
wenig	weniger	der wenigste = 'little', 'less', 'least'

Some examples of these in the texts are: *eines unserer größten Umweltprobleme* — 12.1.2; *der findet unser System auch besser* — 7.2.2; *nächstes Jahr* — 8.2.2; *das Lebensalter . . . in dem die meisten zu uns kommen* — 7.1.4; *man kann ja gar nichts Anderes mehr machen* — 7.2.2; *in bester Form* — 9.2.2; *weniger Technik* — 13.1.1; *mehr Lebensqualität* — 13.1.1.

(d) *Forms of Comparative Statement*

1. Expressing equality: *so . . . wie* or *ebenso . . . wie* are used, equivalent to English 'as . . . as': . . . *haben ebenso geschwärmt, wie die Roggenbucks* — 3.1.3 = 'were just as keen as the Roggenbucks'.

2. Expressing superiority, equivalent to English comparative followed by 'than': *ich dachte immer, daß deutsche Lehrer strenger sind, als bei uns* — 11.1.2; *mehr als 175 000 Kilometer* — 12.1.2; *sie wird größer sein, als in der Bundesrepublik* — 13.1.2.

An older form of the language used *denn* in comparisons of this kind, and this is still sometimes found in fixed expressions: for example, *mehr denn je* = 'more than ever'; *da sie ihr ferner sind denn je* — 9.1.3 = 'when they are farther than ever from it'.

3. Inferiority is expressed by *nicht . . . wie: eine politische Partei . . . ist noch nicht so wichtig hier, wie in der Bundesrepublik* (see Key to Exercises, page 164).

4. Progression, as in English 'smaller and smaller' is rendered by *immer* + comparative: *. . . wird die Lebensqualität immer geringer* — 12.1.2; *immer mehr Umweltbelastung* — 12.1.2; *immer schlechter* — 12.2.1.

5. Proportion, as in English 'the more . . . the more', is rendered by *je mehr . . . desto mehr: je mehr man hat, desto mehr will man haben* = 'the more one has, the more one wants'.

6. After the verb *sein*, the superlative may either take the form with the definite article or with *am*.

7. The absolute superlative is used, not to imply a comparison with anything else, but to express the highest degree of what is being described: *möglichst bald nach dem Verlassen der Schule* — 8.1.2. Similar use is found with *äußerst* — e.g. *äußerst schnell*.

8. Note the following group of adverbial superlatives: *höchstens* — 'at the most'; *wenigstens* — 'at least'; *frühstens* — 'at the earliest'; *spätestens* — 'at the latest': *du hast wenigstens mal deine Ruhe* — 1.2.2; *die Entzündung wird frühstens erst in einer Woche zurückgehen* — 10.2.2.

7 The Personal Pronoun

7.1 Forms

	Nom	Acc	Dat
I	ich	mich	mir
you (familiar, sing.)	du	dich	dir
he	er	ihn	ihm
she	sie	sie	ihr
it	es	es	ihm
we	wir	uns	uns
you (familiar, plural)	ihr	euch	euch
you (polite)	Sie	Sie	Ihnen
they	sie	sie	ihnen

7.2 Uses

(a) *Sie, du and ihr*

The familiar forms of the second person ('you') are used when addressing relatives, close friends, children and animals. See, for example, text 8.2.2, where the interviewer addresses Petra as *du*. When *du* or *ihr* are used in letters, they are used with capital letters, as also are the other parts of speech associated with them: *was Du mir von Deiner Familie und Eurem Haus geschrieben hast* — 1.1.2.

Sie is the most normal form of address to strangers, adults and acquaintances: *ich möchte Sie bitten* — 3.1.4; *bei Ihnen* — 3.1.4.

(b) *Third Person*

In using the third person pronoun, care must be taken to see that it agrees with the gender of the noun referred to — for example: *schräg gegenüber hielt die Linie 901. Sie war vorher* . . . — 2.1.3. Here *sie* refers to the feminine noun *die Linie*. Note also: *das Kind fühlt sich hier nicht fremd, denn es ist mit seiner Mutter gekommen* — 7.1.4, where *es* refers to *das Kind*.

(c) *Some Uses of es*

(See also Grammar Summary section 12.10 on impersonal verbs and 12.10 (d), (e) on *es ist/es gibt*.)

1. *es* is used to refer, in advance, to a following clause beginning *wie: das Ehepaar empfindet es als besonders wohltuend, wie ihnen das Haus entgegenkommt* — 3.1.3. Here *es* refers to the whole meaning of the *wie* clause. The best rendering of this sentence in English would be: 'the couple feel that the way the house meets their wishes is particularly beneficial'.

2. *es* is used as a pronoun of general reference. For example, in the sentence *Ferien in Familie — Roggenbucks geniessen sie und können es sich schöner nicht vorstellen* — 3.1.3, *sie* refers to *die Ferien*, and *es* refers, not to any particular noun, but to the whole experience of spending the holidays in such a place. This might be translated: 'Roggenbucks enjoy the family holiday and can not imagine anything nicer'. Note also: *die Autofahrer haben es gut* — 4.1.2 = 'car-drivers are lucky'.

3. *es* is used as a general all-purpose subject with *sein* and *werden*, just like 'it' in English: *von hier aus ist es nicht mehr weit* — 2.1.3; *zehn Kilometer waren es* . . . — 2.1.3; *wieder wurde es grau* — 2.1.3; *es ist wie im Interhotel* — 3.1.3.

4. *es* is used as the subject of verbs describing the weather: *es regnete* — 2.1.3.

5. There are a number of expressions, similar to impersonal expressions, where *es* stands for the following clause: *es fiel uns also leicht, 14 Tage . . . zu verbringen* — 4.1.2. For other such expressions, and forms of *es geht*, see Grammar Summary section 12.10.

(d) *Use of damit, darauf, etc.*

There are a group of prepositions which are followed by the pronouns of the third person when people are referred to, but when the reference is to objects, a compound form *da* + preposition is used instead of the pronoun. The prepositions concerned are as follows:

normally taking dative — *aus, bei, mit, nach, von, zu;*
normally taking accusative — *durch, für, gegen, um;*
taking either dative or accusative — *an, auf, hinter, in, neben, über, unter, vor, zwischen.*

For example, in text 11.1.2 *viele von ihnen* refers to people, but in 14.3 you read: *und nehmen davon kaum noch Notiz*, where *davon* means 'of it' or 'of that'. Other examples are *und damit immer mehr Umweltbelastung* — 12.1.2; *danach eine Pause?* — 3.1.2; *heute wachsen Seerosen darauf* — 2.1.3; *dazu gehören ein Kinobesuch, ein gemütlicher Abend* — 14.3. For use of *dazu* see also Grammar Summary section 14.1(d). Further uses of these compound forms with a following clause (*dafür, daß* . . .) are discussed in section 12.16.

Note the use of *daher* to mean 'hence', 'therefore': . . . *müssen sich daher entscheiden* — 8.1.2.

(e) *Reflexive Pronouns*

These have the same form as the personal pronouns except for the use of *sich* as the reflexive of the second person polite form *Sie*, and the third person forms *es, sie, er*. The reflexive pronoun used with a verb may be in the accusative or dative. For example, in the sentence: *als ich das erste Mal in einer deutschen Universität war, habe ich mich sehr gewundert* — 11.1.2, the reflexive pronoun *mich* is in the accusative case, as it is the direct object of *wundern*. The same is true of the examples: *die Menschen in den Städten wollen sich bewegen* — 13.1.1.

But if the reflexive verb has another direct object, the reflexive pronoun becomes the indirect object, in the dative case. For example, the reflexive verb *sich etwas kaufen* means 'to buy something for oneself'. Therefore, *ich brauche das Geld, um mir ein Moped zu kaufen* — 9.2.2 means 'I need money to buy myself a moped', where *Moped* is the direct object of the verb *kaufen* and *mir* is the indirect object, dative of the reflexive pronoun *mich*. Note the other examples: *ich sehe mir nämlich auch gern gute Filme an* — 9.2.2; *das habe ich mir immer gewünscht* — 1.2.2. These examples use the reflexive verbs *sich (etwas) ansehen* and *sich (etwas) wünschen*. The full forms of the reflexive verbs referred to here are:

sich wundern — 'to be surprised'	*sich einen Film ansehen* — 'to see a film'
ich wundere mich	ich sehe mir einen Film an
du wunderst dich	du siehst dir einen Film an
er/sie/es wundert sich	er/sie sieht sich einen Film an
wir wundern uns	wir sehen uns einen Film an
ihr wundert euch	ihr seht euch einen Film an
Sie wundern sich	Sie sehen sich einen Film an
sie wundern sich	sie sehen sich einen Film an

A further point to note is that the reflexive pronoun does not necessarily appear with a verb. It can be used after a preposition to refer back to the subject of the sentence: *hinter sich* — 12.2.1. The word *einander* is a so-called reciprocal reflexive, meaning not 'oneself', but 'one another': *man kennt einander* — 6.2.2 = 'one knows one another/each other'.

8 Miscellaneous Adjectives and Pronouns

8.1 Demonstrative Adjectives and Pronouns

(a) *der, die, das* with all the forms of the definite article may be used as a demonstrative adjective if stressed.

(b) *der, die, das* are also used as demonstrative pronouns, especially when used as a stressed form of the personal pronoun: *wenn der . . . nach Hause kommt* — 7.2.2; *der findet unser System auch besser* — 7.2.2; *die brauchen auch mal Freizeit* — 7.2.2. In these examples, *der* and *die* are stressed forms of *er* and *sie*. *das* is widely used as a general neuter demonstrative pronoun: *das ist ja wie ein Arbeitstag* — 7.2.2; *das glaube ich* — 1.2.2. Sometimes *das* can be used as a general pronoun meaning 'they' — for example, in reference to children in text 3.1.3: *das hopst und kichert*.

(c) *dieser* ('this') and *jener* ('that') may be used as adjectives or pronouns: *dieser Vorteil ist nicht von Dauer* — 8.1.2; *alle diese tollen Angebote* — 6.1.1; *für diese Zeit* — 9.1.4. *Dieser* and *jener* take the same endings as *der, die, das* — for example: *diese Abgase . . . von diesem Problem* — 12.2.1. A further use is for *dieser* to mean 'the latter', and *jener* 'the former': *da diese aber oft nicht . . .* — 14.3 = 'as the latter . . .', referring to the *ausländische Gäste* in the previous sentence of the passage.

(d) *derselbe, dieselbe, dasselbe* are used to mean 'the same': *sie besitzen nicht dieselbe Autorität* — 11.1.2; *ich fahre auch aus demselben Grund* — 1.2.2.

8.2 Interrogative Pronoun

(a) *Forms*

N	wer? — who?	was? — what?	
A	wen?	was?	
G	wessen?	wessen? (more usually *wovon?* in modern German)	
D	wem?	—	

(b) *Uses*

1. In the nominative *wer?* and *was?* are used like English 'who?' and 'what?': *Tagesfamilie — was ist das?* — 1.1.2; *was versteht man unter einem Zehnkampf?* — 9.1.1; *was ist Wandern?* — 9.1.3. In the other cases *wen?* and *wem?* are equivalent to English 'whom'. Note the use of nominative and dative forms in text 9.2.2: *wer will da mit wem ins Kino gehen? Wessen?* means 'whose?': *wessen Buch ist das?*
2. When the interrogative pronoun referring to an object is used with one of the prepositions listed in Grammar Summary section 7.2(d), a compound question form is made with *wo* + preposition. For example, *mit wem fahren Sie?* means 'with whom are you travelling?' and *womit arbeiten Sie?* means 'what are you working with?'
3. *was!* may also be used as an exclamation.
4. *wer* may sometimes have the sense of 'whoever', 'somebody who': *wer schnell ist, hat den Vorteil!* — 6.1.1. In such a position it is a general relative pronoun, and not an interrogative. It stands for persons, either male or female.

8.3 Interrogative Adjective

(a) *Forms*

	Masc.	Fem.	Neut.	Plural
N	welcher?	welche?	welches?	welche?
A	welchen?	welche?	welches?	welche?
G	welches?	welcher?	welches?	welcher?
D	welchem?	welcher?	welchem?	welchen?

(b) The forms of *welcher?* are used like an adjective agreeing with the following noun. It is equivalent to English 'which?' or 'what?', as in the following sentences: *welche Kinder sind auf sie angewiesen?* — 1.1.2; *in welches Café wollen wir gehen?* — 4.2.2.

The genitive forms are not often used in modern German, but they have the endings of *der, die, das* in the genitive when they occur. There is one example only in this book: *welcher Art ist diese Unterhaltung?* — 3.1.4 = 'of what kind . . . ?'

(c) A further form of interrogative adjective is *was für (ein)?* meaning 'what sort of?'; *was für Sport- und Wandermöglichkeiten gibt es?* — 3.1.4. Note that *was für?* is invariable and does not affect the case of the following word. The two words may be separated — e.g. *was ist das für ein Auto?* or *was für ein Auto ist das?*

was für may also appear as a subordinating conjunction: *egal, was für Pläne Sie haben* — 2.1.2 = 'it does not matter what plans you have'.

8.4 Relative Pronoun

(a) *Forms*

It is possible to use *welcher* (see above) as a relative pronoun. More commonly, the following forms are used:

	Masc.	Fem.	Neut.	Plural
N	der	die	das	die
A	den	die	das	die
G	dessen	deren	dessen	deren
D	dem	der	dem	denen

(b) *Uses*

1. The relative pronoun in English is 'which' or 'who' in a sentence such as 'the man who owns the dog' or 'the ball which is lost'. The word to which the relative pronoun refers — that is, in this case, 'man' or 'ball' — is called the antecedent. In German it is important to remember that the relative pronoun agrees with its antecedent. For example: *an der Bushaltestelle stehen viele Leute, die zur Schule fahren* — 7.1.3. Here the relative pronoun *die* is plural because the antecedent to which it refers is *die Leute*. Having decided what the gender and number of the antecedent are, one must then decide what function the relative pronoun is performing in its clause. Is it subject, object, in the genitive or used with a preposition? In the sentence already quoted, the relative clause is *die zur Schule fahren* and the relative pronoun is in the nominative, subject of the verb *fahren*. Here are some more examples where the relative pronoun is subject of its clause: *eine Familie, die tagsüber Kinder betreut* — 1.1.2; *Leif beschreibt seinen Schulalltag, der mit dem Leben anderer Schüler doch vieles gemeinsam hat* — 7.1.3. Note that in this last example the relative pronoun is subject of its own clause and is therefore in the nominative, even though the antecedent, *Schulalltag*, is the object of the main clause verb. Compare the following example: *wir haben einen eignen Schulbus, der uns direkt zur Schule bringt* — 7.1.3. The relative pronoun can sometimes be omitted in English, but never in German.
2. Here are some examples of relative pronouns from the texts in cases other than the nominative: *weil auch der steife Preuße Humor hat, den der Bayer nicht versteht* — 11.2.2. In this case the subject of the relative clause is *der Bayer* and the relative pronoun *den* is object of the verb *versteht*.

In the dative case the relative pronoun is very often preceded by a preposition: *ich habe Ihre Adresse aus einem Hotelverzeichnis entnommen, in dem alle Hotels . . . aufgelistet sind* — 3.1.4; *ein Prospekt von ihrem Hotel, aus dem ich die genaue Lage . . . entnehmen kann* — 3.1.4; *eine gemütliche Stadt, in der es sich gut leben läßt* — 14.3.
3. When the antecedent is *alles, etwas, nichts, vieles* or *das*, the relative pronoun is *was: gute Vorstellungen von dem, was kommt* — 8.2.2; *alles, was wir brauchen* — 5.2.2; *alles, was er sich . . . vorstellt* — 14.3. *was* is also the relative if it refers to the whole of the preceding clause, and not just to a single word. The English equivalent is 'what' or 'that which': *Silka zeigt ihr, was sie gerade entdeckt hat* — 7.1.4; *was Du mir . . . geschrieben hast* — 1.1.3; *. . . zu hören, was du so machst* — 5.1.3. If a verb in the clause preceding the relative clause is normally followed by

a dependent preposition, it is necessary to retain this preposition in the relative clause structure. For example, *berichten über* means 'to report about', and the relative clause construction is therefore: *sie berichten darüber, was ihnen auffällt* - 11.1.2 (see also Grammar Summary section 12.16).

4. In the cases where the relative pronoun should be *was*, according to the previous examples, but where the relative pronoun is combined with a preposition, the combination *wo* + preposition is used: *die Titelverteidiger erkämpften . . . den WM-Titel, wobei sie drei neue Bahnrekorde erzielten* – 9.1.2.

5. This form of *wo* + preposition is often used for the dative forms of relative pronouns when the antecedent is an object and not a person. Such use is not obligatory, however: *ein großes Lastauto, mit dem er durch das ganze Zimmer robbt* – 7.1.4.

6. The forms *wo, wohin* and *woher* may all appear as relative pronouns, comparable to English 'where': *sie stellen ihren Wagen ab, wo sie ihn loswerden können* – 4.1.2; *Duisburg begann für uns dort, wo die Linie 79 zur Hochbahn wird* – 2.1.3; *im Erzgebirge, wo wir in einer Jugendherberge übernachtet haben* – 10.1.2.

7. For the use of *wer* as relative pronoun, see Grammar Summary section 8.3(b)5.

8.5 Further Miscellaneous Adjectives and Pronouns

(a) *alles, alle*

alles ('everything') is the most usual form to be found in the singular: *vielleicht wird ja auch alles gut* – 8.2.2. It may also be found inflected in the singular, in certain expressions: *vor allem junge Leute* – 13.1.1. Usually, when English 'all' needs to be translated into the singular in German, *ganz* is most frequently used: *den ganzen Tag Schule* – 7.2.2 = 'school all day' or 'school the whole day'. *alle* in the plural means 'everybody', or translates English 'all'. *alle* is inflected in the genitive and dative cases, as will be seen from the examples below: *mit allen Annehmlichkeiten* – 2.1.2; *wo die Linie . . . alle Straßen überquert* – 2.1.3; *aus allen Himmelsrichtungen* – 3.1.2; *alle anderen riskieren ihr Leben* – 4.1.2. After *alles*, the adjective is written with a capital letter and ends in *e: alles Preußische* – 11.2.2 = 'everything Prussian'. The plural *alle* is followed by the weak endings of the adjective: *alle Norddeutschen* – 11.2.2.

(b) *anders* means 'else' in the combination *niemand anders* – 'nobody else', and *wer anders?* — 'who else?' It can be used to mean 'different': *ganz anders die Frankfurter* – 4.1.2. As an adjective, *anders* loses the final *s*, and takes adjectival endings: *. . . sagen die anderen* – 14.3. Note that *ander-* is always written with a small letter, even when it is an adjectival noun.

(c) *sonst* is commonly used with the meaning of 'else', 'otherwise': *sonst sind die Töpfe zu klein* – 5.2.2.

(d) *beide*, when preceded by the definite article, is inflected like any other adjective, and means 'two': *die Kopien meiner beiden letzten Zeugnisse* – 8.1.3. Used without the article, *beide* means 'both', either as an adjective: *auf beiden Seiten* – 13.1.2, or as a pronoun, *wir beide* = 'both of us'.

(e) *einer, eine, eines* are used as pronouns to mean 'one', 'anyone', 'someone': *an die Fußgänger denkt kaum einer* – 4.1.2 = 'hardly anyone . . .'; *das Auto ist . . . eines unserer größten Umweltprobleme* – 12.1.2 = 'the car is one of our greatest environmental problems.'

(f) *ein bißchen* means 'a little': *ich habe schon selbst ein bißchen für die Zeitung gearbeitet* – 1.2.2; *mir war auch ein bißchen übel* – 10.1.2.

(g) *ein paar* means 'a few' and remains uninflected: *ich wandere mit ein paar Freunden* – 9.2.2; *ich schreibe dir ein paar Schmerztabletten auf* – 10.2.2.

(h) *einige* can occur in the singular meaning 'a few things': *weil ich einiges versäumt habe* — 10.1.2. It most frequently occurs in the plural, either standing alone as a pronoun to mean 'some', 'a few', or as an adjective with a following noun. Compare: *einige unterhalten sich* — 7.1.3 and *für einige Stunden* — 9.1.3. In cases other than the nominative, *einige* takes the same endings as *diese*: *seit einigen Jahren* — 8.1.2. When followed by another adjective, this takes strong endings: *einige gute Bücher.*

(i) *etwas* is indeclinable and is used in the following ways:

1. to mean 'something', 'anything': *so etwas wäre unmöglich* — 11.1.2; = 'something like that would be impossible'; *wir haben schon etwas anderes vor* — 9.2.2; *man hat nie etwas von der Anonymität . . . gespürt* — 1.1.3; *. . . daß etwas nicht ganz in Ordnung war* — 10.1.2.

2. to mean 'a little' when followed by an adjective: *dann wirst du dich etwas besser fühlen* — 10.2.2.

3. When followed by an adjectival noun, *etwas* means 'something', and the adjective takes strong endings (see also Grammar Summary section 4(e)): *wie wäre es mit etwas Orientalischem* — 5.2.2; *etwas Extrafeines* — 5.2.2; *etwas Bestimmtes* — 4.2.2.

(j) *irgend* is an indefinite adverb which can be used as follows: *irgend jemand* = 'somebody or other'; *irgend etwas* = 'something or other'; *irgendwann* = 'sometime or other'; *irgendwie* = 'somehow or other'. Note also: *hast du irgendwelche Schmerzen?* — 10.2.2 = 'have you any pains at all?'

irgendein is an indefinite adjective meaning 'some . . . or other': *irgendein Norddeutscher* — 11.2.2 = 'some North German or other'.

(k) *jeder* is declined like *dieser*, and means 'each', 'every': *jede Epoche* — 13.1.1; *jeden Samstag* — 3.1.2; *in jedem Jahr* — 4.1.3. Note the phrases *jeder Art* — 13.1.1 = 'of every kind'; and *auf jeden Fall* — 8.2.2 = 'in any case'. (Compare: *auf keinen Fall* — 1.2.2 = 'on no account').

As a pronoun, *jeder* means 'everyone': *immer noch bezeichnet mich jeder als Preußen* — 11.2.2.

(1) *jemand*, 'somebody', and *niemand*, 'nobody', are used just like their English equivalents. There are inflected forms (*jemanden, jemandem*), but it is quite correct in modern German for these words to remain invariable. Note the inflected forms used in text 9.2.2: *ich suche noch jemanden zum Bergsteigen . . . ob du jemanden zum Skilaufen brauchst.*

(m) *kein* is declined like *ein* in the singular, and like *diese* in the plural. It means 'no', 'not a' in the following examples: *keine richtige Familie* — 11.1.2; *über 1000 Geschäfte lassen keinen Wunsch unerfüllt* — 3.1.2; *keine Freizeit* — 7.2.2; *fast keine Hochhäuser* — 1.1.3. *Kein* is almost always used instead of *nicht ein*. *Keiner* is a pronoun meaning 'nobody'.

(n) *man* is equivalent to the English 'one' in a general sense: *man kann viele Lehrgänge besuchen* — 8.2.2 = 'one can attend lots of courses; *um fünf Uhr kann man hier schon einkaufen* — 4.1.3. Other possible ways of translating *man* into English might be to use a vague general term like 'people', or 'they': *man sagt* = 'they say', or 'people say': *bei uns zu Hause sagt man . . .* — 11.1.3. The reflexive pronoun for *man* is *sich*. *Man* is very widely used (see particularly text 7.2.2), and might also be rendered by 'you', or by a passive construction: *man lernt . . . mehr als hier* — 7.2.2 = 'you learn more than here'; *wenn man den ganzen Tag lang in der Schule ist* = 'if you have to spend the whole day in school.'

(o) *mancher* is declined like *dieser* and means 'many a': *mancher Japaner* — 14.3.

(p) *nichts* is invariable, and means 'nothing'. An adjective after *nichts* has a capital letter and strong endings: *nichts Verrücktes* — 5.2.2.

(q) *solcher* is declined like *dieser*: *solche Träume* — 8.2.2 = 'such dreams'. It may be used in the plural, as in this example, or in the singular: *solches Wetter* = 'such weather'.

(r) *so* combines with *ein* to mean 'such as . . .': *mit so einer großen Familie* – 1.2.2. *so* combines with *etwas* to mean 'such a thing', or 'something like that': *so etwas wäre in meiner Heimat unmöglich* – 11.1.2. *so* is frequently used with *viel*, or a following adjective, as an intensifier: *weil ich so spät aus der Schule komme* – 7.1.3 = 'so late'; *Sonne und Schnee konnten noch so sehr locken* – 3.1.3; *so viel Freiheit* – 11.1.2; *so viele Bürgerinitiativen* – 13.1.1. *so* can be used with the force of *also* to mean 'therefore', 'and so': *so mußte ich zum Arzt gehen* – 10.1.2. *so* may be used as an adverb to mean 'in such a way': *so kann man Millionen von Bürgern treffen* – 3.1.3; *jede Erzieherin muß es so betreuen, als wäre es ihr eigenes* – 7.1.4 = 'each nursery nurse must look after it just as if it were her own'.

(s) *viel, wenig*

1. *viel* and *wenig* may be used as pronouns meaning 'much' or 'little'. They may be uninflected: *Deutschland kann wenig tun* – 12.2.1, or, alternatively, they may appear in the forms *vieles, weniges: . . . der mit dem Leben anderer Schüler doch vieles gemeinsam hat* – 7.1.3 = 'has a lot in common . . .'. The inflected form may be used when referring to a number of things all connected together, and could be translated 'a lot of things'.

2. *viel* and *wenig* may be followed by a noun in the singular or plural. In the plural the forms are *viele* and *wenige* in nominative and accusative, and *vielen*, *wenigen* in the dative. As stated above, the singular forms are generally uninflected, though one exception is *vielen Dank* – 9.1.4. Note the following examples of singular and plural use: *so viel Freiheit* – 7.2.2; *in vielen Stadtbereichen* – 12.1.2; *in wenigen Jahrzehnten* – 2.1.3; *die wenigen Menschen* – 4.1.2.

viel and *wenig* can be intensified by *sehr: in unserem Stadtviertel gab es sehr viele Einfamilienhäuser* – 1.1.3.

3. *viel* and *wenig* may be used in the singular or plural with a following adjective + noun. In this case, the adjective takes strong endings: *viele liebe Grüße* – 1.1.3.

4. *viele* and *wenige* can be used as pronouns to mean, respectively, 'many people' and 'few people': *viele wollen . . . nicht mehr in der Stadt wohnen* – 12.1.2; *viele von ihnen* – 11.1.2.

5. *viel* may be used to intensify a following adjective in the comparative: *viel billiger* – 3.1.3 = 'much cheaper'.

6. Compound forms of *viel* and *wenig* may be written as either one or two words, *so viel* and *soviel; so wenig* and *sowenig*. In general, the rules are as follows:

(i) with *so* they are written as one word in certain set phrases: *soviel wie möglich* = 'as much as possible'. They are written as two words if *so* is an adverb intensifying *viel: da hatte man nicht so viel Freiheit* – 7.2.2.

(ii) with *zu*, they are written as one word if the stress falls on *viel* or *wenig: ich finde das zuviel* – 7.2.2. They are written as two words if *viel* is inflected, e.g. in the plural: *zu viele Hausaufgaben*. They are also written as two words if the stress falls on *zu: Sie haben wirklich zu wenig gemacht!* = 'you really have done *too* little!'

(iii) with *wie, wiewenig* is always written as one word; *wieviel* is one word, but *wie viele* is two: *wie viele Kinder betreut sie?* – 1.1.2; *wieviel Leute?* – 5.2.2. *wieviel* may introduce a question, as in these examples, or introduce a relative clause: *laß uns mal ausrechnen, wieviel wir brauchen* – 5.2.2.

7. For effect, conversation may use stronger adverbs than *viel*, for example: *es hat alles riesig Spaß gemacht* – 10.1.2 = 'it was all enormous fun.'

189

9 Numerals

9.1 Cardinal Numerals – Forms

0 null	11 elf	22 zweiundzwanzig
1 eins	12 zwölf	23 dreiundzwanzig
2 zwei	13 dreizehn	30 dreißig
3 drei	14 vierzehn	40 vierzig
4 vier	15 fünfzehn	50 fünfzig
5 fünf	16 sechzehn	60 sechzig
6 sechs	17 siebzehn	70 siebzig
7 sieben	18 achtzehn	80 achtzig
8 acht	19 neunzehn	90 neunzig
9 neun	20 zwanzig	100 hundert *or* einhundert
10 zehn	21 einundzwanzig	101 hunderteins

102 hundertzwei	2000 zweitausend
103 hundertdrei	1 000 000 eine Million
121 hunderteinundzwanzig	2 000 000 zwei Millionen
200 zweihundert	
1000 tausend	
1001 tausendundeins	

3 234 756 drei Millionen zweihundertvierunddreißigtausendsiebenhundertsechsundfünfzig

1986 neunzehnhundertsechsundachtzig

9.2 Some Notes on the Use of Cardinal Numbers

(a) *eins* is used with final *s* when counting, but loses this *s* in compound numerals, e.g. *einundzwanzig.* When used with a noun, it is declined like *ein: die eine Stunde* – 7.1.4. When used with *Uhr, ein* is never inflected: *kurz nach ein Uhr.*

(b) *zwei* sometimes occurs as *zwo*, particularly when giving telephone numbers, and when there might be some confusion with *drei*.

(c) Cardinal numbers have a form ending *er* to denote decades: *neu in den siebziger Jahren . . . die schnelle industrielle Entwicklung in den 50er und 60er Jahren* – 13.1.1. Note that this form is invariable. It is also used when denoting value. For example, when buying postage stamps, you could say either: *zwei sechziger Briefmarken*, or, *zwei Briefmarken zu sechzig.*

(d) *Million* is used only as a noun and takes plural endings: *Hamburg hat 1,6 Millionen Einwohner* – 4.1.3; *Millionen von Bundesbürgern* – 9.1.3. *hundert* and *tausend* may also be used as nouns, as in *Hunderte von Kilometern* – 12.2.1, and they are then written with a capital letter. Otherwise, they are adjectives with a small letter: *hundert Kilometer.*

(e) Cardinal numbers may be qualified by *etwa, rund, ungefähr* (all meaning 'approximately'), *über* ('over'), *knapp* ('barely'): *über 1000 Geschäfte* – 3.1.2; *von den rund 1500 Gästen* – 3.1.3; *die rund 570 Herbergen* – 9.1.3; *ungefähr 10 Minuten* – 7.1.3.

(f) Where English inserts 'or' between two numbers, German has a comma. Compare: '80 or 90 years ago'; *vor 80,90 Jahren.*

(g) In writing large numbers and decimals, German follows the normal continental usage of a comma for the decimal point: *1,6 Millionen* – 4.1.3: *88,8 Prozent aller Kinder* – 7.1.4. When speaking these two examples would be expressed: *ein Komma sechs Millionen; achtundachtzig Komma acht Prozent.* In writing thousands it is usual to leave a space between the thousands and the figures following: *175 000 Kilometer* − 12.1.2. In writing numerals out in full, only millions are written separately; otherwise, even long numbers are written as a single word: *hundertfünfundsiebzigtausend*.

(h) Age is expressed as in text 7.1.3: *ich bin vierzehn Jahre alt*. Note also the compounds for age: *die neunjährige Nicolle* − 3.1.3.

9.3 Ordinal Numerals

The ordinal numbers are formed by adding *te* to cardinals from 2 to 19, and *ste* to cardinals from 20 upwards. The following are the only variations: *der erste* ('the first'); *der dritte* ('the third'); *der siebte* ('the seventh'); *der achte* ('the eighth'). Ordinals take the usual adjectival endings: *am ersten Tag . . . am zweiten Tag* − 9.1.1; *als dritte Möglichkeit* − 8.1.2. When making a list of items, two possibilities exist, as shown in text 8.1.2: *zum zweiten . . . viertens*. Note also in 8.1.2: *daß Ungelernte . . . als erste entlassen werden* = 'that unqualified people are sacked first'. The same construction is found in text 3.1.3: *als erstes eroberten (sie) die Schwimmhalle* = 'the first thing they did . . .'.

9.4 Fractions

(a) *Hälfte* means 'half' when used as a noun. Linked to another numeral the form is: *eineinhalb* (1½); *zweieinhalb* (2½); etc. Another possibility for 1½ is *anderthalb*.
(b) The other fractions are formed by adding *l* to the final *te* of the ordinals. They are all neuter nouns: *ein Achtel* (1/8) *Liter Kaffee . . . ein Viertel* (¼) *Teelöffel Nelkenpfeffer* − 5.1.2. Fractions may form compounds with following nouns in certain cases: *eine Viertelstunde; ein Viertelpfund; ein Dreiviertelkilo*.

9.5 Uses of *mal* and *Mal*

(a) *mal* is compounded with cardinal numerals to make 'once', 'twice', etc.; *nur einmal in der Woche* − 6.2.2, *ich bin nur zweimal umgezogen* − 1.1.3; *dreimal täglich* − 10.2.2. *einmal* may also have the sense of 'once upon a time', as in the beginning of a fairy story: *es war einmal . . .*, and in text 2.1.3: *Essen war einmal die größte Bergbaustadt*. There is also a compound *diesmal* = 'this time': *wollen wir nicht diesmal etwas kochen?* − 5.2.2. Note also the common expression *zunächst einmal* = 'first of all'. Note also *zuerst einmal* and *erstmal: jetzt haben wir erstmal Sommer* − 9.2.2 = 'summer is just beginning'.
(b) *Mal* is written as a separate word with a capital letter to mean 'time', 'occasion': *als ich das erste Mal in einer deutschen Universität war* − 11.1.2; *das erste Mal bin ich . . . umgezogen* − 1.1.3.
(c) Note that *nicht einmal* or *nicht mal* mean 'not even': *ich habe nicht mal Lust zum Lesen* − 1.2.2.

9.6 Other Uses of Numerals

(a) Dates are expressed as follows: *auf der Stadtmauer von vierzehnhundertachtzig* (1480) − 3.1.2; *seit Eröffnung des Hauses neunzehnhundertachtzig* (1980) − 3.1.3. Note from this last example that the English preposition 'in' does not need to be translated with dates; note also text 14.2: *elfhundertsechzig (1160) erhielt Schwerin das Stadtrecht*. For letters see page 247.
(b) Telephone numbers are usually given in pairs of numerals: 94 32 86 = *vierundneunzig zwounddreißig sechsundachtzig* (for use of *zwo* see 9.2(b) above).

(c) Prices in Marks and Pfennigs are expressed: *12,85 DM = zwölf Mark fünfund-achtzig* or *zwölf fünfundachtzig.*

10 Particles

Particles are the little words, such as *denn, doch, mal, ja, aber*, which occur very frequently, particularly in the spoken language, and give spoken German much of its flavour. The use of such particles is difficult for foreigners, and it is not always easy to explain their force and meaning in a sentence. Listen to the dialogues on tape, and study the texts of the dialogues, so as to understand the particles when used in context. The following list of particles is arranged alphabetically, and attempts to give an explanation of the main uses, with examples taken from the texts in the book, in most cases.

(a) *aber*

1. Used to give emphasis: *das ist aber gut!* — 'that *is* good!'
2. Used with the sense of 'however': *. . . habe ich mich dann aber sehr gewundert* — 11.1.2; *lebt aber in Süddeutschland* — 11.2.2.
(b) *allerdings* can be used to agree with a statement made by another person, thus meaning 'that is certainly true'.

(c) *auch*

1. used with its main sense of 'also', 'too': *sie denken auch an den Fußball* — 11.1.1; *wir auch* — 3.1.3.
2. Used with the negative: *ich auch nicht* — 1.2.2 = 'nor me!'
3. Used with *oder* to mean 'or else': *in der Gruppe oder auch ganz alleine* — 7.2.2.

(d) *dabei*

1. 'at the same time': *die Kinder sagen frei ihre Meinung und können dabei sogar den Eltern widersprechen* — 11.1.2; *die dabei freigesetzten Schadstoffe* — 12.1.2.
2. Idiomatic use: *wir helfen Ihnen dabei* — 2.1.2; *dabei geht es unserer Umwelt immer schlechter* — 12.1.2. In these examples *dabei* has the meaning 'in this matter' or 'with this matter'.
3. Used to mean 'present', 'a member of the group': *da muß die Mama einfach dabei sein* — 7.1.4.
(e) *denn* (see Grammar Summary section 13.1(a) for use as a conjunction). For use as 'than' in a comparison see paragraph 6(c)2. Inserted in a question, *denn* makes the question less abrupt, or expresses an interest: *wo kommst du denn her? . . . wohin fährst du denn?* — 1.2.2; *was sind denn deine Eltern von Beruf?* — 1.2.2; *wo fehlt es denn?* — 10.2.2.

(f) *doch*

1. 'yet', 'nevertheless': *doch schnell versiegen die Tränen* — 7.1.4.
2. 'after all', 'all the same', 'despite everything': *nach 4 oder 5 Stunden läßt die Konzentration doch unheimlich nach* — 7.2.2; *das lange Stehen strengt doch sehr an* — 8.2.2; *du weißt doch, daß* — 9.2.2.
3. Used to intensify a statement: *Mensch, du weißt doch . . .* = 'surely you know . . .'; *das macht doch Spaß* — 5.2.2; it may also strengthen an imperative in the same way: *geh doch lieber . . .* — 9.2.2.

4. Used to contradict a negative statement or question: *gibt es in Deutschland keine richtige Familie mehr? Doch!* — 11.1.2; *kann man . . . nicht zwingen? Doch!* — 12.2.1.

(g) *eben* can be used to explain something: *dort ist es eben billiger* — 6.2.2 = 'the thing is, it's cheaper, you see?' *nun ist es eben alles teurer* — 6.2.2.

(h) *eigentlich* means 'actually': *Jugendliche verdienen zunächst eigentlich ganz gut* — 8.1.2. *eigentlich* is also used to soften the force of a question: *wie heißt er, eigentlich?* It can also be used to soften the force of a negative reply: *eigentlich nicht* — 4.2.2.

(i) *einmal, mal*

For uses of *einmal* = 'once', see Grammar Summary section 9.5. In colloquial use the shorter form *mal* is often used with the following meanings:

1. With an imperative, corresponds to 'just': *kommen Sie mal nach Ulm!* — 3.1.2; *spazieren Sie mal auf der Stadtmauer!* — 3.1.2; *schreib mir mal!* — 10.1.2.

2. In other positions 'just' will again be the nearest English translation: *mal rauskommen aus der Stadt* — 9.1.3 = 'just to get out of the town'. *mal* is frequently combined with *ja: da muß man ja auch mal lernen* — 7.2.2, and with *doch: erzähl mir doch bloß mal!* — 13.2.1.

3. Other idiomatic uses include expressions of time: *zunächst einmal* — 7.1.4 = 'first of all'; *später mal* — 8.2.2 = 'later on'; *erst mal* — 8.2.2 = 'first of all'.

In some cases there will be no obvious translation of *mal* or *einmal*, and it is best to find the most idiomatic English rendering: *da hast du wenigstens mal deine Ruhe* — 1.2.2 = 'well, at least you've got peace and quiet'; *können wir drei nicht auch einmal so etwas machen?* — 9.2.2 = 'couldn't we three do something like that as well?'

(j) *etwa*

1. 'approximately', 'about': *etwa 100 Kilometer von der Nordsee entfernt* — 4.1.3; *in etwa einer Stunde* — 2.1.3; *bis etwa ein oder zwei Uhr nachmittags* — 7.2.2.

2. After *nicht, etwa* implies 'you surely don't mean to say that . . .': *du willst doch nicht etwa zu Hause sitzen* — 9.2.2.

3. In a question, *etwa* expresses a possibility or chance: *ist dein Vater etwa ein Journalist?* — 1.2.2 = 'could your father be a journalist, by any chance?'

(k) *freilich* is used in much the same way as *allerdings*.

(l) *ja*

1. Its first meaning is 'yes', and it may also be compounded for emphasis: *jawohl!; ja, freilich!*

2. *ja* can express a wide range of feelings, including surprise and indignation: *den ganzen Tag Schule — das ist ja wie ein Arbeitstag bei den Erwachsenen* — 7.2.2; *das ist ja lustig* — 1.2.2.

3. *ja* expresses certainty, conviction: *ich habe ja auch noch andere Interessen* — 7.2.2 = 'I've certainly got other interests'; *Haushalt und Familie machen ja auch viel Arbeit* — 8.2.2.

4. *ja auch mal* can appear as a single group: *man muß ja auch mal an die Lehrer denken* — 7.2.2 = 'you've just got to think of the teachers as well'.

(m) *nämlich*

1. Used just like English 'namely'.
2. Used to mean 'you see': *ich habe nämlich noch drei Geschwister* — 1.2.2.

(n) *noch*

1. 'still', 'yet': *sind Päße noch gültig?* — 2.1.1; *noch vor zehn Jahren* — 2.1.3.
2. *noch* may have the meaning of 'more', 'further', 'as well': *dann muß ich noch weiter lernen* — 8.2.2. Note the use with numerals: *noch zwei Karten* — 9.2.1 = 'two more tickets'; *noch ein Doppelzimmer* — 3.1.4.
3. *noch nicht* = 'not yet': *Ihr Reiseweg steht noch nicht fest* — 2.1.2. *noch nie* = 'never yet': *wir waren noch nie im Harz* — 9.1.4.
4. *immer noch* is a stressed form of *noch*: *. . . ist immer noch nicht langsamer geworden* — 11.2.2 = '. . . has *still* not got any slower!'

(o) *nun*

1. Is used to mean 'now', but not with so definite a sense as *jetzt*. Compare: *ich spiele nun mal so gern Volleyball* — 9.2.2 and *jetzt haben wir erstmal Sommer* — 9.2.2.
2. *nun* can mean 'well' and 'now' in a conversational sense: *ob Sie nun mit der Bahn kommen . . .* — 3.1.2 = 'now, whether you are coming by train . . .'; *nun, ich will Dir einige Tips geben* — 5.1.3.

(p) *nur* means 'only': *nur Ihr Reiseweg steht noch nicht fest* — 2.1.2; *die wollen nur von mir bedient werden* — 8.2.2. *nur* can also be used with *nicht* to mean 'not only': *es gibt nicht nur frische Fische* — 4.1.3.

(q) *schon*

1. 'already': *um fünf Uhr kann man hier schon einkaufen* — 4.1.3.
2. 'even': *schon von weitem begrüßt Sie das weltbekannte Münster* — 3.1.2.
3. *schon* gives a persuasive note to a statement or question: *das macht schon Spaß* — 1.2.2 = 'that really is fun, you know'. *Wer will schon Kartoffelsuppe essen?* — 5.2.2 = 'who do you think wants to eat potato soup?'

(r) *so*

See Grammar Summary 8.6(r)

(s) *überhaupt* used with a negative means 'not at all': *hat überhaupt keine Freizeit* — 7.2.2 = 'has no free time at all'.
(t) *übrigens* — 'by the way': *übrigens, ich heiße Karen* — 1.2.2; *was gibt es übrigens zu trinken?* — 5.2.2.
(u) *wirklich* means 'really', 'truly': *. . . erhält man wirklich eine gute Ausbildung* — 8.2.2.

(v) *wohl*

1. *wohl* can be used as an adjective to mean 'in good health', but it is never used in front of a noun.

2. As a particle, it means 'admittedly', 'certainly': *das wohl wichtigste Argument* — 8.1.2 = 'the most important argument, admittedly, . . .'.

11 Expressing Time

11.1 Time o'clock

(a) 'What is the time?': *wieviel Uhr ist es?* or *wie spät ist es?* To ask, 'at what time . . .?': *um wieviel Uhr . . .?* — 4.2.2.

(b) *Expressing Time*

1. On the hour: *es ist ein Uhr; es ist zwei Uhr*; etc.
2. Quarter and half hours: 10.15 — *es ist Viertel nach zehn*; 3.45 — *es ist Viertel vor vier* or *es ist dreiviertel vier*. 9.30 — *es ist halb zehn*. Note that when expressing the half hour, German, unlike English, says half way towards the following hour. Here are further examples: 4.30 — *halb fünf;* 7.30 — *halb acht.*
3. Minutes to and past the hour. Note examples from text 7.1.3: *die erste Stunde beginnt um zehn Minuten nach acht* (8.10); *fünf Minuten vor neun Uhr ist die Stunde zu Ende*. In this latter example, it would be quite enough to say *fünf vor neun* or *fünf Minuten vor neun*. Here are further examples taken from *Leifs Stundenplan* in Chapter 7: *die vierte Stunde dauert von zehn Minuten vor elf bis fünfundzwanzig Minuten vor zwölf; die sechste Stunde beginnt um fünfundzwanzig vor eins und ist um zehn nach eins zu Ende.*
4. Prepositions to express exact or approximate time. As will be seen from the examples above, 'at' with a time is expressed in German by *um: um halb acht gehe ich aus dem Haus* — 7.1.3. Approximate time can be expressed by using *gegen: gegen 18 Uhr* — 9.2.2. Another possibility for approximate time is *etwa: von acht Uhr früh bis etwa ein oder zwei Uhr mittags* — 7.2.2. Note also, in the same chapter, *kurz nach sechs Uhr* = 'shortly after six o'clock'.
5. The 24 hour clock is normally used for travel timetables, theatre performances, and generally more often than in English. Thus, 9.30 a.m. is *halb zehn morgens* and 9.30 p.m. is either *halb zehn abends* or *einundzwanzig Uhr dreißig*. Note that a train leaving at 20 minutes past midnight would leave at 0.20 = *null Uhr zwanzig.*

11.2 Dates

(a) Asking the date: *der wievielte ist heute?* or *den wievielten haben wir heute?*
(b) Giving the date: 'February 1st' = *es ist der erste Februar* or *wir haben den ersten Februar* 'June 23rd' = *der dreiundzwanzigste Juni*. At the head of a letter, the date is expressed as follows: *den 11.01.1986* (text 8.1.3); *den 12. Juni* (text 9.1.4). The *den* is optional, and this date may be written *12. Juni*. Other ways of writing the date are: 12.7.86; or 12.vii.86.

(c) *'Today', 'Yesterday', 'Tomorrow'*

heute means 'today': *heute ändert sich Essen wieder* — 2.1.3; *heute ist Donnerstag* — 7.1.3. *heute* can be combined with other parts of the day to have the following meanings: *heute abend* — 4.2.2 = 'this evening'; *heute nacht* — 3.2.2 = 'tonight'; *heute morgen* — 'this morning'. In the same way, *gestern* ('yesterday') and *morgen* ('tomorrow') can be used: *gestern abend* — 'yesterday evening'.

Note particularly the different uses of *morgen: morgen früh* = 'tomorrow morning'; *morgen in der Frühe* = 'early tomorrow morning'; *morgen abend* — 9.2.2 = 'tomorrow evening'.

11.3 Expressing Duration, Definite Time, etc.

(a) Duration of time is expressed in the accusative case: *den ganzen Tag Schule* — — 7.2.2; it is possible, with such statements, to add an optional *lang* after the statement of time: *eine Woche lang* — 11.1.2; *den ganzen Tag lang* — 7.2.2. Note the expression of duration in the future: *kommen Sie mal auf ein Wochenende!* — 3.1.2 = 'come for a week-end'.
(b) Definite time is also expressed in the accusative: *jeden Tag* — 6.2.2; *nächstes Jahr* — 8.2.2. An alternative to the accusative is the use of a preposition with the dative: *in jedem Jahr* — 4.1.3; *am Sonntagmorgen* — 8.1.3. The preposition *am* is usually used with days of the week and parts of the day: *und am Abend?* — 3.1.2; *am letzten Sonntag im September* — 12.1.2.
(c) Indefinite time and repeated actions are expressed by the genitive case: *eines Tages* — 13.1.2 = 'one day'; *ich bin mittags immer total erschöpft* — 7.1.3 = 'every mid-day'; *freitags* — 9.2.2 = 'every Friday'.

(d) *'Ago', 'Before', 'After'*

1. 'ago' is expressed by *vor* followed by the dative: *vor 80 Jahren* — 2.1.3; *vor einem Monat* — 5.2.2.
2. 'before' may be a preposition (*vor*), adverb (*vorher*) or conjunction (*bevor*).
(i) As a preposition: *vor dem Krieg*: 'before the war'.
(ii) *vorher* means 'previously': *sie war vorher . . . vorbeigefahren* — 2.1.3; *vorher war es eine Siedlung* — 14.2.
(iii) *bevor* must be followed by a subordinate clause: *bevor ich mitreden kann* — 13.2.1.
3. 'after' also has three possible forms: preposition (*nach*); adverb (*nachher*); and conjunction (*nachdem*).
(i) As a preposition: *nach 45 Minuten . . . nach ungefähr einer Stunde* — 7.1.3.
(ii) *nachher* has the meaning 'afterwards'.
(iii) *nachdem* must be followed by a clause: *nachdem er sich gewaschen hat . . . .*
(e) *erst* may have two meanings (see also Grammar Summary section 9.3).
1. 'at first', 'first of all' (= *zuerst; zunächst*): *zum Glück bin ich erst in Berlin eingestiegen* — 1.2.2.
2. 'not until': *erst dann . . .* — 1.1.2; *Steffen stieg erst im September . . . in den Bob* — 9.1.2.
(f) *Use of an, in, um, zu in time phrases*
1. *an* is used with days of the week and dates: *am ersten Tag* — 9.1.1; *am Sonntagmorgen* — 4.1.3; *am Abend* — 3.1.2 (*an + dem* = *am*).
2. *in* (*in + dem* = *im*) is used with *Augenblick, Stunde, Woche*, and with months, years and seasons: *im Juni* — 8.1.3; *in wenigen Jahrzehnten* — 2.1.3; *im September vergangenen Jahres* — 9.1.2: *in der ersten Stunde* — 7.1.3; *im Winter mild, im Sommer oft mit frischen Winden* — 4.1.3; *im Dezember* — 9.2.2.
  in can be used, as in English, to refer to the coming end of a period of time: *die Schule fängt in zwei Tagen wieder an* — 10.1.2; *erst in einer Woche* — 10.1.2 = 'in a week at the earliest'.
3. *um* is used mainly to indicate time o'clock, but can also be used with a date to mean 'approximately': *um 1800* —2.1.3.
4. *zu* is used with certain festivals: *zu Weihnachten* = 'at Christmas'. *zu* is particularly used with *Zeit: zu keiner Zeit* — 9.1.3 = 'at no time'. Also common is *zur*

Zeit — 14.2, which means 'at the present time', and which may also be written as one word, *zurzeit*. Note that in text 9.1.3 there is also an example using *in: in einer Zeit, da . . . .* The difference between *in* and *zu* is usually that *in* denotes a longer period, whereas *zu* is a more specific point of time.

(g) *Translating 'for'*

1. For a period of time already completed in the past, or which will take place in the future, use the accusative as described in paragraph 11.3(a): *sie waren eine Woche lang zu Gast* — 11.1.2.
2. If the speaker is describing a period of time which began in the past, but the effects of which are still continuing, use *seit* + Present tense: *Achim lebt seit 10 Jahren in Süddeutschland* — 11.2.2 = 'Achim has been living for 10 years . . .'; *ich bin schon seit einigen Jahren mittlerer Leistungskader* — 13.2.1 = 'I have been for some years . . .'.
3. Looking forward to the future, use *für* or *auf: kommen Sie auf ein Wochenende nach Ulm* — 3.1.2. *für* is also used in the present, instead of the simple accusative described in (g)1 above: *ab und zu kommt Silka für einen Moment zu ihr gelaufen* — 7.1.4.

(h) *Omission of Preposition*

No preposition is used with *Anfang, Mitte* or *Ende: Anfang März; Mitte Januar; Ende August.*

12 The Verb

12.1 Conjugation of the Auxiliary Verbs *haben, sein, werden*

(a) *haben — 'to have'*

Indicative	Subjunctive
Present tense	
ich habe	ich habe
du hast	du habest
er/sie/es hat	er/sie/es habe
wir haben	wir haben
ihr habt	ihr habet
Sie haben	Sie haben
sie haben	sie haben
Imperfect tense	
ich hatte	ich hätte
du hattest	du hättest
er/sie/es hatte	er/sie/es hätte
wir hatten	wir hätten
ihr hattet	ihr hättet
Sie hatten	Sie hätten
sie hatten	sie hätten
Perfect tense	
ich habe gehabt (etc.)	ich habe gehabt (etc.)
Pluperfect	
ich hatte gehabt (etc.)	ich hätte gehabt (etc.)

Future

ich werde haben	ich werde haben
du wirst haben	du werdest haben
er/sie/es wird haben	er/sie/es werde haben
wir werden haben	wir werden haben
ihr werdet haben	ihr werdet haben
Sie werden haben	Sie werden haben
sie werden haben	sie werden haben

Future Perfect

ich werde gehabt haben (etc.) ich werde gehabt haben (etc.)

Conditional   *Conditional Perfect*

ich würde haben   ich würde gehabt haben OR ich hätte gehabt

du würdest haben   *Imperative*

er/sie/es würde haben   hab(e)! haben Sie! habt!

wir würden haben   *Participles*

ihr würdet haben   Past: gehabt

Sie würden haben   Present: habend

sie würden haben

(b) *sein* — 'to be'   *werden* — 'to become'

Indicative	*Subjunctive*	*Indicative*	*Subjunctive*
	Present		*Present*
ich bin	ich sei	ich werde	ich werde
du bist	du sei(e)st	du wirst	du werdest
er ist	er sei	er wird	er werde
wir sind	wir seien	wir werden	wir werden
ihr seid	ihr seiet	ihr werdet	ihr werdet
Sie sind	Sie seien	Sie werden	Sie werden
sie sind	sie seien	sie werden	sie werden
	Imperfect		*Imperfect*
ich war	ich wäre	ich wurde	ich würde
du warst	du wär(e)st	du wurdest	du würdest
er war	er wäre	er wurde	er würde
wir waren	wir wären	wir wurden	wir würden
ihr wart	ihr wär(e)t	ihr wurdet	ihr würdet
Sie waren	Sie wären	Sie wurden	Sie würden
sie waren	sie wären	sie wurden	sie würden
	Perfect		*Perfect*
ich bin gewesen	ich sei gewesen	ich bin geworden	ich sei geworden
	Pluperfect		*Pluperfect*
ich war gewesen	ich wäre gewesen	ich war geworden	ich wäre geworden
	Future		*Future*
ich werde sein	ich werde sein	ich werde werden	ich werde werden

Future Perfect   *Future Perfect*

ich werde gewesen sein (etc.)   ich werde geworden sein (etc.)

Conditional   *Conditional*

ich würde sein   ich würde werden

Conditional Perfect   *Conditional Perfect*

ich würde gewesen sein   ich würde geworden sein

Imperative   *Imperative*

sei! seien Sie! seid!   werde! werden Sie! werdet!

Participles   *Participles*

Present: seiend (rarely used)   werdend

Past: gewesen   geworden

12.2 Conjugation of Weak Verbs

Weak verbs are those which form the Imperfect by adding *te* to the stem, and have a past participle ending in *-t* — e.g.: *holen, holte, geholt.*

holen — *'to fetch'*

	Indicative	Subjunctive	Passive
Present	ich hole	ich hole	ich werde geholt
	du holst	du holest	du wirst geholt
	er holt	er hole	er wird geholt
	wir holen	wir holen	wir werden geholt
	ihr holt	ihr holet	ihr werdet geholt
	Sie holen	Sie holen	Sie werden geholt
	sie holen	sie holen	sie werden geholt
Imperfect	ich holte	ich holte	ich wurde geholt
	du holtest	du holtest	du wurdest geholt
	er holte	er holte	er wurde geholt
	wir holten	wir holten	wir wurden geholt
	ihr holtet	ihr holtet	ihr wurdet geholt
	Sie holten	Sie holten	Sie wurden geholt
	sie holten	sie holten	sie wurden geholt
Perfect	ich habe geholt (etc.)	ich habe geholt	ich bin geholt worden
Pluperfect	ich hatte geholt (etc.)	ich hätte geholt	ich war geholt worden
Future	ich werde holen	ich werde holen	ich werde geholt werden
Future Perfect	ich werde geholt haben	ich werde geholt haben	ich werde geholt worden sein
Conditional	ich würde holen		ich würde geholt werden
Conditional Perfect	ich würde geholt haben		ich würde geholt worden sein
Imperative	hol(e)!		
	holt!		
	holen Sie!		
Participles	Present: holend		
	Past: geholt		

12.3 Conjugation of Strong Verbs

Strong verbs change the vowel of the stem in the Imperfect and sometimes also in the past participle.

tragen — *'to carry'*

Present Indicative	Subjunctive
ich trage	ich trage
du trägst	du tragest
er trägt	er trage
wir tragen	wir tragen
ihr tragt	ihr traget
Sie tragen	Sie tragen
sie tragen	sie tragen

For compound tenses and passive voice, compare with the verbs already given in 12.1 and 12.2 – e.g. *ich habe getragen, ich werde tragen*, etc.

Imperative	*Participles*
trag(e)!	Present: tragend
tragt!	Past: getragen
tragen Sie!	

12.4 Conjugation of Mixed Verbs

A small number of verbs have the weak endings *-te* for the Imperfect and *-t* for the past participle, but change the vowel in the Imperfect like a stong verb – for example: *brennen* – 'to burn'; Imperfect *brannte*; past participle *gebrannt*.

12.5 Notes on Verb Forms

(a) *Stem Ends in a Sibilant*
In this case the second person singular of the Present Tense adds only *-t: schließen, du schließt: lesen, du liest; waschen, du wäscht.*

(b) *Stem Ends in d or t*

In this case the stem is always followed by *e* inserted before the ending: *reden, du redest, er redet, wir haben geredet.*

(c) *Vowel Changes in Present Tense of Strong Verbs*

In the second and third persons singular of the Present Indicative, strong verbs show the following vowel changes:
long *e* changes to *ie: lesen, ich lese, du liest, er liest.*
short *e* changes to *i: helfen, ich helfe, du hilfst, er hilft.*
    a changes to *ä: waschen, ich wasche, du wäscht, er wäscht.*
    au changes to *äu: laufen, ich laufe, du läufst, er läuft.*
    o changes to *ö: stoßen, ich stoße, du stößt, er stößt.*
Note the following common exceptions to the above rules: *gehen, du gehst, er geht; kommen, du kommst, er kommt; stehen, du stehst, er steht.*

(d) *Forms of the Imperative*

1. The second person singular (*du*) adds *e* to the stem to form the Imperative, but this *e* is optional, and is often dropped in both written and spoken German: *frag mich* – 9.2.2; *geh doch* – 9.2.2. The *e* is never added to the stem of strong verbs which change *e* of the stem to *ie* or *i: nehmen, nimm!; sprechen, sprich!* Sometimes *du* is included for emphasis: *mach du mal einen Vorschlag* – 5.2.2. In the great majority of cases, however, the pronoun is not used in the Imperative.
2. The second person polite form (*Sie*) has the same form as the Present tense, but the verb and pronoun are reversed: *wählen Sie . . . denken Sie daran* – 2.1.2. The pronoun *Sie* is *always* included.
3. The second person plural familiar form (*ihr*) has the same form of the verb as the Present tense, with the pronoun omitted: *kommt!; lest!*
4. The infinitive may be used with the force of an Imperative: *gleich kommen* – 6.1.1; *in die Schüssel geben* – 5.1.2. This form is particularly common in recipes.
5. The inverted form of the first person plural is a form of the Imperative equivalent to English 'let us . . .'; *sagen wir zehn* – 5.2.2 = 'let's say ten'; *gehen wir ins Café* – 4.2.2 = 'let's go into the café'.

(e) *Verbs with no ge- in the Past Participle*

1. Verbs with inseparable prefixes: *besuchen, besucht; benutzen, benutzt.*
2. Foreign borrowings ending in *ieren: arrangieren, arrangiert.*

12.6 Use of the Auxiliaries *haben* and *sein*

(a) The following verbs are conjugated with *haben* when they form the Perfect, Pluperfect and other compound tenses:
1. All verbs taking a direct object (transitive verbs): *Sie haben Großbritannien ausgewählt* — 2.1.2; *ich habe viele deutsche Freunde kennengelernt* — 11.1.2.
2. All reflexive verbs: *ich habe mich dann aber sehr gewundert* — 11.1.2.
3. Most impersonal verbs: *es hat geregnet.*
4. Intransitive verbs not listed in (b) below: *ich habe schon selbst gearbeitet* — 1.2.2; *meine Eltern und ich haben in einer Wohnung gelebt* — 1.1.2.
(b) A number of verbs are conjugated with *sein* in compound tenses:
1. verbs of motion: *ich bin erst in Berlin eingestiegen* — 1.2.2; *tagsüber sind wir viel gewandert und gerodelt* — 10.1.2.
2. Plus the following group of verbs:
begegnen — 'to meet'; *gelingen* — 'to succeed'; *bleiben* — 'to remain'; *sein* — 'to be'.
　　Strong verbs taking *sein* as an auxiliary are given in the list of strong verbs which follows.

12.7 Principal Parts of Strong Verbs

Infinitive	3rd sing. Present	Imperfect	Past Participle	Meaning
backen	bäckt	backte	gebacken	to bake
befehlen	befiehlt	befahl	befohlen	to command
beginnen	beginnt	begann	begonnen	to begin
beißen	beißt	biß	gebissen	to bite
biegen	biegt	bog	gebogen	to bend
			ist gebogen	to turn
bieten	bietet	bot	geboten	to offer
binden	bindet	band	gebunden	to tie
bitten	bittet	bat	gebeten	to ask
bleiben	bleibt	blieb	ist geblieben	to stay
braten	brät	briet	gebraten	to roast; to fry
brechen	bricht	brach	gebrochen	to break
brennen	brennt	brannte	gebrannt	to burn
bringen	bringt	brachte	gebracht	to bring
denken	denkt	dachte	gedacht	to think
dürfen	darf	durfte	gedurft	to be allowed to
essen	ißt	aß	gegessen	to eat
fahren	fährt	fuhr	ist gefahren	to travel
fallen	fällt	fiel	ist gefallen	to fall
fangen	fängt	fing	gefangen	to catch
finden	findet	fand	gefunden	to find
fliegen	fliegt	flog	ist geflogen	to fly
fliehen	flieht	floh	ist geflohen	to flee
fließen	fließt	floß	ist geflossen	to flow
frieren	friert	fror	hat gefroren	to freeze; to be cold
			ist gefroren	to freeze over

geben	gibt	gab	gegeben	to give
gehen	geht	ging	ist gegangen	to go
gelingen	gelingt	gelang	ist gelungen	to succeed
genießen	genießt	genoß	genossen	to enjoy
geschehen	geschieht	geschah	ist geschehen	to happen
gewinnen	gewinnt	gewann	gewonnen	to win
gießen	gießt	goß	gegossen	to pour
gleichen	gleicht	glich	geglichen	to resemble; to be like
gleiten	gleitet	glitt	ist geglitten	to slide
greifen	greift	griff	gegriffen	to seize
haben	hat	hatte	gehabt	to have
halten	hält	hielt	gehalten	to hold; to stop
heben	hebt	hob	gehoben	to raise
heißen	heißt	hieß	geheißen	to be called; to mean
helfen	hilft	half	geholfen	to help
kennen	kennt	kannte	gekannt	to know
klingen	klingt	klang	geklungen	to sound
kommen	kommt	kam	ist gekommen	to come
können	kann	konnte	gekonnt	to be able
kriechen	kriecht	kroch	ist gekrochen	to crawl; to creep
laden	lädt	lud	geladen	to load
lassen	läßt	ließ	gelassen	to let; to leave
laufen	läuft	lief	ist gelaufen	to run
leiden	leidet	litt	gelitten	to suffer
leihen	leiht	lieh	geliehen	to lend
lesen	liest	las	gelesen	to read
liegen	liegt	lag	gelegen	to lie
meiden	meidet	mied	gemieden	to avoid
messen	mißt	maß	gemessen	to measure
mögen	mag	mochte	gemocht	to like
müssen	muß	mußte	gemußt	to have to
nehmen	nimmt	nahm	genommen	to take
nennen	nennt	nannte	genannt	to name
pfeifen	pfeift	pfiff	gepfiffen	to whistle
raten	rät	riet	geraten	to advise; to guess
reiben	reibt	rieb	gerieben	to rub
reißen	reißt	riß	gerissen	to tear
reiten	reitet	ritt	ist geritten	to ride
rennen	rennt	rannte	ist gerannt	to run
riechen	riecht	roch	gerochen	to smell
ringen	ringt	rang	gerungen	to wrestle
rufen	ruft	rief	gerufen	to call
scheiden	scheidet	schied	geschieden	to separate
scheinen	scheint	schien	geschienen	to shine; to seem
schieben	schiebt	schob	geschoben	to push
schießen	schießt	schoß	geschossen	to shoot
schlafen	schläft	schlief	geschlafen	to sleep
schlagen	schlägt	schlug	geschlagen	to hit; to strike
schließen	schließt	schloß	geschlossen	to close
schneiden	schneidet	schnitt	geschnitten	to cut
schreiben	schreibt	schrieb	geschrieben	to write
schreien	schreit	schrie	geschrien	to shout
schreiten	schreitet	schritt	ist geschritten	to stride
schweigen	schweigt	schwieg	geschwiegen	to be silent

schwimmen	schwimmt	schwamm	ist geschwommen	to swim
sehen	sieht	sah	gesehen	to see
sein	ist	war	ist gewesen	to be
senden	sendet	sandte	gesandt	to send
singen	singt	sang	gesungen	to sing
sinken	sinkt	sank	ist gesunken	to sink
sitzen	sitzt	saß	gesessen	to sit
sollen	soll	sollte	gesollt	to be obliged to
sprechen	spricht	sprach	gesprochen	to speak
springen	springt	sprang	ist gesprungen	to jump
stehen	steht	stand	gestanden	to stand
steigen	steigt	stieg	ist gestiegen	to climb
sterben	stirbt	starb	ist gestorben	to die
tragen	trägt	trug	getragen	to carry
treffen	trifft	traf	getroffen	to meet
treiben	treibt	trieb	getrieben	to pursue an activity
treten	tritt	trat	ist getreten	to step
trinken	trinkt	trank	getrunken	to drink
tun	tut	tat	getan	to do
vergessen	vergißt	vergaß	vergessen	to forget
verlieren	verliert	verlor	verloren	to lose
wachsen	wächst	wuchs	ist gewachsen	to grow
waschen	wäscht	wusch	gewaschen	to wash
weisen	weist	wies	gewiesen	to point
werden	wird	wurde	ist geworden	to become
werfen	wirft	warf	geworfen	to throw
wissen	weiß	wußte	gewußt	to know
wollen	will	wollte	gewollt	to want
ziehen	zieht	zog	gezogen	to pull
zwingen	zwingt	zwang	gezwungen	to force

12.8 Use of Tenses

(a) *Present Tense*

1. There is no equivalent in German to the continuous form of the Present tense. Therefore, *ich stehe* may be translated 'I stand' or 'I am standing'. Note, for example, text 7.1.1: *ich esse . . . ich gehe . . . Am Bus stehen viele Leute*. In the context of the passage, this would be translated: 'I eat . . . I go . . . . Many people are standing at the bus-stop'.
2. The Present tense is used with *seit* where English has Perfect tense continuous (see Grammar Summary section 11.3(g)2).
3. The Historic Present can be used to add a little drama to a narrative which is really about events in the past: *es ist Silkas erster Tag . . . (sie) fühlt sich hier nicht fremd* — 7.1.4.
4. The Present tense is widely used instead of the Future tense: *nächstes Jahr habe ich meine erste Prüfung; danach muß ich noch weiter lernen . . . und dann kommt die Hauptprüfung* — 8.2.2; *Ostern ist bald hier* — 10.1.2.

(b) *Future Tense*

As just stated above, the Future may often be replaced by the Present. When used, the Future is formed by using the auxiliary verb *werden* + infinitive, which goes to the end of the clause: *sie werden bald ihre Schule verlassen* — 8.1.2; *ich werde arbeiten* — 9.2.2; *vielleicht werde ich an den Wochenenden zelten* — 9.2.2.

(c) *Imperfect Tense*

1. The Imperfect is used with *seit* to translate a sentence such as: 'she had been working there for three years' = *sie arbeitete seit drei Jahren dort*.
2. The Imperfect is the standard past tense of German narrative prose, equivalent to the English Past Definite. See the examples in text 2.1.3: *unsere Fahrt begann . . . wir parkten . . . oben wartete die Linie 79 . . . laut und schwankend fuhr die Bahn . . .* , etc. This is exactly equivalent to: 'our journey began . . . we parked . . . the tram travelled . . .', etc.
3. The Imperfect is used to describe a habitual or repeated action in the past, equivalent to 'used to' in English: *ich war in einer Ganztagsschule . . . da hatte man nicht so viel Freiheit* — 7.2.2 = 'I used to be . . . we used to have . . .'.

(d) *Perfect Tense*

1. The Perfect is the standard past tense of German conversation and of letter-writing. This means that, in speech, the Perfect expresses the English Past Definite, for which the Imperfect is used in written narrative: *habe ich mich dann aber sehr gewundert* — 11.1.2 = 'then I was really astonished'; *zum Glück bin ich erst in Berlin eingestiegen* — 1.2.2 = 'luckily, I did not get in until Berlin'.
2. The Perfect is also used, in both speech and writing, to record events which took place in the past, but whose influence is still felt in the Present. This is the same usage as the English Perfect tense: *ich habe viele Deutsche kennengelernt* — 11.1.2 = 'I have got to know a lot of Germans'; *es ist mit seiner Mutter gekommen* — 7.1.4 = 'it [the child] has come with its mother'; *das habe ich mir immer gewünscht* — 1.2.2 = 'that is what I have always wanted'. English makes a clear distinction between Past Definite and Perfect, which is not at all clear in German conversational usage. For example, the statement in text 11.1.2: *in Brilon habe ich eine richtige deutsche Familie kennengelernt* could mean either 'I got to know a real German family' [completed action in the past] or 'I have got to know a real German family' [and I am still in touch with them].

(e) *Passive Voice*

The Passive is formed in English by the auxiliary verb 'to be' + past participle. The active sentence 'my father reads the book' can be expressed in the Passive as 'the book is read by my father'. The tenses of the Passive are then formed by varying the tenses of the auxiliary verb, 'has been read', 'will be read', etc.
1. The Passive is formed in German by the auxiliary *werden* + past participle at the end of the clause (see Grammar Summary section 12.2 for full conjugation). As in English, it is the auxiliary verb which then changes to show changes of tense. The 'agent', expressed with 'by' in English ('by my father'), is usually rendered by *von* (see paragraph (v), below). Note the following examples of the various tenses:
(i) Present Passive: *jährlich werden vierzig Millionen Tonnen Kraftstoff durch unsere Motoren gepumpt und verbrannt* — 12.1.2 = '. . . are pumped out and burned up by our engines'; *unser U-Bahn und Busnetz wird täglich von Millionen Londonern benutzt* — 2.1.2 = '. . . is used daily by millions of Londoners'; *sie werden . . . genannt* — 9.1.1 = 'they are called . . .'.
(ii) Imperfect Passive: the Imperfect of the last example in the previous paragraph would be: *sie wurden . . . genannt* = 'they were called'.

(iii) Perfect Passive: In this construction the past participle of *werden* loses its initial *ge*: *die schöne Kinderkrippe ist im Dezember eröffnet worden* — 7.1.4 = 'the attractive crèche has been opened/was opened in December'; *fremdsprachliche Einflüsse sind oft kommentiert worden* — 13.1.2. It may be helpful to look at this sentence more closely, as Passive constructions sometimes give difficulty:

Fremdsprachliche	Einflüsse	sind	oft	kommentiert	worden
Foreign language	influences	have	often	commented upon	been

Therefore, each element of the English sentence ('have been commented upon') is found in the German: *sind . . . kommentiert worden*. The past participle + *worden* come together at the end of the sentence: *. . . eröffnet worden; . . . kommentiert worden*. Thus, in a subordinate clause only one word actually changes position, the auxiliary *ist* or *sind: . . . die . . . festgelegt worden sind*.

(iv) The Passive infinitive (*gesehen werden*) can be used like the Indicative infinitive: *um Leute zu sehen, und von Leuten gesehen zu werden* — 4.1.2 = 'to see people and to be seen by people'.

(v) As stated earlier, the agent of the Passive voice is usually *von*. There are occasions, however, when *durch* is used. The difference is that *von* usually indicates a more direct agent. Compare two examples in text 12.2.1: *. . . werden vom Wind getragen . . . durch den Regen ausgelöst*. See also Grammar Summary sections 14.2(b) and 14.1(d).

2. *The Passive of State*. It has been explained that the usual form of the Passive in German is *werden* + past participle. There is also a Passive formed with *sein* + past participle, which describes a state, rather than an action: *noch vor zehn Jahren war der Fluß sehr verschmutzt* — 2.1.3; *die Vorstellung ist ausverkauft* — 9.2.2.

3. The Passive may be avoided in German, either by using an active construction: (*mein Vater liest das Buch*, instead of *das Buch wird von meinem Vater gelesen*), or by using *man*, meaning 'one': *man lernt an einem Tag mehr als hier* — 7.2.2 could be translated either 'one learns more in a day than here' or 'more is learned in a day than here'. Note also: *so kann man Millionen von Bundesbürgern antreffen* — 9.1.3 = 'millions of federal citizens can be encountered'.

(f) *Pluperfect tense*

The Pluperfect in English is formed by 'had' + past participle. In German the Imperfect of the auxiliary *sein* or *haben* is used: *sie war vorher . . . vorbeigefahren* — 2.1.3 = 'it had previously travelled past . . .'; *in der zweiten Woche hatte ich mir dann eine herrliche Erkältung zugelegt* — 10.1.2; *vorher war es eine Siedlung . . . gewesen* — 14.2.

12.9 Separable and Inseparable Prefixes

(a) The inseparable prefixes are *be-, emp-, ent-, er-, ge-, miß-, wider-, ver-, zer-*. None of these prefixes exist in the language separately from the verbs to which they are joined. The inseparable prefixes are always unstressed. The past participles of inseparable verbs do not begin *ge*. Examples from the texts of inseparable verbs in various tenses are: *Autos zerschneiden die Landschaft* — 12.1.2; *jährlich werden vierzig Millionen Tonnen Kraftstoff . . . verbrannt* — 12.1.2; *ich habe Ihre Adresse aus einem Hotelverzeichnis entnommen* — 3.1.4; *hast du das vergessen?* — 9.2.2.

(b) The following prefixes may be separable or inseparable, and differ in stress accordingly: *über-, unter-, durch-, voll-, wieder-, hinter*. Note the difference in stress between **über**setzen (separable) and über**setzen**. As a general rule, it can be said that these prefixes are separable when the verb retains its original, physical meaning – for example, **über**setzen = to carry someone over' – and inseparable when the verb has a more figurative meaning: über**setzen** = 'to translate'. Note the following examples from the texts: *in einem Großkaufhaus werden die meisten . . . übernommen* – 8.2.2; *nicht so überfüllt* – 1.2.2; *meine Freunde und ich möchten . . . übernachten* – 9.1.4.

(c) Separable prefixes are any not mentioned in (a) and (b) above. Most separable prefixes exist as words in their own right, usually prepositions such as *auf, aus, mit*, etc. The separable prefix always carries the main stress of the verb. Note the following uses of separable verbs:

1. In a main clause the prefix comes at the end of the clause: *mittags fängt das Leben an* – 7.1.3; *es fing alles ganz harmlos an* – 10.1.2.

2. In a subordinate clause, where the verb moves to the end of the clause, the verb joins up with the separable prefix: *. . . wie ihr Töchterchen sich hier zurechtfindet* – 7.1.4; *so mußte ich zum Arzt gehen, der eine Mittelohrentzündung feststellte* – 10.1.2.

3. When used in the past participle form, *ge* is inserted between the prefix and the participle: *Sie haben Großbritannien ausgewählt* – 2.1.2; *wie gut sind die Spaziergänge ausgezeichnet?* – 3.1.4; *bis ich von zu Hause fortgezogen bin* – 1.1.3.

4. Where the infinitive is used with *zu*, the usage is as follows: *ohne umzusteigen* – 2.1.2; *. . . daß Badesachen mitzubringen sind* – 3.1.3.

5. Where the infinitive is not used with *zu* (for example, after a Modal verb), the simple infinitive form is used: *könnten Sie mir bitte den Preis mitteilen?* – 3.1.4; *der Teig muß leicht vom Löffel abreißen* – 5.1.2.

6. Note the prefixes *hin* and *her*, either used alone or in conjunction with a preposition to indicate the direction of movement – for example, *hineinsteigen* (movement away from the speaker), *hereinkommen* (movement towards the speaker).

12.10 Impersonal Verbs and Expressions

Impersonal expressions include the following:
(a) Phrases about the weather: *es regnete* – 2.1.3.
(b) Miscellaneous expressions – for example, the use of *es geht: und so ging es weiter* – 2.1.3; *wie geht's?* – 11.2.2; *wie geht es dann weiter?* – 8.2.2; note also: *es tut mir leid* – 10.1.2 = 'I am sorry'; *es hat mich sehr gefreut, zu hören . . .* – 5.1.3; = 'I was very pleased to hear'. Further examples are the use of *werden* impersonally: *hinter Lohausen . . . wurde es leiser . . . wieder wurde es grau* – 2.1.3; *es wird alles zu teuer* – 5.2.2. Finally, in this section, note *es fehlt: wo fehlt es denn?* – 10.2.2 = 'what's the problem, then?'; *es fehlen nur noch Kleinigkeiten* – 13.2.1 = 'only bits and pieces are still missing'.
(c) There are many examples of expressions with the impersonal *es*, where this pronoun anticipates a following clause which is the real subject of the sentence. For example: *für mich ist es wichtig, solche Träume zu haben* – 8.2.2. Here *es* really stands for the infinitive phrase *solche Träume zu haben. Es ist wichtig, . . .* is an example which can stand for other, similar, expressions: *es fing alles ganz harmlos an* – 10.1.2; *es fiel uns also leicht, vierzehn Tage . . . zu verbringen* – 4.1.2. *es* may also anticipate *alles* in the same way: *es hat alles riesig Spaß gemacht* – 10.1.2 = 'everything was fantastic fun'. Finally, in this section, *es* may stand for a following noun, which it precedes for the sake of emphasis: *es ist vor allem der Wortschatz, der betroffen ist* – 13.1.2.

(d) *'there is'*

German has two possible ways of translating 'there is':
1. *es gibt* + accusative is used to make a general statement *es gibt nicht nur frische Fische . . . es gibt auch Schallplatten* — 4.1.3; *es gibt Linienverbindungen zu 1100 Häfen* — 4.1.3; *es gibt noch andere Gründe* — 8.1.2. *es gibt* is invariable. Note the question form: *gibt es Passagierdampfer?* Note also the Imperfect tense: *in unserem Stadtviertel gab es sehr viele Einfamilienhäuser* — 1.1.2.
2. *es ist* or *es sind* usually describe a situation in more specific terms than the general *es gibt. zehn Kilometer waren es bis nach Gelsenkirchen* — 2.1.3.
(e) The Passive voice may occur in impersonal expressions — for example: *es wird behauptet* — 14.2; *nach der ersten Stunde wird gemeinsam gesprochen* — 7.1.4. In this latter example *es* has been omitted, but the basic construction is: *es wird gesprochen* = 'there is some talking'.
(f) As in the example just mentioned, *es* may be omitted with some expressions: *mir war auch ein bißchen übel* — 10.1.2; *mir scheint . . .* — 10.2.2.
(g) *es scheint* = 'it seems' is one of the commonest impersonal expressions: *es scheint ihnen keine Zeit mehr zu bleiben* — 12.2.1.

12.11 Modal Verbs

(a) *Forms*

There are six Modal auxiliary verbs, used mainly together with the infinitive of another verb. The forms of the Modals are as follows:

Infinitive	Present tense	Meaning of 1st person
können	ich kann, du kannst, er kann wir können, ihr könnt, Sie können sie können	I can; I am able
dürfen	ich darf, du darfst, er darf wir dürfen	I may; I am allowed to
mögen	ich mag, du magst, er mag wir mögen	I like
müssen	ich muß, du mußt, er muß wir müssen	I must; I have to
sollen	ich soll, du sollst, er soll wir sollen	I am to
wollen	ich will, du willst, er will wir wollen	I want to

(b) *Uses*

Modal verbs are almost always used with a dependent infinitive, without *zu*. Note the various examples which follow of the Modal verbs in various tenses.
1. *können*
(i) Present tense: *die Kinder können sogar den Eltern widersprechen* — 11.1.2 = 'the children can even contradict their parents'. In subordinate clauses the Modal moves to the end of the clause, coming after the dependent infinitive: *damit die Räder rollen können* — 12.1.2; *. . . in dem Hotelgäste ihr Menü zusammenstellen können* — 3.1.4.
(ii) Imperfect: *Sonne und Schnee konnten noch so sehr locken* — 3.1.3 = 'sun and snow could entice as much as they liked'; *ich konnte sogar eine Woche lang nicht zur Schule gehen* — 10.1.2.

(iii) Perfect tense: when used in the Perfect tense, Modal verbs have the infinitive form instead of the past participle, thus giving the effect of two infinitives coming together: *ich habe heute nicht kommen können.*

(iv) Future: *du wirst wahrscheinlich auch eine Zeitlang . . . schlecht hören können* — 10.2.2. Here, again, two infinitives come together at the end of the sentence, but the auxiliary verb is *werden.*

(v) Imperfect Subjunctive: The form *könnte(n)* is frequently used with the sense of 'could' or 'would be able to': *zum zweiten könnten sie eine Ausbildung . . . beginnen* — 8.1.2 = 'secondly, they could [might] begin some training'; *wir könnten eine Riesenpizza backen* — 5.2.2. This form of the verb is also used to express a polite request: *wir wären Ihnen sehr dankbar, wenn Sie uns Prospekte schicken könnten* — 9.1.4; *könnten Sie mir bitte den Preis mitteilen?* — 3.1.4 = 'could you please let me know the price?'

2. *dürfen*

(i) Present tense: *die deutschen Schüler dürfen frei ihre Meinung sagen* — 11.1.2 = 'German pupils may / are allowed to speak their opinions freely'; *darf ich mitkommen?* — 9.2.2 = 'may I come?' Note that when *dürfen* is used in the negative, it means 'must not': *der Zuckerguß darf nicht zu dünn werden* — 5.1.2 = '. . . must not become too thin.' See also the notes on *müssen.*

(ii) The use of the other tenses is as described for *können.*

3. *mögen*

(i) In the Present tense *ich mag* expresses liking: *ich mag reiten* = 'I like riding'.

(ii) A very common use of *mögen* is in the Imperfect Subjunctive form *möchte(n)*, with the meaning of 'would like': *sie möchten nicht mit der neuesten Mode imponieren* — 4.1.2 = 'they would not like to impress with the latest fashion'. *möchte* may also be used in conjunction with *gern: meine Freunde und ich möchten gern . . . übernachten* — 9.1.4.

4. *müssen*

(i) Present tense: *man muß ja auch mal an die Lehrer denken* — 7.2.2.

(ii) Imperfect: here, the English translation is 'had to': *so mußte ich zum Arzt gehen* — 10.1.2; *ich mußte alle ständig bitten, lauter zu sprechen* — 10.1.2.

Note that with *müssen*, and with the other Modals, the infinitive is sometimes understood, but not expressed: *heute abend muß sie zum Elternaktiv* — 13.2.1 = *. . . muß sie . . . gehen.*

5. *sollen* may be translated 'am to', 'should'. Like *müssen*, it conveys an obligation, and in the Present tense it is not always easy to make a distinction between *sollen* and *müssen*. The distinction is really between 'should' and 'must'. Note the following examples:

(i) Present tense: *jedes Kind soll sich bei uns wohlfühlen* — 7.1.4 = 'every child should feel happy here'; *soll ich erst zu dir kommen?* — 4.2.2; *wo soll ich da anfangen?* — 13.2.1.

(ii) In the Imperfect tense, *sollen* has the meaning 'ought to': *das sollten Sie frühzeitig prüfen* — 2.1.1 = 'you ought to check that in good time'.

6. *wollen*

(i) Present tense: *auf jeden Fall will ich früh selbständig werden, will meine eigene Wohnung haben* — 8.2.2 = 'in any case, I want to be independent early, and I want to have my own flat'. Other examples: *willst du nicht lieber verreisen?* — 9.2.2; *das will ich auf keinen Fall werden* — 1.2.2; *Leute, die neue Wege gehen wollen* — 13.1.1.

(ii) Imperfect: *sie wollten auf der längsten Straßenbahn der Welt fahren* — 2.1.3 = 'they wanted to travel . . .'.

(iii) Note that the Present of *wollen* can be used to make a proposal: *wollen wir nicht eine Party geben?* — 5.2.2. Note also that the infinitive can be omitted with *wollen: . . . wenn ich zum Café will* — 4.2.2.

12.12 Use of the Infinitive

(a) Verbal noun: *Schwimmen wird . . . großgeschrieben* — 3.1.3 = 'swimming is very important'; *das lange Stehen im Geschäft* — 8.2.2 = 'standing for a long time in the shop'. The verbal noun is the infinitive used with neuter gender and a capital letter as a noun. It may often be translated by the English gerundive ending in '–ing'. For example: *ich habe nicht mal Lust zum Lesen* — 1.2.2 = 'I don't even want to do any reading'.

(b) *Infinitive Used without zu*

The infinitive is used as directly dependent on another verb, and without an intervening *zu*, in the following cases:

1. After Modal verbs, as described already in paragraph 12.11(b), above.
2. After the verbs of perception, *sehen, hören, fühlen: ich sehe ihn kommen; ich höre sie singen.*
3. After *lassen*, meaning 'to let', 'to allow' and also 'to have something done'. Note the following examples: *abkühlen lassen* — 5.1.2 = 'allow to cool'; *laß mal sehen . . . laß mich mal deine Temperatur messen* — 10.2.2. In the Perfect tense *lassen* forms a construction like a Modal verb: *er hat ein Haus bauen lassen* = 'he had a house built'; *sie hat sich die Haare schneiden lassen* = 'she had her hair cut'.
4. After *gehen: Jugendliche, die möglichst bald arbeiten gehen* — 8.1.2.

(c) The Infinitive is used with *zu* in most cases not mentioned in the previous paragraph.

1. After verbs other than those listed above: *ich versuche . . . immer nett zu sein* — 8.2.2; *sie lernen früh, über ihr eigenes Leben zu entscheiden* — 11.1.2; *manchmal habe ich mir gewünscht, ein Einzelkind zu sein* — 1.2.2.
2. Where the infinitive is the real subject, after an introductory *es* (see paragraph 12.10(c) for further explanations): *es fiel uns also leicht, vierzehn Tage . . . zu verbringen* — 4.1.2.
3. Where the infinitive phrase is the complement of *sein: mein Traum für die Zukunft wäre, . . . eine Boutique aufzumachen* — 8.2.2. This usage is comparable with English: 'it would be my dream to open . . .'.
4. After *um* (*um . . . zu* = 'in order to') and *ohne* (*ohne . . . zu* = 'without').
(i) *ich brauche das Geld, um mir ein Moped zu kaufen* — 9.2.2.
(ii) *ohne sich beim Lehrer zu verabschieden* — 11.1.2 — 'without taking leave of the teacher'. Note that the German construction *ohne . . . zu* + infinitive is equivalent to English 'without + –ing'.
5. Note the use of *sein + zu* + infinitive in the following construction: *sie sind schnell zu erreichen* — 14.2 = 'they may be reached quickly'.

(d) See Grammar Summary section 12.5(d) for the use of the infinitive to give instructions in formal announcements, recipes, etc.: *erwärmen . . . abkühlen lassen* — 5.1.2.

12.13 Participles

(a) *The present participle* is formed by adding *d* to the infinitive: *umweltbelastend* — 12.1.2; *wohltuend* — 3.1.3; *schwankend* — 2.1.3. The main use of the present participle in German, as in the three examples just given, is as an adjective. The verbal use of the English present participle ending '–ing' is unusual in German.

(b) *The Past Participle*

1. Also occurs frequently as an adjective: *das weltbekannte Münster* — 3.1.2; *in beliebten Wandergebieten* — 3.1.3; *die Zahl neu gebildeter Wörter* — 13.1.2.
2. Occurs in participial expressions: *die Schuhe geschnürt, den Rucksack geschultert* — 3.1.3 = 'with shoes laced up and rucksack on shoulder'; *zwei Zimmer, verbunden durch eine Tür* — 3.1.3.
3. The past participle used as an adjective may, by extension, be used as an adjectival noun. For example, *ausgebildet* is the past participle of *ausbilden* ('to train'). In text 8.2.2 the past participle is used as an adjectival noun: *die meisten Ausgebildeten* = 'most of the trained personnel'.
4. A particular use of the past participle is after *kommen: ab und zu kommt Silka für einen Moment zu ihr gelaufen* — 7.1.4 = 'from time to time Silka comes running to her for a moment'.
5. The past participle is, of course, widely used in a variety of compound tenses, as described elsewhere in this summary.

12.14 The Subjunctive

The forms of the Subjunctive are given with the verb tables in Grammar Summary sections 12.1, 12.2 and 12.3. The Subjunctive is always regular in formation. Traditionally, the purpose of the Subjunctive has been to express doubt or uncertainty, as opposed to the certainty of the Indicative mood. Increasingly, in modern German, there is a tendency to avoid the Subjunctive, particularly in the spoken language. The Present Subjunctive, in particular, is felt to be affected in speech, and its form, in any case, often coincides with that of the Indicative. Similarly, the form of the Imperfect Subjunctive of weak verbs is the same as that of the Indicative, so that if a Subjunctive flavour is required, it may be conveyed by the use of Modal verbs, as will be described below. The main uses to note are as follows.

(a) *Conditional Sentences (wenn Clauses)*

1. *wenn ein Student nicht mehr hören will, geht er aus dem Raum* — 11.1.2. In this sentence, although *wenn* states a condition ('if . . .'), there is not any real doubt involved, so what looks like a condition is expressed in the Present tense of the Indicative.
2. *Ich würde mich sehr freuen, wenn Sie mir Gelegenheit zu einer persönlichen Vorstellung geben würden* — 8.1.3 = 'I would be very pleased, if you would give me the opportunity for a personal introduction'. As in English, the German main clause is in the Conditional, and the *wenn* clause may be either in the Conditional, as here, or in the Imperfect Subjunctive. It is often possible for the Imperfect Subjunctive to replace the Conditional in this way: *wir wären Ihnen sehr dankbar, wenn Sie uns einige Prospekte schicken könnten* — 9.1.4 = 'we would be very grateful if you could send . . .'; *das Beste wäre . . .* — 10.2.2 = 'the best thing would be . . .'; *wären Sie bereit . . .?* — 6.2.2 = 'would you be ready . . .?'
3. Despite the point just made, the Conditional is often used to render the form expressed in English by the auxiliary 'would': *wir würden am 25. Juni eintreffen* — 9.1.4 = 'we would arrive . . .'; *ich würde gern . . . 2 Wochen bei Ihnen verbringen* — 3.1.4. The auxiliary verb *würde(n)* goes, as usual, to the end of the subordinate clause: *so daß sich der Deutsche in West und der Deutsche in Ost eines Tages kaum mehr verstehen würden* — 13.1.2.
4. Note that it is possible to express conditions by omitting *wenn*, and inverting verb and subject: *hat ein Student Verspätung, so fragt ihn der Professor nicht*

nach dem Grund — 11.1.2 = 'if a student is late . . .'. If this was expressed as a more doubtful condition, and not as a fact, the Imperfect Subjunctive could be used: *hätte ein Student Verspätung, so würde ihn der Professor nicht nach dem Grund fragen.*

5. The Conditional (or Imperfect Subjunctive) may appear, even if the full condition is not expressed: *es wäre schön!* — 12.2.1, meaning 'it would be nice [if . . .]'.

(b) *'as if' Clauses*

'as if' may be translated *als ob* or *als wenn* with the following verb in the Subjunctive. It is also possible, as with *wenn* clauses, to omit *wenn* or *ob* and invert the verb and subject: *. . . als wäre es ihr eigenes* — 7.1.4 = 'as if it were her own'. In speech, *als ob* and similar clauses are often used with the Indicative.

(c) *damit Clauses*

damit introduces a subordinate clause meaning 'in order that'. Such clauses will often be found with the Indicative: *damit die Räder rollen können* — 12.1.2; *damit die Sendung schnell zum richtigen Empfänger kommt* — 6.1.2. But in more literary German the Subjunctive is more common.

(d) Certain expressions which have a negative sense may be followed by a Subjunctive: *kaum ein Mensch, der nicht eine Nacht in einer Jugendherberge geschlafen hätte* — 9.1.3 = 'there is hardly a single person who has not slept a night in a youth hostel'. Other such expressions which may be found with a Subjunctive are: *nicht daß; ohne daß.*

(e) For particular uses of the Subjunctive of Modals (*möchte; könnte*), see the section on Modal Verbs (12.11).

(f) *Subjunctive of Indirect Speech*

1. *Statement*

Indirect statements such as 'he said that . . .', 'he explained that . . .' should, technically, be followed by the Subjunctive, though here, again, usage in conversation often avoids the Subjunctive: *warum haben uns die Preußen erklärt, sie tränken nur deshalb so viel von unserem Bier, weil es so viel schwächer als das norddeutsche sei?* — 11.2.2. Here the reported speech is introduced by the verb *erklärte.* Such a verb may either be followed by *daß* and a clause, or *daß* may be omitted, as in this example, and the direct word order follows the comma after *erklärte.*

2. *Indirect questions* are introduced by *ob*, which may correctly be followed by the Subjunctive: *die Entwicklungen führten bereits zu der Frage, ob die Teilung des Landes nicht auch zu einer Teilung der Sprache führe* — 13.1.2 = '. . . the question whether . . . might lead to . . .'. In modern English, 'might' is often the indication of the sort of doubt conveyed by a Subjunctive. Here, again, as in so many examples quoted, the Subjunctive is less and less used in speech: *meine Frage ist nun, ob es manchmal zu früh ist* — 11.1.2; *frag mich im Dezember, ob du jemanden zum Skilaufen brauchst* — 9.2.2.

12.15 Verbs Followed by the Dative

(a) There are a number of verbs where the dative can be expected — for example, *geben* ('to give something *to* someone'), *schicken* (to send something *to* someone). Such verbs have a direct and indirect object: *wenn Sie uns einige Prospekte schicken könnten* — 9.1.4. The dative also occurs after such verbs as *sagen, schreiben: was Du mir geschrieben hast* — 1.1.2; *schreib mir mal* — 10.1.2; *man sagt den Politikern direkt die Meinung* — 13.1.1.

(b) The following verbs also take the dative: *auffallen* ('to strike'); *sie berichten darüber, was ihnen auffällt* — 11.1.2; *dienen* ('to serve'); *fehlen* ('to be missing'); *gehören* ('to belong'), may be used with a dative, or with the preposition *zu: das gehört zum Privatbereich* — 11.1.2; *Protestbewegungen gehören zum Alltag* — 13.1.1; *glauben* ('to believe'): *wir glauben dir auch so* — 9.2.2; *gefallen* ('to please'): *was gefällt Ihnen* — 6.2.2; *helfen* ('to help'): *wir helfen Ihnen dabei* — 2.1.3; *widersprechen* ('to contradict'): *. . . und können dabei sogar den Eltern widersprechen* — 11.1.2. Note also *danken* ('to thank'); *folgen* ('to follow').

(c) The verb *vorziehen* ('to prefer') takes two objects, one direct and one indirect ('to prefer one thing to something else'): *die Preußen haben noch immer alles Preußische dem Bayerischen vorgezogen* — 11.2.2 = 'the Prussians have always preferred everything Prussian to anything Bavarian'.

12.16 Verbs Followed by Prepositional Constructions

Many verbs are used in close conjunction with a particular prepositional construction — for example: *was denken Ausländer über die Deutschen* — 11.1.1; *. . . sie denken an den Fußball und an das deutsche Bier; sie halten die Deutschen für fleißig*; etc. Such constructions are straightforward when there is a noun directly dependent on the preposition (as with *denken über* and *denken an*), or an adjective (as with *halten für*). But when such verbs are followed by a clause, a way has to be found to incorporate the preposition into the construction. For example, *berichten über* means 'to report about', so 'they report about their stay' would be translated: *sie berichten über ihren Aufenthalt*. But, if the English has a clause: 'they report about what strikes them', then the German construction is: *sie berichten darüber, was ihnen auffällt* — 11.1.2. That is to say, the preposition forms a compound with *da* and acts as antecedent to the *daß* clause. Note these further examples: *eine Möglichkeit besteht darin, daß sie . . . eine Arbeitsstelle annehmen* — 8.1.2; *40 Mitarbeiter sorgen dafür, daß 144 Kinder ein zweites Zuhause haben* — 7.1.4; *es gab Diskussionen darüber, ob das Deutsche West und das Deutsche Ost . . . nur Varianten . . . seien* — 13.1.2.

12.17 Use of Anticipatory *es*

In some constructions verbs that are followed by *zu* + infinitive, or by clauses beginning with *daß* or *wie*, include *es* in the construction which anticipates the following clause: *das Ehepaar empfindet es als besonders wohltuend, wie ihnen das Heim entgegenkommt* — 3.1.3.

12.18 A small number of verbs take the genitive case: *Genf erfreut sich einer größeren Popularität* — 14.3.

13 Conjunctions

13.1 Co-ordinating Conjunctions

(a) *und, aber, sondern, denn*

These conjunctions are followed by the normal word order — that is, they link two main clauses: *das Kind fühlt sich hier nicht fremd, denn es ist mit seiner Mutter gekommen* — 7.1.4: *spazieren Sie mal auf der Stadtmauer oder erleben Sie den Ulmer Wochenmarkt* — 3.1.2.

(b) *aber* is followed by the main clause word order when it stands at the head of the sentence: *aber wir haben eine Vierzimmerwohnung* — 1.2.2. It may also occur within a sentence with the meaning 'however': *es ist aber auch eines unserer größten Umweltprobleme* — 12.1.2.

(c) *sondern* means 'but' and is used after a negative: *er ist nicht Engländer, sondern Deutscher.*

(d) *weder . . . noch* = 'neither . . . nor'; *entweder . . . oder* = 'either . . . or'.

13.2 Subordinating Conjunctions (for *daß*, See Paragraph 15(b)2)

All these conjunctions begin clauses which have their verb at the end.

(a) *Conjunctions of time*

nachdem ('after'); *wie* ('as'); *sobald* ('as soon as'); *bevor* or *ehe* ('before'); *seitdem* or *seit* ('since'); *bis* ('until'); *als, da, wenn* ('when'); *während* ('while'). Note the following points.

1. 'When' is translated *als* when it refers to a single event in the past: *als wir die Nachricht erhielten* — 3.1.3; *wenn* is used if a habitual action is referred to ('whenever') or to actions in the present: *wenn Ausländer an die Deutschen denken* — 11.1.2; *wenn du an Zukunft denkst* — 8.2.2; *wenn ich Dir das alles schreibe* — 1.1.2. Note that the question form of 'when?' is *wann?* in either direct or indirect questions.

2. 'Until' is rendered by *bis: bis die Linie . . . uns zum Endpunkt brachte* — 2.1.3, 'Not until' is *erst: Steffen stieg erst im September in den Bob* — 9.1.2.

3. 'Since' may be *seitdem* or *seit: seit ich von der Klassenfahrt zurück bin* — 10.1.2; *seitdem die Grünen so populär geworden sind* — 12.2.1.

4. *wie* expresses 'as': *wie er die Straße hinunterging* — 'as he was going down the street'.

5. *während* = 'while': *während wir unser Eis essen* — 4.2.2.

(b) *Conjunctions of Place*

wo ('where') *wohin* ('where to'); *woher* ('where from'). Also *worauf; worin*; etc.: *sie stellen ihren Wagen ab, wo sie ihn loswerden können* — 4.1.2; *. . . zum Aldi Supermarkt, wo wir . . . einkaufen* — 6.2.2.

(c) *Conjunctions of Manner and Degree*

wie ('as', 'like'); *als ob* ('as if'); *. . . zu hören, wie es dir geht* — 5.1.3; *wie* may be linked to an adjective to mean 'how . . .': *als ich las, wie oft Ihr umgezogen seid* — 1.1.2. Similarly, *wie* may be followed by an adverb and have the meaning 'as': *wie schon lange versprochen* — 14.2 = 'as was long ago promised'.

(d) *Causal Conjunctions*

da ('as'); *weil* ('because'); *da ich mit dem Wagen ankommen werde* — 3.1.4 = 'as I shall be coming by car'; *weil ich so spät aus der Schule komme* — 7.1.3. Note that there is a tendency in modern German for the verb to come rather earlier in the clause than might be expected: *weil man da einfach mehr Zeit hat für Sport, Musik* — 7.2.2. It would be grammatically quite correct to put the verb *hat* at the end of this sentence, but colloquial German may differ from the written rules.

(e) *Consecutive conjunction* – *so daß* ('with the result that . . .'); *so daß wir schon im voraus planen können* – 9.1.4.

14 Prepositions

14.1 Prepositions Taking the Dative

(a) *aus; bei; mit; nach; von; zu; seit; gegenüber.*

Examples: *aus der Stadt* – 9.1.3; *aus allen Himmelsrichtungen* – 3.1.2; *bei Köstlichkeiten* – 3.1.2; *von weitem* – 3.1.2.

(b) *bei* has a number of meanings, notably 'at the house of': *bei meiner Familie* – 1.1.2; *bei uns* – 5.1.3. *bei* is also used in a number of phrases: *bei starker Hitze* = 'when the temperature is high' – 5.1.2; *beim 100-Meter-Lauf* – 9.1.1; *bei . . . idealen Witterungsverhältnissen* – 9.1.2. *bei* can mean 'in the region of': *bei Rostock* – 1.2.2, and is used particularly with shops and traders: *bei unserem Fleischer* – 6.2.2. *bei dem (beim)* is used with the verbal noun: *beim Einkaufen* – 6.2.2 = 'when shopping'.

(c) *nach* can mean 'after': *nach ungefähr einer Stunde* – 7.1.3. When used with the names of towns and countries, *nach* means 'to': *nach Großbritannien . . . nach London* – 2.1.2. It is also used with this sense in the expression *nach Hause* – 7.1.3 = '[to] home'.

(d) *zu* is used to mean 'to' in a large number of expressions: *noch ehe es zur Krippe kommt* – 7.1.4; *jeden Morgen fahre ich zur Schule* – 7.1.3. Note that *zu Hause* – 11.1.2 means 'at home', and may sometimes be used as a noun: *von diesem Zuhause* – 1.1.2, or as an adverb: *bis ich von zuhause fortgezogen bin* – 1.1.2. *zu* is sometimes used where the dative case would, itself, be enough to convey the meaning: *ich versuche zu meinen Kunden immer nett zu sein* – 8.2.2. *zu* is also used in expressions of time: *zu keiner Zeit* – 9.1.3 = 'at no time'; *ich besuche zur Zeit die Klasse 9* – 8.1.3 = 'at the present time'. In the compound form *dazu*, *zu* is used to show how one thing goes with another: *dazu trinken wir Tee* – 5.1.3; *dazu kam noch Fieber* – 10.1.2. Finally, note *zu Fuß* – 12.1.2 = 'on foot'.

(e) *von* translates most of the English uses of 'from': *von vielen deutschen Groß-städten* – 2.1.2. It may also be rendered 'of', and in this sense is often used in modern German to avoid using the genitive case: *viele von meinen Klassenkamera-den* – 7.1.3; *für die Dauer von einer Stunde* – 7.1.4. *von* is the most frequently used preposition to indicate the agent in a Passive voice construction: *unser Busnetz wird täglich von Millionen von Londonern benutzt* – 2.1.2. (See also paragraphs 12.8(e); 14.2(b).)

(f) *mit* is used with forms of transport: *mit der Bahn* – 3.1.2; *nicht gern mit dem Zug* – 1.2.2. An occasional alternative to *mit* in this sense is *per: per Bus* – 4.2.2.

(g) *aus*, besides its usual sense 'out [of]', is used with materials to mean 'made of': *Teller aus Porzellan* – 4.1.3. *aus* is also used with a place-name or country to mean 'from': *aus Süddeutschland* – 11.2.2. *die Schule ist aus* – 5.1.3 = 'school is over'.

(h) *außer* means 'apart from': *außer mir* – 1.2.2 = 'apart from me'.

14.2 Prepositions Taking the Accusative: *bis; durch; für; gegen; ohne; um*

(a) *bis* can mean 'until': *von acht Uhr früh bis etwa ein oder zwei Uhr nachmittags* – 7.2.2. *bis* may also mean 'as far as', and in this sense may often be used together with *nach* or *zu: bis nach Dortmund . . . bis zum Endpunkt* – 2.1.3. When used in this way, the dative occurs because of *nach* or *zu*. Note the use with numerals:

vier bis fünf Kinder — 1.1.2 = 'four or five children'; *von 20 bis 25 Kilometern* = '20 to 25 km'. In conversation, *bis dann* — 4.2.2 means 'see you soon'.

(b) *durch* means through: *durch die monotone Vorstadt* — 2.1.3; *durch die Parks* — 13.1.1. *durch* may also be used as the preposition with the agent of a Passive construction: *verbunden durch eine Tür* — 3.1.3 (see explanation in paragraphs 12.8(e); 14.2(b)). *durch* often translates 'by' when the agent is inanimate, as in the example 'linked by a door', whereas *von* usually has an animate agent: *von Millionen von Londonern benutzt* — 2.1.2. *durch* may also mean 'as a result of': *durch intensive Nutzung westdeutscher Fernsehsendungen* — 13.1.2 = 'as a result of intensive use of West German TV programmes'.

(c) *gegen* = 'against': *Bürger demonstrieren gegen neue Straßen* — 13.1.1.

(d) *ohne* = 'without': *ohne Chemie* — 13.1.1.

(e) *für* = 'for': *der Preis für die schnelle industrielle Entwicklung* — 13.1.1 (see also Grammar Summary section 11.3(g)3).

(f) *um*. For use in expressions of time see Grammar Summary sections 11.1(b)4; 11.3(f)3. Besides these uses in expressions of time, and its general sense of 'around', *um* is used in several verbal constructions: *Uwe bewirbt sich um einen Ausbildungsplatz* — 8.1.3. Note also *bitten um* ('to ask for'). Note also: *nicht alle Länder haben Angst um ihre Wälder* — 12.2.1 = '. . . are afraid about their forests'.

14.3 Prepositions Taking the Dative or Accusative

(a) The following prepositions take the dative when they refer to a fixed position, and the accusative when they indicate some sort of motion: *in; auf; über; unter; vor; hinter; neben; zwischen*.

Examples: *auf* dative: *auf der Stadtmauer . . . auf dem Marktplatz* — 3.1.2.
accusative: *eine schöne Aussicht auf die Elbe* — 4.1.3.
in dative: *im Kloster Wiblingen* — 3.1.2 (*im = in + dem*).
accusative: *Steffen . . . stieg in den Bob* — 9.1.2; *eine schöne Aussicht in das flache Land* — 4.1.3.

(b) *unter* may mean 'under': *unter dem Jan-Wellem-Platz* — 2.1.3. It can also mean 'among': *unter 29 Bobs* — 9.1.2. Note also the use of *unter* with *verstehen*: *was versteht man unter einem Zehnkampf?* — 9.1.1 = 'what is understood by the term decathlon?' In certain expressions *unter* can mean 'during': *unter der Woche* — 5.1.3.

(c) To translate 'on', *auf* is used when the meaning is 'on top of' and *an* if the meaning is 'on the side of'. Compare: *es liegt an der Elbe und auf einem Berg* — 4.1.3. With days of the week, 'on' is rendered by *am* (*an + dem*): *am letzten Sonntag im September* — 12.1.2; *an den Wochenenden* — 9.2.2; *am Montag . . . am Donnerstag* — 11.2.2.

(d) *auf* and *über* are both used with verbal constructions, and in such cases are followed by the accusative: *. . . daß ich so lange nicht auf Deinen Brief geantwortet habe* — 10.1.2; *was denken Ausländer über Deutschland?* — 11.1.1; *auf den französischen Krimi habe ich mich gefreut* — 9.2.2.

(e) Besides meaning 'on' (see above) *an* can mean 'to' (see paragraph 14.5(c)) or 'at': *an einer Berufsschule* — 1.2.2.

(f) Note some further uses of *auf: auf die Namen* — 9.1.4 = 'in the names of . . .'; *kommen Sie auf ein Wochenende* — 3.1.2 = 'come for a week-end'; *stolz auf* — 13.2.1 — 'proud of'.

(g) *über* has the following meanings:

1. 'over': *die Bahn fuhr über die Ruhr* — 2.1.3.
2. 'over' in the sense of 'more than', used with numerals (see paragraph 9.2(e)).
3. 'via': *über Oostende nach Dover* — 2.1.2.
4. 'about' 'concerning': *Informationen über das Gebiet* — 3.1.4.

(h) *vor* usually means 'in front of'. It can also be used with expressions of fear and protection: *Angst haben vor* . . . = 'to be afraid of'; *der Schutz des Individuums vor dem Super-Wissen des Computers* — 13.1.1. (See also paragraph 11.3(d)1.)

14.4 Prepositions Taking the Genitive

The following prepositions are normally followed by the genitive: *während* ('during'); *wegen* ('because of'); *statt* ('instead of'); *trotz* ('in spite of'): *wegen des Waldsterbens* (Key to exercise 12.2(ii)); *während der Schulferien* (Key to exercise 8(iii)4).

14.5 Translating 'to'

Reference has already been made in the sections on *nach, zu* and *an* to the translation of English 'to'. This section now summarises use for this difficult question.
(a) *in* is used when it is implied that one is going 'into' a building: *in den Unterricht* — 11.1.2 = 'to lessons'; *ins Kino* — 9.2.2; *ins Theater* — 3.1.2.
(b) *auf* is used in a number of fixed phrases: *eine Aussicht auf die Elbe* — 4.1.3; *er geht auf die Straße; auf die Toilette* or *aufs Klo. auf* can be used with *Schule* and *Universität* to mean 'going to' in the sense of 'attending': *er geht noch auf die Schule; sie ist auf der Uni.*
(c) *an* mean 'up to': *sie geht ans Fenster. an* is used with names of rivers to mean both 'on' and 'to': *an der Elbe* — 4.1.3; *kommen Sie an die Donau* — 3.1.2. *an* is also used with other destinations which extend over some length: *im Juli* . . . *fahre ich an die Ostsee* — 9.2.2.
(d) *nach* is used with towns, countries and continents (see Grammar Summary section 14.1(c)).
(e) *zu* is always used for going to a person: *Silka kommt zu ihr gelaufen* — 7.1.4. It is the most widely used preposition for going to places: *zur Disco* — 9.2.2; *zur Schule* — 1.2.2. (See also Grammar Summary section 14.1(d).)

15 Word-order

Earlier sections on the various parts of speech have given information about word-order. This section aims to sum up the main rules for word-order in German.

(a) *Main Clauses*

1. The normal order is subject + verb + complement/object/adverb: *die erste Stunde* (subject) *beginnt* (verb) *um 8.10 Uhr* (prepositional phrase).
2. In questions, the subject and verb are inverted — that is, instead of *du hast*, one says, *hast du?: Hast du schon genaue Vorstellungen?* — 8.2.2; *besteht die Möglichkeit . . . ?* — 3.1.4.
   Note that in conversation, questions may be put using the direct word order, without inversion, but with a questioning intonation pattern: *du ruderst?* — 9.2.2.
3. If the main clause starts with something other than the subject, the verb and subject are inverted — that is to say, the verb always comes as the second main item in the main clause: *ab und zu* (adverbial expression) *kommt* (verb) *Silka* (subject) — 7.1.4; *ganz anders* (adverbial expression) *verhält sich* (verb) *Markus* (subject) — 7.1.4. To say that the verb comes in second place does NOT mean that it is the second word. The first place in the sentence might be a short phrase,

as in the example above, or even a whole clause. Consider also the following examples from text 11.1.2:

	1	2	3
	bei uns zu Hause	*sagt*	*man . . .*
	so etwas	*wäre*	*in meinem Heimatland unmöglich.*

Here is an example where a complete subordinate clause occupies first place in the sentence, followed by the main clause verb in second place:

	1	2	3	4
	wenn ein Student nicht mehr hören will,	*geht*	*er*	*aus dem Raum.*

The placing of a phrase in the first position of the sentence may be for variety and interest, or it may be for reasons of emphasis: *aber jetzt glaube ich* = 'but *now* I believe . . .'; *besonders interessant war für mich* = 'it was *particularly* interesting for me'; *mir macht Rudern auch Spaß* — 9.2.2. In conversation, a response may begin with a verb, because the word *das* is omitted: *kann ich verstehen* — 1.2.2. Compare: *das glaube ich* — 1.2.2, where *das* might also be omitted in speech.

(b) *Subordinate Clauses*

1. The verb goes to the end of the clause after all subordinating conjunctions (listed in paragraph 13.2) and in relative clauses:

(main clause)	(subordinate clause 1)	(subordinate clause 2)
sie berichten darüber,	*was ihnen auffällt,*	*wenn sie uns besuchen* — 11.1.2.

And here is a case of the subordinate clause preceding the main clause:

als ich das erste Mal in einer deutschen Universität war, habe ich mich dann sehr gewundert — 11.1.2.

2. *daß* introduces a subordinate clause after many verbs: *ich weiß, daß . . .; ich glaube, daß . . . .* The verb goes to the end of the clause, after *daß: aber jetzt glaube ich, daß das Gegenteil stimmt* — 11.1.2. Note that in sentences which include a comparison the verb of the *daß* clause does not normally go right to the end of the sentence in modern German: *ich dachte immer, daß deutsche Lehrer strenger sind als bei uns* — 11.1.2. In indirect statements ('they say that . . .') *daß* may be omitted, in which case the normal main clause word-order occurs: *bei uns zu Hause sagt man, die Deutschen haben besonders viel Disziplin* — 11.1.2. Note that the same usage is possible after *hoffen* ('to hope'): *ich hoffe, du hast den Winter gut überstanden* — 10.1.2.

3. As stated above, *wissen* is usually followed by *daß*. It may, however, be followed by *ob* if there is no certainty, but some doubt: *es wäre für mich wichtig zu wissen, ob Sie einen bewachten Parkplatz haben* — 3.1.4. The same distinction is made in English between 'I know that . . .' and 'I do not know whether. . .'.

4. The point was made in paragraph 2, above, that the verb does not always go to the very end of the sentence in modern German. In the spoken language of the dialogues in this book, you will find a number of examples of the verb coming earlier in the sentence than might be expected, according to the rules of the written language.

(c) Separable prefixes go to the end of the clause. See Grammar Summary section 12.9(c).

(d) Participles and infinitives go to the end of the clause: *viele wollen . . . nicht mehr in der Stadt wohnen* — 12.1.2; *in Brilon habe ich eine richtige deutsche Familie kennengelernt* — 11.1.2. When constructions with infinitives and participles occur in subordinate clauses, the finite verb goes to the very end of the clause, after the infinitive or participle — for example, main clause word-order: *er will schriftliche Nachrichten versenden*. In a subordinate clause this becomes: *wer schriftliche Nachrichten versenden will* — 6.1.2. A further example: *er hätte eine Nacht in einer Jugendherberge geschlafen* is main clause word-order. In a relative clause this becomes: *kaum ein Mensch, der nicht eine Nacht in einer Jugendherberge geschlafen hätte* — 9.1.3.

(e) *Position of Complements, Objects, Adverbs*

1. Object pronouns occur in the sentence as soon as possible after the subject and verb: *das kommt mir sehr fremd vor* — 11.1.2; *besonders interessant war für mich die Stellung der Eltern* — 11.1.2. In a subordinate clause this may mean that a pronoun — for example, a reflexive pronoun — is at some distance from its verb: *so daß sich der Deutsche in Ost und der Deutsche in West eines Tages kaum mehr verstehen würden* — 13.1.2.

2. Order of direct and indirect objects ('to give something to someone').

(i) Two nouns: dative precedes accusative: *irgendein Norddeutscher hat einem bayerischen Freund einen Ratschlag gegeben.*

(ii) Noun and pronoun: pronoun precedes noun: *geben Sie mir das Buch; geben Sie es dem Mann.*

(iii) Two pronouns: accusative precedes dative: *geben Sie es ihm.*

3. Adverbs and adverb phrases usually occur in the order time — manner – place: *sie werden bald* (time) *ihre Schule* (place) *verlassen* — 8.1.2; *auf jeden Fall will ich früh selbständig werden* — 8.1.2 (time preceding adjective); *kommen Sie mal auf ein Wochenende an die Donau* — 3.1.2 (time preceding place). When the verb *sein* is followed by an adverb of time + an adjective, the adjective comes last: *ich war eine Zeitlang krank* — 10.1.2; *ich war den ganzen Tag müde* — 10.1.2. This is different from the English order: 'I was ill for a while'; 'I was tired the whole day'.

4. *Position of nicht*

(i) The neutral position for *nicht* is early in the sentence, so that it negates the whole statement: *ob die Teilung des Landes nicht auch zu einer Teilung der Sprache führe* — 13.1.2.

(ii) In simple sentences *nicht* normally stays close to the verb: *ich habe nicht mal Lust zum Lesen* — 1.2.2; *ich fahre nicht gern mit dem Zug* — 1.2.2.

(iii) If there are object pronouns they come earlier in the sentence than *nicht*: *ich kann mir gar nicht vorstellen* — 1.1.2.

(iv) In a question where verb and subject are inverted, *nicht* comes after the subject: *warum gehen wir nicht zur Disco?* — 9.2.2.

(v) Note the phrase: *ich auch nicht* = 'nor me'.

(vi) When *nicht* qualifies an adjective, it remains close to that adjective: *es war wirklich nicht schön* — 10.1.2.

(vii) With a Modal verb construction, *nicht* usually stays close to the dependent infinitive: *kann man die Fabriken nicht zwingen?* — 12.2.1.

(f) *Analysis of Complex Sentences*

Word-order remains one of the main problems of learning German for many students. The rules given in the preceding paragraphs about main clauses and subordinate clauses may be learned, and well known, and still some of the sentences of more complicated passages can prove difficult to decipher. The passage in 13.1.2 contains several of these complex sentences, one of which it might be helpful to examine more closely.

Erfahrungen der letzten Jahre zeigen, daß die Leute in der DDR, vermutlich durch intensive Nutzung westdeutscher Fernsehsendungen, im Hinblick auf neue Wörter in der Bundesrepublik kaum Schwierigkeiten haben.

Look first for the main statement of the sentence:

Erfahrungen der letzten Jahre zeigen (main clause) = 'Experiences of recent years show'; *daß die Leute in der DDR kaum Schwierigkeiten haben.* = 'that the people of the GDR have hardly any difficulties'.

Now look to see what it is that they do not experience as a difficulty:

im Hinblick auf neue Wörter in der Bundesrepublik = 'with regard to new words in the Federal Republic'.

There remains one phrase: *vermutlich durch intensive Nutzung westdeutscher Fernsehsendungen* which is the phrase that adds most to the difficulty of the sentence, in that it interrupts the progress of the subordinate clause. *Vermutlich* means 'presumably', and this gives the clue to the meaning of the whole phrase, which guesses at a reason for the fact that GDR citizens do not have problems with West German vocabulary: 'presumably because of their intensive watching of West German TV programmes'. And so the whole sentence in English reads as follows:

'Experiences of recent years show that people in the GDR, presumably because of their intensive watching of West German TV programmes, have hardly any difficulties with regard to new words in the Federal Republic.'

16 Spelling and Punctuation

16.1 Spelling

(a) All nouns are written with a capital letter.

(b) *Sie* (second person polite 'you') and all parts of speech connected with it are written with a capital: *Ihr Reiseweg steht noch nicht fest. Wir helfen Ihnen dabei* — 2.1.1. Otherwise, pronouns are written with a small letter, except for *Du, Ihr* in letter-writing (see Grammar Summary section 5.6).

(c) Indeclinable adjectives formed from the names of towns are written with a capital letter: *eine Hamburger Kuriosität* — 4.1.3.

(d) *deutsch* is written with a small letter when an adjective: *sie denken ans deutsche Bier* — 11.1.1. It also has a small letter when referring to the language, after the preposition *auf: auf deutsch* = 'in German'. It has a capital when it is an adjectival noun referring to the people: *was denken Ausländer über die Deutschen?* — 11.1.1. It also has a capital when referring to the language, except after *auf* (see above): *Deutsch* — 7.1.1 = 'German'; *das Deutsche* — 13.1.2 = 'the German language'.

(e) Time phrases are treated like adverbs, and written with a small letter: *freitags* — 1.2.2; *mittags* — 7.1.3. There is a certain amount of latitude in such expressions (for example, *zur Zeit* or *zurzeit*). If it is clear that a noun is involved, it is usual to retain the capital letter: *jeden Morgen* — 7.1.4.

(f) *Use of Hyphen*

The hyphen is used when two or more compound words have their final component in common: *Gas- und Wasserinstallateur . . . Kaufmann im Groß- und Außenhandel* — 8.1.1. Note the use of the hyphen in other positions such as: *U-Bahn* — 2.1.2; *Jan-Wellem-Platz* — 2.1.3; *100-Meter-Lauf . . . 110 Meter-Hürdenlauf* — 9.1.1; *Zweier-Bobs . . . WM-Titel* — 9.1.2.

(g) *Use of ß*

This letter, a relic of the old gothic alphabet, is called *'es-tset'*, *eszett* or *scharfes S*. It is used in some positions instead of *ss*.
1. At the end of a word: *daß; muß.*
2. If *ss* is followed by a consonant: *mußten.*
3. After a long vowel: *heißen*. But note that *ü* is a short vowel; therefore: *müssen.*

16.2 Punctuation

(a) *The comma*

1. In sentences where two main clauses are linked by *und* or *oder*, a comma precedes *und/oder* if the second clause has its own subject: *das müssen wir wissen, und das müssen wir ändern* — 12.1.2.
2. Always put a comma before *aber; sondern; doch; jedoch: nicht die Tatsache, daß Millionen Menschen es betreiben, sondern . . .* — 9.1.3.
3. Always divide up subordinate clauses with commas (see the many examples in the texts).
(b) The colon is used to introduce direct speech: *er sagt: ,,ich kann nicht kommen".*
(c) Inverted commas. The form for book titles is as in English: *'Das Brot der frühen Jahre'*. For direct speech, the German form for inverted commas is: *,, "*
(d) Full stop is used in abbreviations: *z.B. = zum Beispiel*. When the abbreviations are used to form a new word, however, there are no full stops: *BRD* (pronounced 'bay-air-day'); *DDR* (pronounced 'day-day-air').
(e) The exclamation mark is normally used after the greeting at the head of a letter: *Lieber Herbergsvater!* — 9.1.4 (see also section on letter writing, page 247).

Index to Grammar Summary

Opposite each entry given in this index the simple numerals refer to texts and chapters where examples of usage may be found. For example, 12.1.2 refers the reader to the relevant text of Chapter 12. If the numeral is in italic type, it refers to the text where that particular point is given more detailed treatment in the exercises of that chapter. If the numeral is in bold type, it refers to the section of the Grammar Summary where the point is explained.

221

Guide to Pronunciation

This short summary of German pronunciation can do no more than offer a brief introduction to the pronunciation of standard High German. This is the pronunciation normally heard on radio and TV, and on the stage, and spoken by many native German speakers. Regional variations in pronunciation are quite widespread, particularly in South Germany, Austria and Switzerland, but the pronunciation described here is a norm which is very widely understood, and to which even regional speakers approximate.

Any guide to pronunciation is bound to be of limited value unless linked to the chance to hear the sounds described. However close to the sounds of English certain German sounds may be, it is only by hearing the sound pronounced that important differences can be noted and imitated. The descriptions given here should, therefore, be read in conjunction with the tape accompanying the book, or listening to broadcasts, native speakers, etc.

1. Stress

1.1 Stress within the Word

Each German word of more than one syllable has a syllable which carries a heavier stress than the rest of the word. Throughout the vocabularies of this book, the stressed vowel or vowel combination is printed in bold type. As a very general rule, the first syllable is most commonly stressed, but there are important exceptions to this rule:

(a) words whose first syllable contains an unstressed *e* — for example: *gegében*; *bekómmen*.

(b) Words beginning with the unstressed prefixes *ent*, *ver*, *zer*, etc. (for a full list see the section of the Grammar Summary dealing with inseparable verbs (section 12.9)). For example: *zerschnéiden*; *verbíeten*; *entschéiden*.

(c) Many words borrowed from other languages — for example: *Präsidént*; *Elephánt*; *Hotél*.

(d) A number of German place-names: *Berlín*; *Hannóver*.

The frequency of first syllable stress can be seen by the way the stress changes as compound nouns build up — for example: *Belástung, Úmweltbelastung*; *Búrger*, *Búndesbürger*.

1.2 Sentence Stress and Intonation

In the normal musical pattern of sentence pronunciation, particular words of importance carry a heavier emphasis than others. Small words, such as prepositions and articles may be contracted or glossed over, and particular nouns, verbs or adjectives carry the emphasis. As in English, attention can be drawn by stress to a particular word in a statement — for example, *mein Vater heißt Heinrich*

227

would normally carry the stress on *Vater*. In particular circumstances, however, one might say *meín Vater heißt Heinrich* (my father and not yours), or *mein Vater heißt Heínrich* (and not Fritz).

In addition to such stressing of words within the sentence, there are the musical patterns of intonation, which may be summarised as follows:

(a) The pattern used to make statements, give commands or put questions containing a specific question word such as *wer?* or *wo?*

For example, in dialogue 2 of Chapter 1 we hear:

Ich fahre nicht gern mit dem Zug.

Wo kommst du denn her?

(b)

This rising intonation is used for general questions — for example:

Ist dein Vater etwa ein Journalist? It can also be used as an alternative to pattern (a) for questions with a specific question word.

(c) Another variation of the rising intonation is used for incomplete statements, or leading to the end of a subordinate clause, when there is the sense that more is to follow — for example:

wenn man am gleichen Tag zurückkommt, ...

These patterns may be varied by the wish to stress a particular word.

2. Vowels

In general, the difference between German vowels and English vowels is that the German vowels are pure and do not 'slide' into diphthongs as English vowels often do. German is also spoken with more energy and tenseness than English, which seems rather lazy and slack in comparison.

To the five vowels of English are added the three vowels with Umlaut. Each of these eight vowels has short and long forms, making 16 sounds. Two sounds coincide (short ä and short e), but unstressed e is added, thus keeping the total number of vowel sounds to 16. To these 16 vowels are added the three diphthongs ei, au and eu/äu to complete the list of vowel sounds described below.

Letter	Nearest English sound	Forms of spelling	Examples
i (long)	like ee in 'meet'	i ie ih	Stil, viel, ihr
i (short)	like i in 'gift'	i	dick, Kind
e (long)	like a in 'made'	e ee eh	leben, steht, Meer
e (short)	like e in 'bed'	e ä	Mensch, fällt
ä (long)	no real equivalent but like long e above	ä äh	Käse, während
a (long)	like a in 'calm'	a ah aa	kam, Jahr, Staat
a (short)	like a in 'fan'	a	dann, Wand

(note that this is the sound which precedes r in German, e.g. *Arbeit*).

o (long)	like o in 'go'	o oh oo	wo? Ohr, Boot
o (short)	like o in 'cod'	o	Post, Dorf
u (long)	like oo in 'mood'	u uh	gut, Ruhr
u (short)	like oo in 'good'	u	dumm, Wurst
e (unstressed)	like a in 'opera'	e	Besuch; and unstressed e ending diese, etc.
ü (long)		ü üh	fühlen

This vowel gives particular problems to speakers of standard English, though it appears in Scottish and a number of English dialects. Put the lips into the position to pronounce oo as in 'food'. Keep the lips in that position and produce the sound for ee as in 'meet'.

ü (short) is formed in the same way, but shorter in pronunciation, and rather closer to the English sound i as in 'gift'.

		ü	dünn, füllen
ö (long)	like ur in 'urn'	ö öh	Vögel, Föhn
ö (short)	similar but shorter	ö	können
ei	like i in 'bike'	ei	mein, reich
au	like ow in 'sow'	au	blau, faul
eu	like oy in 'boy'	eu äu	neun

3. Consonants

3.1 Voiced and Unvoiced Pairs

One important distinction which will help to explain the German consonants is the distinction between voiced and unvoiced consonants. For example, in the pair of consonants p/b, p is produced with a puff of breath only, whereas for b the vocal chords are vibrated also — that is to say, it is voiced. The same applies to the pairs of consonants t/d, k/g, f/v, s/z and to the voiced/unvoiced pronunciation of ch. The importance of this distinction is that voiced consonants do not occur in final position, so that whenever d, g and the others are final, they are pronounced like the corresponding unvoiced consonant. For example, *Hand* (pronounced *Hant*), *brav* (pronounced *braf*), *halb* (pronounced *halp*). The unvoiced g at the end of words may be pronounced as k or as ch. For example, *billig* may sound like *billik* or *billich*. Both pronunciations are acceptable, and the variation depends on region and individual speaker.

3.2 Glottal Stop

The glottal stop is, strictly speaking, a form of consonant, so it can be dealt with here. There is no indication in spelling of a glottal stop, but it is a significant feature of German pronunciation, giving the spoken language some of that energy and tenseness referred to earlier, compared with the more relaxed pronunciation of English. The glottal stop is a slight catch in the throat which occurs, even if only slightly, before words beginning with a vowel. Some forms of English have a glottal stop — for example, the Cockney pronunciation of 'butter', where tt is dropped and replaced by a catch in the throat 'bu–er'. In German combinations such as *war ich*, *da ich*, the glottal stop prevents the two words from running on smoothly, as might be the case in a similar English combination of sounds. Note that the glottal stop does not occur in the compounds with *auf*, *aus*, *unter*, etc.,

229

such as *hinauf*, *hinunter*, *heraus*. In the combinations with *da*, the lack of the glottal stop is shown in the spelling, by the addition of r: *darunter*, *darauf*.

3.3 Pronunciation of Individual Consonants

Bearing in mind the points made already about voiced/unvoiced distinctions, English speakers should encounter no great difficulty in pronouncing the pairs p/b, t/d, k/g, f/v. Nor should there be problems with m, n and h, which are all quite close to the English pronunciation. The main point to note with regard to the above sounds is that German v is pronounced as f (*Vogel* sounds like *fogel*). The English v sound is represented in German by w (*will* sounds like *vill*).

The following notes refer to sounds which might give difficulty.

Written form	*Description of sound*	*Examples*
l	German always has a clear l, in whatever position, and never the 'dark' l which occurs particularly at the end of English words such as 'well'. The tip of the tongue should touch the teeth ridge and not slip back.	Land, malte, will
s (also ss, ß)	Pronounced as ss when final, or before a consonant within a word.	aus, besser, blaß, Wespe, Liste
s	Pronounced like English z when initial or between vowels.	Sand, sehen, rasen
s	Pronounced like English sh when initial before consonant. Also when an initial sp or st occurs in the middle of a compound word.	Stadt, sparen, stehen gespart, besprechen, Hauptstadt
sch	Pronounced close to English sh, but with the lips more protruded.	Schein, falsch
tsch	Like English ch in church.	deutsch
g/j	Pronounced like s in English 'pleasure'. This sound only occurs in foreign loan-words.	Garage, Journalist
ch	A sound which does not exist in standard English, although it occurs in Scottish 'loch'.	machen, kochen
	There is also an unvoiced form of ch, which has a less rough articulation, and is more of a hissing sound. This occurs after vowels i, ei, eu, and after a consonant.	ich, weich, Milch
j	Pronounced like English y in 'young'. The same sound is heard in the combination ie and -tion in words of foreign origin.	ja, Jahr Linie, Nation (= natsjon)
r	Some speakers use a front-type rolled r. More common is the back-type r formed by forcing the air through a small space between the back of the tongue and the soft palate. At the same time the uvula is vibrated. r is one of the more difficult sounds for English speakers, since the German pronunciation is wholly different from English.	Rand, Beruf, wer
ng	Pronounced like ng in English 'sing', and never with the extra g sound of 'finger'.	Klang, singen
z/tz	Like English ts in 'cats'.	zehn, Katze

It cannot be too often emphasised that all the preceding notes on intonation patterns and sound qualities should be read in conjunction with careful listening to the tape accompanying this book. More information about spelling and pronunciation is contained in section 16 of the Grammar Summary.

P.S. Don't forget to buy your Work Out German cassette!

You see, in addition to this Work Out book, you, as a GCSE student, are offered extra help in German with the Work Out German Cassette.

The approach for using cassettes is based on a view that sees languages best learnt when encountered in an interesting and real context. By using such methods you will find it much easier to learn and revise German – and therefore much easier to get the grade you want in your German GCSE.

The Work Out GCSE German cassette is priced at just £12.99 (including VAT) and you can buy it from any good bookshop.

Viel Gluck!

In case of difficulty tear off the form below and return it to
John Darvill
Macmillan
Houndmills
Basingstoke
HANTS RG21 2XS

or telephone 0256 29242

Please send me my copy of the **Work Out German cassette** 0 333 44852 9

I enclose a cheque/postal order for £12.99 (cassette price, including VAT and postage and packing) payable to Macmillan Education

NAME _____

ADDRESS _____

_____

_____ POSTCODE _____

Part III

THE GCSE EXAMINATION

The GCSE Examination

1. The Context of the GCSE

The Secretary of State for Education and Science announced in the House of Commons on 20 June 1984 that the Government had decided to replace the GCE 'O' level and CSE examinations with a new examination, to be called the General Certificate of Secondary Education (GCSE). He proposed that the first GCSE examinations should be held in the summer of 1988.

The new examination will be administered by five groups, involving both GCE and CSE Boards in each group, as follows:

Group	GCE Boards	CSE Boards
Northern Examining Association	Joint Matriculation Board	Northern Regional Exam Board Yorkshire and Humberside Regional Examining Board North West Regional Examining Board Assoc. Lancs. Schools Examining Board
Midland Examining Group	University of Cambridge Local Exam Syndicate Oxford and Cambridge Schools Exam Board Southern Universities Joint Board	East Midlands Regional Examining Board West Midlands Regional Examining Board
London and East Anglian Group	London GCE Board	London Regional Examining Board East Anglian Regional Examining Board
Southern Examining Group	Associated Exam Board Oxford Delegacy of Local Examinations	Southern Regional Examining Board South-East Regional Examining Board South Western Examining Board
The Welsh Board		

There is complete freedom of choice in the GCSE examination. Schools, colleges and individuals may choose to take the examination of a particular group, without being limited to the regional group operating where they live.

2. Schemes of Examination

2.1 National Criteria and Grade-related Criteria

The GCSE differs from the previous system of examining in that national criteria have been drawn up which lay down, for all subjects, the aims, assessment objectives, content and broad patterns of assessment which must be acceptable to the Secretary of State. Further to the National Criteria, Grade-related Criteria are being drawn up for each subject. These criteria specify more clearly than was previously the case the knowledge, understanding and skills expected for the award of a particular grade. This is in line with the Secretary of State's belief that 'examination grades should have clearer meaning, and pupils and teachers need clearer goals'. The criteria are expressed in positive terms, so as to reflect what candidates know and can do, even at the lowest grades. For all subjects, Grade-related Criteria are described in terms of achievement within particular 'domains' of the subject. Those domains in foreign languages are the four skills of listening, speaking, reading and writing. In the new examination the four skills are equally weighted, and each receives 25 per cent of the total marks.

2.2 Differentiation of Assessment

The Secretary of State declared that 'it is essential that the National Criteria should make the necessary provision for proper discrimination between candidates, so that candidates across the ability range are given opportunities to show what they know and can do'. This differentiation is achieved in two ways:

(a) By differentiated papers. Papers are to be set in two bands, Basic and Higher. (Some latitude is allowed to examining groups. It is also the case that the terminology will vary — for example, General and Extended.) To gain the highest grades, it will be necessary to take Higher papers in all four skills (see 2.3 below.)
(b) By differentiated questions. Within a particular paper, there may be sections which separate out questions according to their level of difficulty.

2.3 Grading and Certification

The GCSE candidates are graded according to a seven-point scale of grades, denoted by the letters A to G. The first three grades — A, B, C — are regarded as equivalent to the same grades in the former GCE 'O' level examination. At the Basic Level it is possible to gain grades E, F and G by achieving the necessary standards in three skills, without offering writing in the foreign language. Grade D can be achieved by adding any further element to the Basic Listening, Speaking and Reading. For Grade C there must be an element of Basic Writing, and for A and B the whole range of papers at Higher Level must be offered. Note that the three Basic tests in Listening, Speaking and Reading are treated as the common core examination to be taken by *all* candidates. Further papers will then be added to this common core.

3.   The Written Examination

The written examination tests the domains of Listening, Reading and Writing. Within each domain, it is suggested that there should be five dimensions on which grading will be based: roles, topics, settings, tasks and levels of performance. The question of roles will be discussed in the section on the Oral examination. Topics and settings refer to, for example, the topics of family, food and drink, holidays, and such settings as the home, a restaurant, a post office. The tasks to be set should be genuine or simulated situations containing features of real communication. The aim is that such tasks should be as authentic as possible, and valuable beyond the classroom. Levels of performance in the tasks will be defined by the Grade-related Criteria when these are eventually introduced.

3.1 Listening Tests

The aim of these tests is that the candidate should show an ability to understand the spoken language in a variety of registers and in a range of situations likely to fall within the candidate's experience. Marks are awarded according to the accuracy with which the candidate conveys the information required by the question.

(a)   *Types of Listening Material*

(i) *Basic Level (Common Core)*

1. Announcements − for example, at tourist sites, railway stations, supermarkets.
2. Information items − for example, weather forecasts, short news items, recorded telephone messages and instructions.
3. Native speakers being interviewed about themselves. Conversations, questions, answers and remarks overheard in practical situations.

(ii) *Higher Level*

As for Basic Level, plus an understanding of formal speech, discussions, more extended dialogues.

(b)   *Types of Task*

(i) Multiple choice. Choices given in English, and the candidate must show understanding of the listening text by selecting the correct response from three or four possibilities.
(ii) Comprehension questions in English. The questions may be guided and specific or, at Higher Level, may be more open.

3.2 Reading Tests

The aim of these tests is that the candidate should show an ability to understand the foreign language in its written form in a variety of registers. As with the listening tests, marks are awarded according to the accuracy with which the candidate conveys the information required by the question.

(a)   *Types of Material*

Varieties of authentic material such as brochures, notices, labels, menus, recipes. Also newspaper articles, magazine anecdotes, narrative prose, letters and written messages.

(b)   *Types of Task*

(i) Multiple choice with items in English.
(ii) Comprehension questions in English, as for Listening Comprehension.

3.3 Writing Tests

The criteria for written work relate to:
(1) Effectiveness of written communication in response to a given stimulus. With what degree of relevance and effectiveness is the task carried out?
(2) Quality of communication, with reference to the range of language (variety of vocabulary, structures) and accuracy.

(a) *Types of Material and Tasks*

(i) *Basic Level (Common Core)*

(Note that writing in the foreign language is not part of the three Basic elements required for the award of Grades E, F, G.) Make up shopping list (from visual stimulus); write a post-card with simple messages; list places of interest in a town (from a map).

(ii) *Higher Level*

1. Send more complex messages. Write an informal letter responding to a letter from a pen-friend, or a letter talking about personal interests, school, family. Formal letters asking for information from an information bureau or hotel.
2. Semi-guided composition, giving a report of an event, telling a picture story or constructing a narrative from an outline.

With regard to the written element of the examination, it should be noted that the National Criteria for French, which can be taken as equally relevant for German, state: '. . . any of the following techniques of assessment would be inappropriate as a compulsory technique of assessment: summary, précis, dictation and prose translation'.

4. The Oral Examination

The aim of the oral examination is to test the candidate's ability to use the foreign language effectively to seek and provide information, to take part in conversations and to express opinions within a range of situations from the candidate's own experience. As regards the general question of social and psychological roles, the main feature at this level is that candidates should be able to distinguish between formal and informal roles — for example, the difference between communicating with teachers, doctors, etc., and with friends, members of the family. The main criteria of assessment are as follows:

(1) Completion of the task in cases where candidates are asked to play a particular role.
(2) Effectiveness and relevance of the communication.
(3) Range of language (vocabulary, structures).
(4) Accuracy of language.
(5) Fluency in comprehension and response.
(6) Pronunciation and intonation.

Types of Task

(i) *Personal Questions*

The candidate answers questions about him/herself, interests, family, travel, holidays, etc.

(ii) *Role Play*

The candidate is asked to play a specific task and to carry out a role — for example, shopping for items, asking the way, dealing with the customs, ordering food in a restaurant, etc.

(iii) *Narrative*

The candidate is asked to tell a story on the basis of information contained in a series of pictures, or other stimulus.

5. Sample Materials

Suggested answers to these materials are given in the Key which comes at the end of this section (page 247). Note that besides the sample materials given here, many exercises in the teaching chapters of this book give practice in similar tasks and techniques.

The sample materials are some of those proposed in the provisional GCSE samples of the Southern Examining Group, whose copyright they are. The suggested answers are, however, entirely the responsibility of the present author and not necessarily answers approved by the Examining Group.

5.1 Listening Tests 🖭

(a) *Basic Level*

(i) In this section you will hear statements, questions or short conversations. There is one question on each item. For every question, four possible answers are printed on the question paper. You must decide which of these answers is the most appropriate.

1. *Wir bringen Ihnen Nachrichten und Neuigkeiten in unserer Sendung.*
   Who is speaking?   A. A newspaper seller.
   　　　　　　　　　B. A radio announcer.
   　　　　　　　　　C. A speaking clock.
   　　　　　　　　　D. A railway station announcer.
2. Where would you hear someone asking this question?
   Hier noch jemand zugestiegen?
   　　　　　　　　　A. In a garage.
   　　　　　　　　　B. On a train.
   　　　　　　　　　C. At a pedestrian crossing.
   　　　　　　　　　D. At a police station.
3. The telephone rings.
   Mann: Schmidt.
   Frau: Kann ich bitte Rudi sprechen?

Mann: *Hier wohnt kein Rudi. Ich glaube, Sie sind falsch verbunden.*
Frau: *Entschuldigung.*
Why did the conversation end so quickly?
      A. Rudi was not at home.
      B. The lady has dialled the wrong number.
      C. Herr Schmidt was too busy to speak.
      D. The lady was using the wrong coins.

(ii) In this section you will hear a radio news item. There are three questions on it.

Amsterdam. Ein 28-jähriger Briefträger mußte heute, ausgerechnet an seinem Geburtstag, 500 Mark Geldstrafe zahlen, weil er 3 Monate vorher Briefe weggeworfen hatte. „Ich hatte Fußschmerzen und wollte bei dem schlechten Wetter möglichst bald nach Hause gehen!" hat er gesagt.

How old was the postman?
      A. 48.
      B. 38.
      C. 18.
      D. 28.

What happened on his birthday?
      A. He got 500 Marks.
      B. He got fined 500 Marks.
      C. He got a lot of letters.
      D. He got very wet.

What had he done three months earlier?
      A. Found a lot of money.
      B. Got home very late.
      C. Thrown some letters away.
      D. Delivered his letters in record time.

(iii) In this section you will hear a conversation. It is followed by three questions.

Frau Habicht is talking to her husband about some shopping he did today.
Frau: Wo ist denn die Bierwurst, die du kaufen solltest?
Mann: Bierwurst? Ich habe vier Scheiben Schinken und 200 Gramm Kalbsleberwurst gebracht.
Frau: Du hast aber Bierwurst in dein Notizbuch geschrieben!
Mann: Ich habe leider mein Notizbuch im Büro gelassen. Tut mir leid.
Frau: Das ist einfach zu viel! Jedes Mal machst du 'was Falsches!

What was the man supposed to buy for his wife?
      A. Beer.
      B. Sausage.
      C. Liver.
      D. Notebook.

Which of the following did he buy?
      A. 200 grams of liver sausage.
      B. Too much ham.
      C. A crate of beer.
      D. 4 slices of cake.

Why did he make the mistake?
      A. He forgot to make a list.
      B. He didn't hear what his wife said.
      C. He left his office too late.
      D. He forgot to take his list with him.

(b) *Higher Level*

Late one night Maria telephones her friend because she has a problem. Listen carefully to their conversation and then answer, *in English*, the questions.

Telefon klingelt.
Mann: (gähnt): Hallo.
Frau: Hier ist Maria. Es tut mir leid, daß ich dich aufgeweckt habe, aber ich dachte, du hättest sie vielleicht gefunden.
Mann: Was gefunden?
Frau: Meine Schlüssel natürlich. Zwei an einem Ring. Den Schlüssel für die Haustür und den anderen zu meiner Wohnung. Sie waren in meiner Handtasche, als ich bei dir ankam, aber jetzt sind sie verschwunden.
Mann: Wo bist du im Moment?
Frau: Ich stehe in der Telefonzelle an der Ecke und kann nicht schlafen gehen, weil der Portier keinen Nachtdienst hat.
Mann: Bleib dort; ich komme sofort.

1. Where have Maria and her friend spent the evening?
2. Why has Maria telephoned?
3. From where is she telephoning?
4. Why can't she get the porter to let her in?
5. What is she to do now?

5.2 Reading Tests

(a) *Basic Level*

(i) The following is a notice seen in the foyer of a cinema. Read it carefully, and then answer, in English, the question.

> Nicht für Jugendliche unter 18 Jahren

What does the notice tell you?
A. The film is not about young people.
B. No 18-year-olds will be allowed in.
C. The film can only be seen by adults.
D. No young people under 18 may buy alcohol.

(ii) Read the following weather forecast for Nordrhein-Westfalen (NRW) from a German newspaper, then select the most suitable answer for each question.

> HEITER
> Ein Hoch mit Kern über der Nordsee ist für NRW wetterbestimmend.
> Vorhersage für heute: heiter bis wolkig und trocken.
> Höchsttemperaturen um 23, in den Hochlagen von Sauerland und Eifel 19 Grad. Tiefsttemperaturen in der Nacht 14 bis 10 Grad.
> Weitere Aussichten: Auch am Wochenende trocken und warm.

1. What is affecting today's weather?
  A. Cold winds from the North Sea.
  B. A low-pressure area over NRW.
  C. Thick clouds over the Sauerland and the Eifel.
  D. A high-pressure area over the North Sea.

2. What is likely to be the highest temperature during the night?
   A. 19°C.
   B. 14°C.
   C. 23°C.
   D. 10°C.
3. What kind of weather can we expect at the weekend?
   A. Cold.
   B. Cloudy.
   C. Dry.
   D. Wet

(b) *Higher Level*

A boy leaves school and gets his first job. Read carefully this account, and then answer, *in English*, the questions which follow.

Fünfzehn Jahre lang hatte Frau Notke mit ihrem Sohn Kurt in einer engen Gasse dicht am Hamburger Freihafen gewohnt. Ihr Mann, der ein tüchtiger Zimmermann gewesen war, war durch einen Straßenunfall gestorben, als Kurt erst sechs Monate alt war. Die Wohnung war ganz klein, und ein Zimmer davon vermietete sie an andere Leute. Sie selbst saß bis tief in die Nacht und nähte Kleider für fremde Damen, aber sie verdiente dabei nicht viel Geld.

Nun sollte Kurt die Schule verlassen. Er wollte zur See fahren, wie jeder echte Hamburger Junge, und träumte von großen Ozeanfahrten, aber die Mutter wollte ihn noch nicht ganz hergeben, besonders da er nicht kräftig war. Sie besorgte ihm eine Stelle bei einer In- und Exportfirma.

Von nun an war Kurt den ganzen Tag im Dienst und konnte nicht einmal mittags nach Hause gehen. Was mußte er jeden Tag für viele Wege machen! Zur Bank, zur Börse und zum Güterbahnhof! Aber am schönsten war es doch, wenn er etwas im Hafen besorgen mußte, denn da war er ja bei seinen geliebten Schiffen. Oft lief er extra im Laufschritt, um nachher ein paar Minuten auf dem Kai sitzen zu können.

1. What had happened to Kurt's father?
2. How old was Kurt at the time?
3. What did Frau Notke do for a living?
4. How else did she make some money?
5. What work did Kurt take up on leaving school?
6. What did he really want to do on leaving school?
7. Why did his mother not grant him his wish?
8. Why could Kurt not go home at midday?
9. What did he find particularly enjoyable, and why?
10. What did he do in order to spend more time there?

5.3 Writing Tests

(a) *Basic Level*

Write a message in German of 20–30 words, based on the following situation:
You arrive in Koblenz with a school party. You call on your German pen-friend, who lives in Koblenz. She/he is out and so you write a message including the following information:

      You arrived by train yesterday. (1 item)
      You are staying at the youth hostel. (1 item)
      You can meet your friend at 3 o'clock tomorrow. (1 item)
      Suggest a meeting place. (1 item)

(b) *Higher Level*

Write a continuous story in German in the past tense, relating the events shown in the following picture sequence. You should write about 120 words. [Note that not all examining groups will make use of the picture story as a form of free composition. Other possibilities are to write a narrative account of an incident, or, most probably, to respond with a letter to a request for information in a letter which you have received from a pen-friend. There are many examples of this form of written response in the exercises of this book.]

5.4 Oral Tests

(a) *Basic Level*

(i) *Role Play*

The candidate will be given a role-play card to prepare before his/her oral test. The examiner will play the part of the shopkeeper, tourist, etc.

You are at a garage in Germany.
1. Say you would like the tank filled.
2. Explain that you have a long journey to make.
3. Say you do not need any oil.
4. Ask whether they sell maps.
5. Ask whether there is a telephone nearby.

(ii) *Questions and Answers*

For example:
　Wie heißt du?
　Wie alt bist du?
　Wo wohnst du?
　Beschreibe dein Haus!
　Was für Hobbys hast du?
　Was machst du in deiner Freizeit?
　Wo warst du letztes Jahr in den Sommerferien?
　Wohin fährst du in den Ferien?
　Erzähl mir etwas über deine Ferien in Deutschland!

(b) *Higher Level*

(i) *Role Play*

As for Basic Level, but more developed. For example:

Study the following situation carefully and be prepared to perform in German the role indicated.

You are a student looking for a summer job and you have heard that a certain farmer, Herr Norbert, in the village of Aarfeld is looking for temporary labour. The examiner will play the role of Herr Norbert or his wife.
1. Check that you are speaking to the right person.
2. Explain why you have called.
3. If a job is available you will need
　(i) to know what work you will be doing and when you can begin;
　(ii) advice on where to stay locally.
4. If you are not offered a job,
　(i) ask whether Herr Norbert is likely to have one for you later;
　(ii) ask whether there is any other farmer who might be able to help you.

(ii) At Higher Level the oral examination may also contain questions on a single picture, or a picture narrative (like the written picture story on page 243), depending on which examining group is setting the paper. In the conversation the following are the main topic areas which might be covered by an oral examiner.
1. Personal information: name, age, date of birth, family.
2. House and home: describe house, furniture, garden, situation in town or village.

3. Routine: time of getting up, going to bed, meals.
4. Life at school or work: daily routine, subjects studied, games and clubs, clothes worn to school or work.
5. Free time: hobbies, spare-time interest, radio and TV likes and dislikes, sport, discos, theatre, cinema.
6. Travel and holidays: countries visited, preferred places for holidays, methods of transport, types of accommodation (hotel, camping), last year's holiday, next holidays.
7. Weather and seasons: describe the weather, which season preferred, describe weather on holiday.
8. Future plans: further study, jobs.

Here is a sequence of possible personal questions. Answers will obviously vary between individual students, but some suggestions are given in the Key.

1. Wie heißen Sie? Wie alt sind Sie? Wann sind Sie geboren? Wie viele Personen sind in Ihrer Familie? Haben Sie Geschwister?
2. Wo wohnen Sie? Wohnen Sie lieber in der Stadt oder auf dem Lande? Beschreiben Sie Ihr Haus! Haben Sie einen großen Garten? Beschreiben Sie Ihr Schlafzimmer!
3. Wann stehen Sie morgens auf? Beschreiben Sie einen typischen Tag! Wann gehen Sie ins Bett?
4. Um wieviel Uhr fängt die Schule an? Welche Fächer studieren Sie in der Schule? Tragen Sie eine Schuluniform?
5. Was machen Sie gern in Ihrer Freizeit? Sehen Sie oft fern? Welche Fernsehsendungen haben Sie am liebsten? Gehen Sie oft abends aus? Haben Sie Musik gern? Spielen Sie ein Instrument? Treiben Sie gern Sport?
6. Wo verbringen Sie normalerweise Ihre Ferien? Waren Sie schon im Ausland? Wo waren Sie letztes Jahr in Ferien? Was haben Sie für dieses Jahr vor?
7. Wie ist das Wetter heute? Welche Jahreszeit haben Sie am liebsten? Warum?
8. Verlassen Sie dieses Jahr die Schule? Was werden Sie nächstes Jahr machen? Werden Sie Deutsch weiterstudieren?

6. Preparing for the Examination

There are a number of general hints which may be helpful in preparing for the sorts of tests explained in the preceding pages.

6.1 The Four Skills

Any adequate preparation for the examination should bear in mind the balance between the four skills of listening, speaking, reading and writing. It would be wrong to concentrate too much on one skill — for example, reading — and neglect the others. On the other hand, if you feel that you are weak in a particular skill, it may be worth concentrating on that area intensively for a time. The listening skill, for example, is sometimes neglected, and yet you will improve markedly in this area if you do some regular and intensive listening practice. It is also worth bearing in mind that we can always recognise, in listening and reading, far more than we can produce in speaking and writing.

6.2 The Listening Tests

(a) With short listening comprehensions there will be certain essential pieces of information to listen for, such as times, places, people. Train yourself to listen for the key item of information, and do not be concerned about understanding every word.

(b) With longer passages of dialogue or narrative, much will depend on whether the instructions for the examination you are taking allow you to make notes during the first or second listening. Whether or not you are allowed to make notes, you should concentrate, on the first listening, on getting the overall gist of the piece. It is often dangerous to get stuck on particular words at this stage, as you may miss important parts of what follows. Remember that you do not need to understand every word in order to answer questions on the listening passages, and also that the meaning of an unusual word may become clear to you when you have heard the whole passage.

6.3 The Reading Tests

(a) With shorter items, such as notices, posters and announcements, the important thing is to locate the key word, rather in the same way as in the short listening tests. You do not need to understand every word to be able to grasp what a notice is saying.

(b) With longer passages, always take time to read the whole passage through with care before starting to answer questions. Much that may seem difficult at first may become clearer within the context of the passage seen as a whole. Some meanings will become evident from the whole passage, and some words may not be essential for answering questions.

(c) The examination you are taking may include a translation from German into English. The important thing about translation of this kind is that your final version should read, as nearly as possible, as a piece of good English. So, although you should stay as close as possible to the original as far as the content is concerned, do not be afraid to turn things round in translation, if you feel that there is a more 'English' way of saying something.

6.4 The Writing Tests

The most commonly used writing tests in the foreign language are letters, or other forms of free composition such as may be provided by the outline of a story or a series of pictures. For all such tests, remember that you will be given credit for effective communication (getting the message across), range of language (vocabulary and structures) and accuracy. Because you choose what you write, and are not forced into using language you don't know, you can avoid using anything you are not sure about. Make use of everything that you know and can use correctly, but do not try to make up words.

Letter-writing is an important skill, and you should know the usual ways of beginning and ending letters in German, and also the other little details about letter-writing. You will find many examples of both formal and informal letters in this book.

(a) Formal Letters

The usual beginning for formal letters is *Sehr geehrte(r)* — for example: *Sehr geehrter Herr Meyer!* (text 8.1.3); *Sehr geehrte Damen und Herren* (text 3.1.4). Note that it is usual to place an exclamation mark in German after this opening phrase of a letter. Another possibility is a comma, in which case the letter continues with a small letter.

The usual ending for this sort of letter is: *mit freundlichen Grüßen* or, if very formal, *Hochachtungsvoll.*

(b) Informal Letters

These begin with the correct form of the adjective *Liebe(r)* — for example, *Liebe Helen!* (text 1.1.3); *Lieber Herbergsvater!* (text 9.1.4). If writing to a whole family, you might write *Liebe Freunde!* or use the name of the family in the plural: *Liebe Schmidts!*

When writing the familiar forms *du* and *ihr* in informal letters, these pronouns, and all their associated parts, are written with capital letters — for example: *Was Du mir von Deiner Familie und Eurem Haus geschrieben hast* . . . (text 1.1.3). Informal letters finish: *Viele liebe Grüße; Herzliche Grüße; Viele Grüße.*

(c) Details of the correct way to address envelopes are given in the publication of the Deutsche Bundespost in text 6.1.3.

(d) The date at the head of a letter is usually written: 10.Dezember 1986, or 10.12.1986. If the place is named it becomes: Berlin, den 10.Dezember 1986.

It is worth noting that, for examination purposes, the beginnings and ends of letters do not normally count as part of the total number of words you are asked to write. It is also worth noting that for all types of letter and free composition there is no great advantage in writing more words than you are asked for. You will not normally be given credit for the extra amount.

6.5 The Oral Tests

You can prepare for many aspects of the oral tests, particularly the personal questions, where the topic areas are clearly laid down. Role play is more difficult to prepare for, since you cannot predict the situation you will meet. However, the topic areas are also those covered by the chapters of this book, and it will be clear, from the samples given, what sort of situation you may expect. You will also have time to prepare your role play before the actual test. Be ready to take the initiative in a role play, by asking questions, and by responding to any unexpected queries from the examiner playing the other role. If you have to deal with a narrative, such as a picture story, study the whole story as you would for a written composition. Make a mental note of the key items of vocabulary you will need, decide which tense you are going to use, and be consistent.

7. Key to Sample Materials

5.1 Listening Tests

(a) (i) 1. A radio announcer. 2. On a train. 3. The lady has dialled the wrong number.

(ii) 28 years old. He got fined 500 Marks. Thrown some letters away.

(iii) Sausage. 200 grams of liver sausage. He forgot to take his list with him.

(b) 1. At the man's house. 2. She has lost her keys. 3. From the telephone box at the corner. 4. Because there is no night duty for the porter. 5. Stay where she is till her friend comes.

5.2 *Reading Tests*

(a) (i) The film may be seen only by adults.
   (ii) 1. A high-pressure area over the North Sea. 2. 14°C. 3. dry.
(b) 1. He died in a road accident. 2. Six months old. 3. She sewed clothes for unknown ladies. 4. She let one of the rooms. 6. He wanted to go to sea. 7. She did not want to give him up completely, especially as he was not particularly strong. 8. Because his work occupied him all day. 9. When he had some errand in the port area. 10. He did his errand at a run, so as to have a few minutes left to sit on the quay.

5.3

(a) Wir sind gestern mit dem Zug angekommen. Wir bleiben in der Jugendherberge. Ich kann Dich morgen um drei Uhr treffen. Am Marktplatz.
(b) Gestern abend hatte ich Freunde eingeladen. Das hat Spaß gemacht! Einige hatte ich schon lange nicht gesehen, und wir haben bis spät in der Nacht geplaudert und getrunken. Erst um zwei Uhr morgens sind die letzten Freunde weggegangen, und ich war total erschöpft. Ich habe mich sofort auf das Sofa gelegt, und ich bin eingeschlafen, ohne mich auszuziehen. Das war wirklich ganz schlimm, als ich um Viertel nach acht aufgewacht bin. Ich hatte einen richtigen Kater, und leere Flaschen standen noch auf dem Tisch oder lagen auf dem Boden. Ich mußte sofort zur Arbeit gehen, ohne zu frühstücken, und ich bin zu spät gekommen, erst um zehn nach neun. Der Manager war sehr böse mit mir und ich mußte mich entschuldigen. Aber ich war noch so müde, daß ich an meinem Schreibtisch eingeschlafen bin.

5.4

(a) (i) 1. Volltanken bitte. 2. Ich muß eine lange Reise machen. 3. Öl brauche ich nicht. 4. Verkaufen Sie Karten? 5. Ist hier in der Nähe ein Telefon?
(b) (i) 1. Entschuldigen Sie bitte! Sind Sie Herr Norbert?
   2. Ich suche Arbeit für die Sommerferien, und man hat mir gesagt, daß Sie Arbeitskräfte brauchen. Hätten Sie vielleicht eine Stelle für mich?
   3. Schön, können Sie mir bitte sagen, was für Arbeit ich machen werde? Und wann kann ich anfangen? Wissen Sie vielleicht, wo ich hier in der Nähe Unterkunft finden kann?
   4. Schade. Ist es vielleicht möglich, daß Sie später eine Stelle für mich haben werden? Oder gibt es vielleicht einen anderen Bauern, der mir helfen könnte?
(Answers will depend to some extent on the part played by the examiner, so the above suggestions are only a rough guide.)
(ii) The following are possible answers for the questions of the oral examination, but the details will obviously vary from student to student.
   1. Ich heiße Peter Smith. Ich bin sechzehn Jahre alt. Ich bin neunzehnhundertsiebzig (1970) geboren. Wir sind sechs Personen in meiner Familie. Ich habe einen Bruder und eine Schwester.
   2. Ich wohne in London. Ich wohne lieber in der Stadt. Mein Haus ist ziemlich klein, mit einem kleinen Garten. Mein Schlafzimmer ist klein, und ich habe nur Platz für einen Schreibtisch, ein Bett und zwei Stühle.

3. Ich stehe morgens um sieben Uhr auf. Ich wasche mich, ich frühstücke, und dann gehe ich zur Schule. Ich esse mein Mittagessen in der Schule, und ich komme um vier Uhr nach Hause. Abends mache ich meine Hausaufgaben und sehe fern. Ich gehe um zehn Uhr ins Bett.

4. Die Schule fängt um neun Uhr an. Ich studiere Sprachen, Naturwissenschaften, Geschichte, Erdkunde und Religion. Wir müssen eine Schuluniform tragen.

5. In meiner Freizeit treibe ich gern Sport. Ich spiele Fußball und Schach, und ich wandere auch gern. Ich sehe jeden Abend fern, und meine Lieblingssendungen sind Dallas und Sportsendungen. Ich habe Popmusik sehr gern, aber ich spiele kein Instrument. Ich möchte gern Gitarre spielen.

6. Wir gehen in den Ferien normalerweise zu meiner Oma. Sie wohnt nicht weit von der See in Südwestengland. Ich war schon zweimal im Ausland, einmal mit einer Schulgruppe in Deutschland und einmal mit meiner Familie in Spanien. Letztes Jahr waren wir in Spanien, aber dieses Jahr werden wir wahrscheinlich wie immer zu meiner Oma gehen.

7. Das Wetter ist heute nicht schön. Es regnet, und es ist kalt. Ich habe den Sommer am liebsten, weil ich gern schwimme und gern in der Sonne liege.

8. Nach meinen Prüfungen werde ich hoffentlich weiterstudieren. Ich werde noch zwei Jahre in der Schule bleiben, und ich werde Chemie, Biologie und Mathematik studieren. Ich möchte dann später zur Universität gehen, aber das hängt von den Prüfungen ab. Ich möchte auch Deutsch weiterstudieren, aber ich weiß noch nicht, ob es möglich sein wird.

Bibliography and Further Information

1. Works of Reference

(a) Dictionaries

Collins German Dictionary (Collins)
Langenscheidt's Standard German Dictionary (Hodder and Stoughton)

(b) Grammars

A German Reference Grammar (Robin T. Hammond, OUP)
German Grammar and Usage (A. E. Hammer, Edward Arnold)

(c) Pronunciation

The Pronunciation of German (P. MacCarthy, OUP)

2. Opportunities for Hearing German

Radio broadcasts from German stations can be received in the United Kingdom, but the speed of delivery may make such broadcasts difficult for English students at intermediate level. The best source of opportunities to hear German is the BBC, with programmes intended both for schools and for adult learners of the language. ITV also broadcasts German programmes for schools.

3. Other Sources of Information about German-speaking Countries

(a) Goethe Institut, 50 Princes Gate, Exhibition Rd, London, SW7 2PG
(b) Embassy of the GDR, Press Department, 34 Belgrave Square, London SW1
(c) Austrian Institute, 28 Rutland Gate, London SW7 1PQ
(d) Swiss Embassy, Cultural and Information Section, 16 Montagu Place, London W1H 2BQ